FATAL
FLOWERS

ALSO BY ROSEMARY DANIELL

A Sexual Tour of the Deep South (poetry)

FATAL FLOWERS

On Sin, Sex, and Suicide in the Deep South

ROSEMARY DANIELL

AN OWL BOOK

HENRY HOLT AND COMPANY   NEW YORK

Published by Henry Holt and Company, Inc.,
115 West 18th Street, New York, New York 10011.
Published in Canada by Fitzhenry & Whiteside Limited,
195 Allstate Parkway, Markham, Ontario L3R 4T8.
A portion of this book first appeared in the *Atlanta Journal-
Constitution*.

Library of Congress Cataloging-in-Publication Data
Daniell, Rosemary.   Fatal flowers.
1. Women—Southern States—Social conditions.
2. Daniell, Rosemary.   3. Southern States—Biography.
4. Southern States—Moral conditions.   I. Title.
HQ1438.A13D35   301.41′2′0975   79-20136
ISBN 0-8050-1027-0 (An Owl Book: pbk.)

Henry Holt books are available at special discounts
for bulk purchases for sales promotions, premiums,
fund-raising, or educational use. Special editions
or book excerpts can also be created to specification.

For details contact:

Special Sales Director
Henry Holt and Company, Inc.
115 West 18th Street
New York, New York 10011

First published in hardcover by Holt, Rinehart and
Winston in 1980.

First Owl Book Edition—1989

Designer: Susan Mitchell
Printed in the United States of America
1   3   5   7   9   10   8   6   4   2

Permission granted to quote from "Hello Mexico (And
Adios Baby To You)" by Billy Sherrill, Steve David, and
Glenn Sutton, copyright © 1978 Algee Music Corp. &
Flagship Music Inc.

Permission granted to quote from "I've Always Been
Crazy" by Waylon Jennings, © 1979 Waylon Jennings
Music, 1117 17th Avenue South, Nashville, Tennessee.

For Melissa Ruth Connell
September 1915–September 1975

With thanks to my daughters, Laura and
Darcy Daniell;
my sister, Anne Webster;
and my editor and friend, Jennifer Josephy

It is a fetish in the South that the sun shines just a little brighter, the moon rays are just a little softer, the breezes blow just a little gentler, the birds sing just a little sweeter, the flowers are just a little prettier, and its climate just a little more salubrious. When going from one section to another, all of us have an idea that we know by instinct just when we cross the line out of the South or into it. . . .

—Southern Cooking,
Mrs. S. R. Dull, 1928

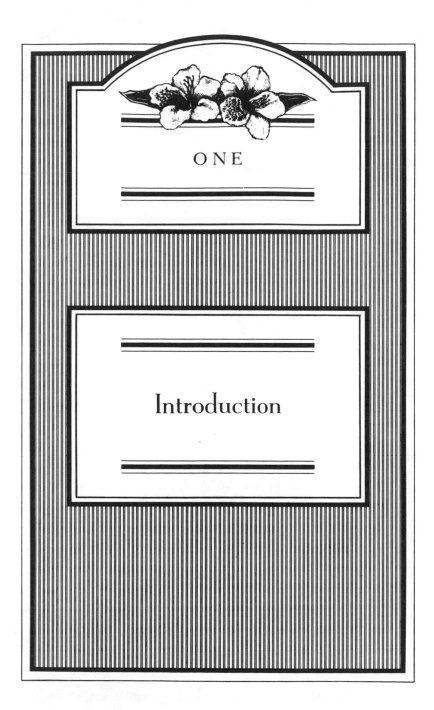

ONE

Introduction

In the backseat of a black limousine, my mother and I speed through darkness. Like Evelyn Mulray's daughter in China-town, *I'm being saved by my glamorous mother from danger-ous men. Pressing my nine-year-old cheek against her shoulder, stroking the cream satin of her blouse, breathing her gardenia perfume, I feel enclosed in a dark cocoon of safety. With a sigh of contentment, I flop my arm across her breasts and discover that, beneath the slippery cloth, one side of my mother's chest is hard, flat—stiff with bandages and adhesive. . . .*

When I woke sobbing in 1974 in my red velour-papered room in the Virginian Hotel in Medicine Bow, Wyoming (population, 450), I didn't know that, as a child, my mother had been driven to school each day in a chauffeured black automobile—just that my dream of her mutilation made me want to rush into the hallway to the hotel's one pay phone to call her at home in North Carolina. Only my fear of the miners, who were the only other guests at the hotel, and whose drunken shouts I still heard from the bar adjoining the café, stopped me. That, and the knowledge that my mother's wound was real, had long since been inflicted, and there was no longer anything I or anyone could do to save her.

A year later, I lay on a lumpy bedspread in a room in the John Milledge Motel in Milledgeville, Georgia, sipping Jack Daniel's and tap water, watching the "Tony Orlando and Dawn" show. I needed to forget, for a few minutes, the poetry workshop I had just conducted at the state prison for women—to forget fifty-five-year-old Jewell's lifelong dream of "staying in one of them motels, just once"; Chain Gang Candy's tale of throwing Clorox into her faithless husband's eyes; and black Doris's story of be-ing railroaded into prison by the white police officer who was the father of five of her six illegitimate children. As I lounged

3

against the cheap veneer headboard, trying to focus on Tony's cheerful sing-along, on the way he lifted women from the audience—plain, fat, pantsuited—to momentary media "life," the phone rang.

My sister Anne's voice came tiredly over the line. Mother had been found unconscious, she said; dressed in a new blue peignoir and her best white-gold costume jewelry, with her favorite bright-red lipstick carefully applied, she had left a scrawled note and an empty bottle of pills beside her bed. Anne would be traveling with her by ambulance to a hospital in Atlanta; would I meet her there as soon as possible? As I faintly registered Anne's irritation that, as usual, I was not on hand for a family crisis, I felt a mixture of relief and numbness that lasted through the minutes of making phone calls, throwing things into suitcases: Mother had finally done what for years she had said she would do. . . .

As I drove through the piny dark, my usual fears of pickups full of red-necks with rifles and a penchant for rape were overlaid by images that wove themselves with the asphalt opening before me. Photographs of Mother, pensively smiling in a black velvet dance dress, holding red roses in her plump arms; standing solemnly with Daddy outside his University of Georgia frat house, dressed in satin-faced cloche and dressmaker coat, her kid slippers fastened with tiny round buttons; or laughing, linking arms in a row of girls, theatrically jutting a knee to show the hemline of her chemise in a local fashion show—"the prettiest girl in Atlanta," I had heard time after time.

Earlier in the day, driving down the Spanish moss–and–dogwood-lined main street of Milledgeville toward the prison, I had passed the college Mother had attended at seventeen—Georgia State College for Women, now the Women's College of Georgia, best known as the alma mater of Flannery O'Connor —and had recalled another picture of her, plump on starchy school food, yet pretty in the required navy pleated skirt and white middy blouse. Grandmother Lee, her mother, had told me that Mother cried so much from homesickness that she was allowed to return home after her first year. She didn't yet know Valentino-dark Daddy, her destiny of two years later—or that

4

he played the saxophone on the roof of the military school across the street to attract the girls.

As I neared the prison, I had recalled that Daddy, too, had visited prisoners. A tire salesman, he had sold truck tires to a warden and had brought supplies for an inmate who made jewelry. The grateful man had given him a matching set of earrings and bracelet which he, in turn, had given to his best girl. For years, after her trousseau lingerie and Persian-lamb coat were gone, the pieces had been Mother's best jewelry. As I turned into the drive leading to the institution, I recalled, through five-year-old eyes, the shiny onyx chunks echoing her jet curls, the glint of filigree as the stones fell from her wrist. . . .

The next morning, allowed into a curtained room in intensive care, I saw that, for once, she wore no jewelry at all—she had become a slight child beneath blue cotton, struggling for breath, cruelly jammed through nose, throat, arms with tubes bubbling red. As I held her small hand in mine, hopelessly whispering "I love you," I noticed that her nails were perfectly filed in her favorite pointed style—and that her face was full, round again. Around eyes as tightly closed as a newborn's, Mother's cheeks and forehead were smoothed for the first time in thirty years of the deep marks of some indescribable inner pain. . . .

The year of Mother's suicide also became the year of Daddy's death from a fast-growing cancer. It was the year during which I found my third and most-desired marriage deteriorating in a way in which I couldn't seem to control, until finally the inevitable separation took place. It was the time when the three children I had borne early, who for years had absorbed much of my consciousness, left home for good—the time, too, during which I sold the house where they had grown up, the house of the coral goldfish pond, the wisteria vines, the hundred-foot pines. It was the year of my fortieth birthday, the near-age of Mother's first breakdown, the time after which I sensed it would be impossible to remain the girl-woman I had been brought up to become.

And it was the year of a long-fantasized—and sometimes dreaded—event: the publication of my first book of poetry. *A Sexual Tour of the Deep South* expresses a lifetime of accumulated feminine rage and a disregard for everything that, in the South, is called "ladylike"; writing it had been a personal thrust toward freedom. But in my hometown of Atlanta, I suddenly found myself controversial, notorious, envied, trashed by local patriarchs, matriarchs, and "feminists," my long-standing job with the Georgia Council for the Arts—and thus my income— threatened.

For the first time, I was without parents, husband, children, youth, and perhaps, an income. As though it had long been hurtling in that direction, my whole life seemed to be falling apart. I experienced the kind of loneliness that felt as though a serrated apple corer had been used to carve out my center. Despite my struggle to live as differently as possible from my mother, I wondered if I would break as she had. It became imperative, if I would find an alternative to madness, to understand her—and thus my own—experience as a Southern woman.

Like Mother, I had absorbed Grandmother Lee's dictum that "You are who you marry." Jimmy Carter, ten years my mother's junior, ten years my senior, recently was reported as recommending that in order to look as young as his wife, Rosalynn, a woman should "get married to a man who will take good care of her." In *The Great Santini,* a novel of Southern family life by Atlantan Pat Conroy, the character Lillian advises her daughter that "a woman has but one job—to be adorable. Everything else is just icing...." Elizabeth Ray, carrying her North Carolina origins to Washington, said that all she had ever wanted was for some man to ask her to marry him. Even after seven years as a feminist, as a descendant of my mother and grandmothers, I found her statement too easy to understand.

For a lifetime, I had dreaded gatherings of the women of Mother's family. One's success as a woman was immediately assessed by Southern standards: an added pound, a less flattering hairdo, the state of one's wardrobe were all commented upon, becoming cause and effect of the failed husband, child, or marriage. That Mother had begun as the prettiest of them made judgment against her, and her own self-condemnation, more severe. (Was this why, as the "prettiest of the granddaughters," I dressed the most sloppily?) A homely aunt with a colorless, yet stable, executive husband, a woman who "didn't have to work," was by all Southern counts more successful than Mother—with her alcoholic first husband, her years of unexpected struggle to support herself and her daughters—could ever be. It was the "right" of each good Southern woman to be supported by a man; the degree of his support was the measure of her goodness.

The most realized of my maternal aunts by these standards was Florance. Three years Mother's junior, freckled and big-boned, she also had the good sense at seventeen to marry an equally plain local boy—a suitor Mother had rejected—who had proceeded with straight-arrow perseverance to "make good." As the wife of a Republican crew-cut vice-president of a major automobile-parts company, the mistress of a two-story house in Ohio, and participant in company jaunts to Hawaii and Mexico ("Though I didn't like Mexico," she declared. "The people look so depressed, and they can't speak our language."), Florance reigns as the family queen of recipes for gelatin salads and new ways with pot roast, of garden-club luncheons and music-club teas.

"Gloria Steinem's too old to wear her hair that way," she commented to me pointedly as we sat planning Mother's funeral in the living room of Lee's house. "She just dresses and acts that way because she's never met the right man." With a pang, I realized how painful my jeans and boots at thirty-five, my disregard of permanent waves and hair rollers must have been for Mother in the face of her siblings' competitiveness. I had felt, in their presence, the discomfort of my ambivalence, a momentary lowering of self-esteem; but for her, I have represented proof of both her own failure and her failure to police her daughter into the proper Southern values. When the question of what Mother should wear in her casket arose, I suggested

7

red, her favorite color, but Florance vetoed my choice in favor of "a soft blue—it's more appropriate." Weak in the presence of so much propriety, I gave in.

At the funeral home, Florance came out of the room where Mother's open casket was displayed to tell me, "She looks real good—her makeup's just right for once, and so is the dress. And they took care of all that swelling from right before she died." I had refused to go back into intensive care after the permanence of her coma, the imminence of her death, were certain. I wanted to remember Mother's small hand in mine. And though later I knew it was caused by the accumulated fluids, the failure of her kidneys, I wanted to remember the smoothness of her face, its final freedom from conflict and failure.

Mother's mother, Lee, had been widowed at thirty-two, left with three young children. Back home with her parents in Villa Rica, Georgia, her days filled with scrubbing out her babies' clothes on a washboard and ironing them, she gratefully married a twice-widowed businessman and landowner who had four children of his own, and she had promptly given birth to two more. It was he who provided the chauffeured car in which Mother rode to school after the family's move to Atlanta, her year at college, and her dressmaker clothes; but years later she told me how shut out she had felt, how abandoned, when she and her younger sisters had had to sit silently, or leave the room, at his frequent and booming commands. "I was always grateful to him," Lee said, "because he gave me and my children a home." For as long as I could remember, until his death, I recall Grandmother Lee waiting on him, indulging his eccentricities about meals, the case of "Co-Cola" he drank each day. Her one pleasure seemed her last child and only son—though when he left home, and the husband she had nurtured over her daughters and herself had died, she continued setting a flawless standard of proper Southern Baptist (the Methodists were on Daddy's side) stoicism for Mother, my sister, and me. The one time she had ever seen Grandmother Lee upset, Anne told me, was when she had discovered Anne kissing a boyfriend good night on the back porch. "Never let a boy kiss you until you're engaged," she had told us: never permit the devaluing of merchandise!

Daddy's mother, Annie, had grown up on a hog farm where Saks Fifth Avenue and Lord & Taylor now stand in Atlanta; in mixed-up dreams I see her standing barefoot on the raw boards of the front porch of a house raised, in the rural Southern tradition, on wooden stilts, calling the hogs with a silk Givenchy scarf around her neck, a new straw hat heavy with rayon flowers on her imperious head. Annie's indulgence, as a wife, had been riding the River car into Atlanta to shop for new scarves, hats, and costume jewelry. She had met her postmaster husband through a letter in the lonely-hearts column of an Atlanta newspaper; he had driven down from North Carolina, and they had married the next day, settling in a community on the edge of town. She had borne him four children but, the opposite of Lee, was known for her neglect of house, young: "Why, she'd just give them a bowl of cereal and get on that River car to go downtown shopping!" Mother told me indignantly. She blamed Daddy's alcoholism on Annie's failure to nurture him properly.

When I was eleven and twelve, we lived at Annie's house because Daddy's gambling debts had made us give up our own. Watching her wring chicken necks in the backyard, helping her scald the still-warm bodies and pluck the feathers, begging to plunge my hands into their entrails in search of half-formed eggs—yet trying, at the same time, not to get in her way—all I had seen was her bitterness. One midnight, I had heard a noise, walked into the dark kitchen, where I saw Annie, her back toward me, staring out the window. Her flesh beneath the robe, uncorseted for once, had appeared weighted with a strange sadness. "Southern men are the only men in this country who have been defeated," a Southern man once said to me. By my teens, I had amended this to Southern women.

Like Mother, I was imprinted with the archetypes of media and literature, and the message was all too clear. Rosalynn Carter—pretty, protected, dependent—is the woman my suicided mother had been born to become. Her failure to achieve this goal was her stigmata, her victimization. Cornelia Wallace;

9

Catherine Marshall, wife of Presbyterian minister Peter Marshall; even Tammy Wynette, who, through her career, met and married her dream "Stand by Your Man" George Jones, were, to women like us, the success stories: power, to a Southern woman, comes through a powerful man. When we were in the same PTA study group, Coretta King sometimes called me to obsess about the problems of going on with her music; after Martin's death, the calls stopped. Ironically, his demise had given her power of her own.

Images of the Carter women—Rosalynn, Lillian, Ruth, and Gloria—suggest the constellation of feminine possibilities acceptable within traditional Southern society. Rosalynn—the Melanie Jimmy says he would have chosen over Scarlett—is the compleat success; that she rarely offers opinions and subdues her anger is proof, by Southern standards, of her quality. Lillian, Jimmy's mother, always liked her bourbon, thought for herself on integration, even temporarily left the Peach Corps for the Peace Corps, and India, though always with Plains and the Carter men behind her. Blonde Ruth embraced the most acceptable outlet for feminine ambition—religious fervor. Yet however successful her mix of pop psychology and down-home evangelism in terms of book sales and lecture tours, it still signals reliance upon God the Father, and by extension, her husband and the structure of patriarchy. Gloria, the rebel, expresses herself through harmless eccentricity—riding motorcycles, refusing beauty parlors. But even she has been punished for her deviation: a son who once threatened to shoot Jimmy and his brother Billy is now in prison in California for armed robbery.

On "The Merv Griffin Show" on December 13, 1976, Billy Carter told Merv that though he often reads five to seven books a week, he would never read a book written by a woman. "Now don't git me wrong," he said, "I've met some nice wimmen. But I ain't never met one I thought had enough sense to write a book." Mother's ambition, passed on to me like a disease, was that we both wanted to become writers. It was a defect that, as Southern women, we sought to overcome—she, by submission to appearances, I, through early marriage and motherhood. We

10

had observed that Carson McCullers, Flannery O'Connor, Margaret Mitchell, and her creation Scarlett O'Hara, had all been punished for their ambition by illness, death, or the loss of love. My favorite story—a true one—was that of a woman in Washington, Georgia, during the nineteenth century who, accused of the murder of her husband, had been condemned to death by jurors whose jealous wives insisted upon it; she had gone to her hanging in the streets of the town known for its antebellum beauty wearing her prettiest silk gown. After hearing and reading stories of what had happened to exceptional Southern women, I shivered: was this the fate that awaited every woman who craved more than the traditional feminine role?

Like transsexual Jan Morris, I had long felt born into the wrong body. At eleven, I had mixed ambitions. I dreamed of marrying the blond boy in church in a baby-blue wedding with six bridesmaids, of becoming the perfect housekeeper and sex partner, and of having six children. But I also imagined writing perfect novels while perfect cakes baked in the oven in my Betty Crocker kitchen. Besides a dark book on sex, Mother had another she had bought for a dollar at Davison's department store in Atlanta; entitled *Writing for Profit*, it included chapters on how to write a novel, short story, play, article, or newspaper story. In spite of poring over her book and my own writing activities—my five-year diary, inscribed each night with a special pen from Japan; my own private version of *My Friend Flicka*, written in pencil on notebook paper held together with shoelaces—I had also internalized the images presented by *Ladies' Home Journal* and *Good Housekeeping*. One of my "books" was a cookbook of totally untested recipes for such delights as "Jell-O Eggs" ("Shake the insides out of eggs, fill them with Jell-O . . ."). At ten, I had found the love stories in *Ladies' Home Journal* so risque and daring that I hid in Mother's room to read them; but at eleven and twelve, at last able to go downtown alone to Atlanta's Carnegie Library, my reading focused on books like Anya Seton's *Dragonwyck,* with its exciting wedding-night rape of the reluctant wife by the brutal husband-landowner, and Frank Yerby's novels of blond pirates and their long-suffering and beautiful women. But I was becoming confused: I identified with both the pirates *and* their women—with the adventuring and plundering, and the sub- mission and languishing passivity. A book at Grandmother An- nie's house, *The New Eugenics,* published early in the century and bound in a dark scrolled leather, presented the ideal female as soft, round, and in dread of her husband's indelicate ad- vances; young girls, the first chapter advised, shouldn't be per- mitted to read too many romances. Grandmother Lee had a book for young girls in which the young virgin keeps her body and thoughts as pure and stain-free as the piece of white satin stored in her hope chest for her wedding day. I burned with fascinated shame as I lay before the fire and read: had I already ruined myself by the reading of romances, my impure thoughts?

By fourteen, the image of my distortion, my feminine de- formity, presented itself to me as a literal penis embedded within my body, conflicting, to my Southern mind, with my short red curls, chunky curves, charm bracelets, and budding breasts. It was as though I contained a shameful secret, the secret of my ambition. Indeed, both my deviance from the norms of Southern womanhood and Mother's lack of it would cost us. With every success, I still struggle with guilt. Among my compelling, if irrational, three-A.M. thoughts are questions: was the publication of my book the cause of my failed marriage, even Mother's death? In the recesses of my mind lives the passive, dependent woman I should have been.

Though Mother had lost her life in the effort to avoid such conflicts, we were not dissimilar: at sixteen, Mother wrote in her diary, "I want to marry a lawyer . . . live in a house with white columns. . . ." Unlike me, she didn't weave her fantasy of be- coming a writer into her domestic one, at least in her diary. But her fantasies, and mine of houses with glass-floored halls with goldfish swimming beneath them, with round libraries and nurseries, were equally extravagant, yet conventional: the houses I sketched in my school tablet were the setting for my marriage to the man who would love and care for me forever.

As a teenager I often soothed my feelings—just as my sister, Anne, did by sucking her thumb—by letting myself believe for

12

a while that Mother's dreams *had* come true, that we did live in the kind of two-story columned house in which many of my classmates had lived, instead of the three-room frame dwelling where Anne and I shared a rollaway bed in the kitchen; that my beautiful mother slept in a canopied bed and wore white satin peignoirs instead of the shredded lingerie left from her honeymoon; that Daddy rushed up the curved staircase, laughing, bearing gifts—instead of stumbling drunkenly over the doorframe. As I listened to the girls in my fourth-grade class talk about the evening dresses they had worn to the premiere of *Gone with the Wind,* I dreamed that I had been there, too, accompanied by my handsome parents.

Understandable fantasies. But why had their frustration been so important to Mother and me that she had been led to madness, me to forty years of failure in self-esteem? As Adrienne Rich declares in *Of Woman Born,* "A mother's victimization does not merely humiliate her, it mutilates the daughter who watches her for clues as to what it means to be a woman. Like the traditional foot-bound Chinese woman, she passes on her own affliction. The mother's self-hatred and low expectations are the binding rags for the psyche of the daughter...."

With Mother's death, I realized that much of my own life had meant energy drained by ambivalence—in attempts to either enter into or escape a seemingly foreordained destiny. My marriage ending, my children gone, my life at least half over, it became imperative that I sort out which parts of myself were rooted in my Southern past, which parts belonged to my present reality. I wanted to know why, in spite of years spent in therapy, feminism, journal keeping and other writing, after traveling and several marriages (the last, to a non-Southern man) and many affairs, I was, and sometimes still am, too much of a Southern woman to feel as comfortable alone as with a man beside me for protection.

When Tammy Wynette sang, "Stand by your man . . . ," I still felt "a little gut wrench" (as a good ole boy described what he likes to give his women). I experienced a pang when a Southern lover asked, "How come your sister turned out so good and you didn't?"—jokingly referring to the fact that Anne's architect-designed house, sports car, and credit cards were supplied by her airline-pilot husband. I had a similar feeling when the same man, eating a soul-food dinner I had cooked—collard greens, black-eyed peas, fried chicken—said, "I'm amazed—I thought only women who didn't do other things [like write!] do this."

I wondered why, at forty, I still slept with a man who said such things, and why in spite of a lifetime of struggle for independence, I still, at moments, wanted—with an intensity I could literally taste—to be taken care of by such a man. Listening to two Southern women friends my age gigglingly connive how to manipulate the married lover of one of them into divorce and remarriage I wondered, if I had remained such a woman—manipulative and coy—would my own marriage have survived? When my lover played his guitar and sang the Baptist hymns with which we had both been brought up, the lyrics that had inflamed my sexual guilt, my self-hate at fourteen, tears of nostalgia filled my eyes.

If Miss Lillian had been my grandmother, as committed to my nurture as she is to Amy Carter's, would I be a writer and feminist today? Could I have been like Bert Lance's wife, La-Belle, believing in a "divine plan" for my life, writing occasional poems to express my religious sentiments? I wondered if my entire life had simply been an attempt to express the ambivalence and rage Mother had never allowed herself—if I had simply been a vehicle, a carrier for her pain.

The key to my confusion seemed to lie in Mother's life. Mother had felt worthless, invisible without the approving attention of a man. She had always listened more closely when a man spoke, even if he was only the grocery clerk. "Yankee women are so smart," she would smile ruefully. "They can talk so much better than we can." Yet implicit in her comment was a hidden one: no Yankee ankle could be so well turned as a Southern woman's, nor could she be bettered at the ultimate skill of sexual manipulation—which for Mother turned out to be her only weapon in a life-or-death contest.

Her talent as a writer had been meaningless in the face of her failure in love and marriage. A week before her death, on her sixtieth birthday—the one beyond which she had always said she wouldn't live—I called her at home in North Carolina. As she described a piece she had recently written, a sketch of childhood remembrances, I noticed a new and frightening resignation in her voice. The hysteria was gone; it was as though the line were dead. "I've already destroyed it," she replied when I said I'd like to read what she had written.

Had she wanted no one to know, after the death she knew was imminent, of the mind that flashed beneath her Southern-belle simperings? After the funeral, as Anne and I went through her papers, the file cabinet of her writings, we found nothing but the puerile romantic and/or Christian sentiments—though I knew, had seen, other pieces, other ideas. (Her copy of my book had disappeared, too; for months, I was tortured by an image of her small hand ripping out the pages one by one, crumpling and throwing them into the fireplace when no one was around; at last, throwing in the binding itself.)

Her courage as a young divorcée supporting two teenage daughters on the salary of an untrained Southern belle meant as little to her as her talent as a writer. Each weekday morning for years, she got up at six-thirty to hail down the Greyhound bus to her job as a clerk-typist in Atlanta, and spent Saturdays cleaning house, carefully planning the expenditure of our $15.00 grocery money, or taking me and Anne downtown to buy a long-planned-for pair of Easter shoes for $6.95 at Butler's.

Yet instead of pride at her resourcefulness, she felt shame. Daddy's midnight calls full of skid-row despair filled her with guilt. When she realized that the man she had been seeing, had been sitting up with until three in the morning despite the fact that she had to rise at six, had no intentions of marriage, she broke down. She suddenly forgot how to type, began crying, and couldn't stop. It was the first of the breakdowns that led her through series after series of electroshock treatments, tranquilizers, and eventually, a suggestion that she be lobotomized.

I wanted to understand Mother's victimization, her frustrations, and most of all, to forgive her. Only a year before her death, at a family Thanksgiving at my house, she had looked venomously at me across the champagne and turkey, with a gaze in which I suddenly saw the full shocking depth of her hatred. The look upon her face was the one I had seen so often as a child in the moment before her palm unexpectedly flashed out to meet my cheek. "I've *nevah*," she snarled—here, her lip curled back, doglike—"been able to make you do *any*thang!"

She referred to the fact that a few minutes before, I had refused to give her the favorite silver bracelet I wore on my arm; but I knew that she also meant that my refusal to be policed by her into what she considered essential values had been another of her unbearable failures—that she considered the "penis" within me, my active will, as much of a deformity as I had at fourteen; that my desire for more than her passive, reactive existence was a threat and perversion. But now I needed to think of her again as that young and innocent girl, her arms full of red roses—to at last understand, to love my mother and thus myself.

The year of Mother's suicide became the year in which this understanding began. It was also a year during which I traveled continuously throughout the Deep South, from Atlanta to Milledgeville to New Orleans to Charlotte to Columbia to Savannah to Macon to Rabun Gap and back. Most of these travels were made because of my work as poet-in-residence, and to give readings from my own poetry.

In each place, I visited women friends and made new ones. As a feminist and poet, my intimate friends were women like myself, women who had attempted radical solutions to our common background—artists, writers, scholars, lesbians, political activists, and entrepreneurs. Because they were like me, I understood their contradictions and the pressures. These women —all of them brilliant, charismatic—had experienced struggles similar to my own, and like me, often still lapsed into the confusion and depletion created by a lifetime of conflict.

But as I met schoolteachers, housewives, beauticians, students, and factory workers, I realized that their apparently simpler choices had in no way saved them from frustration, confusion. It was simply that their responses, out of those available, had been different from those fortunate enough to have the energy or opportunity to break out.

The conflicts of all the Southern women I had met seemed magnified in the lives of the women in prison. At the time of Anne's phone call, I was deeply involved in my work at the state correctional facility for women outside Milledgeville. Because of the town in which I found myself—a town dripping with Spanish moss, antebellum charm, and a fascistic Baptist conservatism—my images of the inmates were already confused with fantasies of my parents' early lives. My poetry reading at the college Mother had attended had just been canceled as "too sensational"; each day I found myself feeling closer to the inmates I had at first feared. I had heard of the woman who had slashed another across the eye with a straight razor, of the night the administration left the building in fear of a riot—indeed, women had been shaken down for weapons on an evening of my workshop.

Yet at the time of Anne's news, in the first moments of shock and disbelief, my impulse had been to call these women—had it been possible—for understanding and support. More than anyone I had known, they knew firsthand of deprivation, fear, loss, and grief; they had truly "lost everything in the oppression," and hearing of Mother's condition, I wanted Doris's plump arms around me, Peggy's empathy, and Maybelle's sweet slow smile, Candy's passionate indignation. Instead of my drive into the night, I craved the structure of walls, even locked doors.

For weeks, I had been moved by the parallels between their lives and Mother's and mine. When Peggy described committing armed robbery to buy whiskey for her boyfriend, I recalled how Mother had gone to work as a clerk-typist to help pay off Daddy's gambling debts—and my own decision to quit school at sixteen to marry for "love." When Doris wrote, "Jealousy is when your grandmother helps your brother go to college, and now he has a house and car, and you're here in prison . . . ," I remembered Mother's upbringing as a helpless belle and my own early fantasies that I would always be taken care of by a man who loved me. At moments, it was as though the years of writing and growth had not occurred, as though I was thrust

17

back in time to share their helplessness, hopelessness, and self-hatred.

What I had once seen as the condition of being female, I now saw as female and Southern. I perceived my mother, grandmothers, sister, daughters—and all the women whose roots I shared—as netted in one mutual silken bondage. Together, we were trapped in a morass of Spanish moss, Bible Belt guilt, and the pressures of a patriarchy stronger than in any other part of the country. (Even in the West, where men are men, and macho, the pioneering woman has long been a tradition.) I wondered what would have become of us had sisterhood, rather than feminine policing and competitiveness, been our ambience.

Like most Southern women, I had grown up feeling that only relationships with men were worth serious pursuit. Because I didn't go to college, I had not even experienced the camaraderie of dormitory life—indeed, had never seen a woman other than my mother or sister naked. (Though at nine, I had watched a teenage aunt dressing for a date; when she pulled on a crotchless girdle, I had seen her pubic hair. Since Mother had the same growth upon her body, I unhappily assumed it to be a family deformity.) The stiff corsets worn by my grandmothers, even on weekdays, had given their bodies the texture of a board and seemed metaphors for their impenetrability. But during the year of Mother's death, with an awareness intensified because of the painful shifts in my own life, in the rush of intimacy between women made possible by the decade, I sought out connections between other women and myself. My grandmothers, my mother, my sister, and I, I was learning, were not isolated sufferers. The female attitudes so often caricatured are real: the manipulative magnolia and the hysterical matron *do* exist. In attempts to escape the ramifications of my roots, I had often caricatured the stereotypes. But now, driven by a search for my own identity, cynicism no longer satisfied me. I wanted —indeed, desperately needed—to understand motivations and choices, to reveal not only weaknesses but strengths: to exonerate, at last, my mother, my Southern sisters, and thus myself.

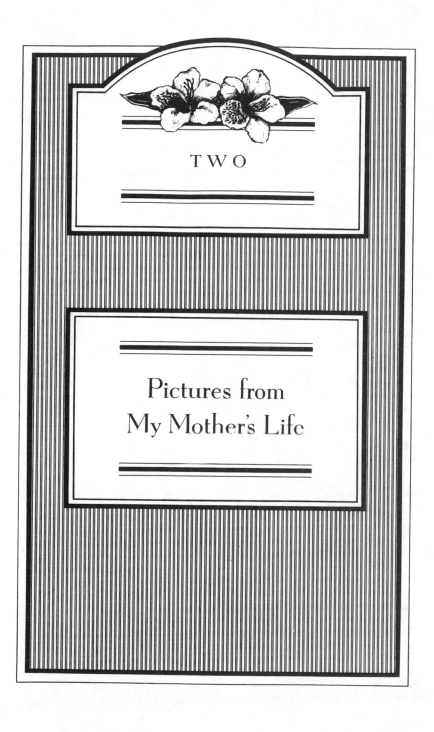

TWO

Pictures from
My Mother's Life

Pictures from my mother's life—images of the people primary to me hold the power to move me backward into a time before I existed. So deeply do I believe myself to have been there, to have shared the experiences of those whose faces and forms were caught on film before I was born, that I project even those born after me into my multilinear time scheme. Driving from Atlanta to Mother's last home in North Carolina, passing through Clayton and Rabun Gap, Georgia—my disorientation growing with the soft beginnings of the Appalachian Mountains —I turned to my sixteen-year-old daughter, Darcy, in the back seat of the car. Noting again that she had dressed for her grandmother's funeral as flashily as a French whore—orange knit midi, orange suede boots—I asked, "Do you remember what Mother was like when she was three?"

I was thinking of a picture I had seen: Mother, crouched at the base of a thick oak, fat-cheeked, peering sullenly toward the camera, her wide forehead cut squarely across by Dutch-boy bangs that emphasized the body structure Grandmother Lee had always described as "built close to the ground." Her gaze is stubborn, her mien serious, echoing remarkably pictures of myself, and later Darcy, at the same age. Despite the fact that Mother had been slightly curvier and shorter, her breasts a bit fuller, her feet a size or two smaller, we three were sisters, replicas, overlapping paper dolls.

In the hospital after Darcy's birth, I saw a moment of my new daughter's future. Jet-curled, curved, she pumped fat calves down and up, driving her tricycle along the drive of our house. Later, what I had imagined became reality. Though she laughed as the streamers of a red velvet sailor hat sped behind her, her face was determined, an amazing likeness of Mother in the photograph.

"Be careful what you want; you might get it" is a common Southern saying. If one's own or another's future could be so clearly seen, could another's past also? In that moment in the car, speeding toward Mother's last social event, I felt as though the three of us had indeed existed simultaneously. Given the infinity of time, the microcosmic nature of the present, and my sense of my mother's life as simply a fragment of my own, that perception may have been as logical as any. Because of her solemn, almost sad gaze, it would be romantic to believe the picture of Mother beneath the oak tree at three to have been made after what she considered the initial and determining tragedy of her life. But it was a tragedy that occurred later, when she was six—a tragedy that, in Bible Belt tradition, had to do with drink.

"Southerners drink more," a displaced New Yorker observed, "because it's so boring down here." A good ole boy might reply that Black Jack is the perfect companion to the gospel songs, storytelling, and contemplations of mortality of which he is fond. Indeed, drinking oneself to death, according to the lyrics of country music, is an acceptable form of male suicide. (Women, too "good" to drink, are allowed promiscuity and hysteria.) When a great-uncle and his nephew were respectively unable to keep their promises to quit drinking to the good Christian women who were their wives, they promptly shot themselves—acts their widows considered appropriate to the nature of their sin.

Daddy's alcoholism had always seemed to me related to the fundamentalist dictum on total abstinence. In Mother's life, drink-related pain began before she was seven with the early death of her father, Huelet Connell. Huelet, Grandmother Lee's first husband, had been killed at thirty-two in an accident in Leeds, Alabama: a "good man" and nondrinker himself, he had taken a cab driven by a drunken driver.

With her father's death, Mother felt she had permanently lost touch with male gentleness and refinement. She loved to tell my sister, Anne, and me how his family had discussed Milton and Shakespeare at the supper table in Villa Rica, Georgia. In addition, his father had been a circuit-riding Methodist minister, providing a direct line to both propriety and God the Father. Mother had always considered the Methodists to be somehow higher on the social scale, more refined than the openly hellfire-and-damnation-shouting Baptists. The intellectual superiority of the family had been borne out, in her view, when Huelet's brother George was made president of Mercer University in Macon, Georgia.

When I visited Macon and Mercer to give readings from my poetry, I, too, felt a twinge of pleasure as I pointed out to my Yankee lover the inscription of my dead uncle's name on the side of a building erected in his honor. Mother would have been pleased at my pride, though had she known the partly carnal nature of my visit, or the feminist content of the poems I had chosen to read, she would have recoiled in shame.

What Mother revered most—polite society, the Ten Commandments, and the written word—began for her in stories of her father's family. That her grandmother, the Methodist minister's wife, was a habitual snuff dipper was an incongruous detail omitted from her recollections. Even before she was born, Mother was destined, like all white Southern women of her generation, to an allegiance to patriarchy, to what was obviously male superiority.

It was an idea to which she clung for a lifetime, and the one that ultimately destroyed her.

The unknowing carriers of this cultural ideal, Lee Darnell and Huelet Connell, had grown up next door to one another in Villa Rica. Until her mid-twenties, as was the custom in staunch Southern families of Scotch-Irish descent, Lee had remained at home doing the family cooking, cleaning, and sewing along with her younger sister, Bunny.

A picture of Lee taken around that time shows a young woman standing beside the front gate of a white picket fence, her bearing dignified, her face inscrutable. Her hair, I have been told, was a fine pink-red—the color echoed today in that of my older daughter, Laura. Her eyes were—and still are at eighty-seven—a clear blue, her fair skin lightly freckled.

A head shot of Huelet around the same time portrays a boy-ish, curly-haired young man sporting the raw haircut and gaunt cheeks—almost as though he is sucking them inward—that seem typical of rural Southern men of the period. Yet with the bones, the curls, he is almost pretty—projecting a girlish delicacy that fits Mother's belief in his inherent gentleness and gentility.

When Lee and Huelet married, they moved to Leeds, Ala-bama, where he had a job with the Southern Railroad. It was 1915, and they began their family, as was customary, immedi-ately. The length of time each child nursed later served as a natural form of birth control, but at the beginning of conjugal life, there was no such protection. Mother—Melissa Ruth Con-nell—was soon born; within two years came Grace; and in two more, Florance.

Lee says that in spite of being a stranger in the small Alabama town, of giving birth at home with little or no anesthesia, of having no washing machine, air conditioning, or electric refrig-eration, she was content. "We didn't have an automobile—not many people did—but I wheeled the babies to the grocery store in their carriage, and sometimes we went somewhere on the streetcar. And there was church once a month, when the local circuit rider came."

After her young husband's sudden death, I envision her mov-ing pragmatically through her grief. The funeral behind her, she must have methodically gathered up the dresses, bloomers, undershirts she had sewn by hand for her three daughters, and the diapers that she washed by hand each day. Though it was common country custom at that time to hang the diapers with-out washing them, trusting to the sun to bleach out ammonia and urine, Lee undoubtedly washed those of her children. Al-ready, she was deeply imprinted with the stoic patience that was a necessary feminine virtue of her time. Ahead was the long train trip—her three youngsters and all their belongings in tow —back to Villa Rica.

Villa Rica was, and is, typical of many small towns throughout Georgia. Though there *are* towns known for columned mansions, live oaks dripping Spanish moss, magnolia-and-azalea-lined squares, Villa Rica is not one of those. Rather, it is a small community that pours as slowly as the regionally produced sorghum syrup along a stretch of dusty railroad track. There are the ubiquitous Baptist and Methodist churches, a few general stores, and the local drugstore.

Traveling, I've often run into such a pharmacy to ask—as local folk, lemon Cokes in hand, swivel necks and stools beside the soda fountain—for a box of Tampax or a tube of Crest; inevitably, too, the clerk's directions have led me among the narrow counters to a stack of boxes that met my fingertips through a grainy veil of red or gray dust. Inevitably, too, I would suddenly need proof of the continued existence of cities, and as I went out the door, would buy from the bright-yellow box a suddenly exotic *Atlanta Journal* or *Constitution.*

In such a town, even today, the silence of a Sunday afternoon, after the ritual of Sunday school and church, the midday meal of fried chicken, biscuits, and cream gravy, is impermeable, a blanket ruffled only by the rotation of the wooden fan inside the fly-specked drugstore, the occasional screech of tires of a car driven by a local teenager. (In rural Georgia every high school annual has a page dedicated to the "outstanding" senior who died in glory on the football field or was killed that year as he attempted to fly, instead of drive, his old Chevy over bumpy country roads.)

Though a half-hearted attempt at a shopping center, complete with Penney's and Sears, may today rise on the highway leading out of town, life revolved, and still revolves, around Sunday-morning and -evening services, Wednesday-night prayer meetings, Friday-night football games, and meetings of secret men's societies, such as the Elks or Masons. Family and personal pride is based not on lineage or achievement but on the regularity of one's church attendance and one's ability to abstain from drinking, smoking, and telling dirty jokes—all virtue a negation of vice!

It is a society that, for women, holds particularly rigid stipulations. If in Plains, Billy Carter enjoys the role of local bad, or "good ole," boy, the same behavior—belting six-packs of beer, hanging out at the local service station or pool hall—would be unthinkable for his wife. In the teachers' lounge of a consolidated county school where I was poet-in-residence for a week, I noticed that the teachers, mostly women, looked less rested, relaxed, unlined than the urban women I knew who slept less and worked harder. As a guest at a dinner for local teachers at the Holiday Inn, I sat across from the Methodist minister and ate dry roast beef and canned cream corn, washed down with the inevitable iced tea, as a visiting Baptist preacher intoned an anecdote about Sherwood Anderson:

" 'Mr. An-nerson,' he said to him, 'you may have written novels showin' the problems of small-town life in America—the narrowness, the bigotry—but sir, you've failed to show us the so-looshions!' " As he concluded his denunciation of artists and intellectuals—"Sherwood An-nerson may have been a great writer, but he was *not* a great man!"—his voice rose and fell with the evangelistic fervor I had heard since early childhood.

The eyes of the teachers—almost all women—widened: in Bremen, Georgia, the voice of the Baptist preacher is the voice of God. I amused myself by thinking what his response would have been had he known he not only had another unsavory writer in his presence, but a woman who wrote feminist poetry. Yet beneath my uncomfortable amusement, I felt sad. I had been in this town five days; these women never left a place where any unpopular action or assertion could wreck the structure of their lives.

"You do, and we'll run you out of town with a shotgun!" had been my stepfather's immediate, only half-joking response when I suggested, at the height of the women's movement, the instigation of a consciousness-raising group in the North Carolina town where he lived with Mother.

It was to an earlier and more rigid version of such a town that Lee traveled with her three daughters after Huelet's death. For two years, she changed diapers, sewed, washed, and ironed within her parents' house—two years broken only by thrice-weekly church services and the summer evenings when the family gathered on the porch to rock and talk till dark. (It is such endless evenings, such years of talk, that give Southerners—like a kind of verbal hope chest—a head start on a lifelong supply of anecdotes.) Occasionally, a churn filled with salty ice, fruit, cream must have been brought out, turns taken at its handle, until Lee or her mother dished out soup bowls full of home-made Georgia peach ice cream, full of delicious little crystals, juicy chunks of fruit. As a scene my sister, Anne, our numerous cousins, and I later repeated, it flashes before me clearly: Mother, Grace, Florance—perhaps a neighbor child or two—fighting over who would lick the icy dasher, then running with cold, full stomachs after lightning bugs, cupping them in palms or jars, stopping off and on to swing from the rubber tire hung from a great oak near the house, until Lee's voice, cutting the dark, called them in to bed.

When Mr. Carroll began to call, there must have been more of such social evenings. Manager of the Chattahoochee Mills near Atlanta, John Carroll was a widower who had already buried two wives and who had four near-grown children of his own. A man of appetites, energy, and power, he was also a reformed alcoholic. It was *his* brother, *his* nephew who shot themselves because of their fondness for drink. Three of his sons, assisted by "good" wives, repeated his pattern of dissolute youth turned hard-driving businessman and patriarch.

On those summer nights, the brawling, rough, overpowering Irishman must have appealed to the controlled young woman who was my mother's mother. She must have thrilled to the gifts with which he showered her—beaded purses, perfume, jewelry—and to their honeymoon trip by train to New Orleans. At seventy, she confided that she had loved him passionately, though it was a passion that would diminish with the responsibilities of a huge household.

By the time I was five or six, Grandmother Lee and Grand-daddy Carroll had moved from the two-story house near the

27

Chattahoochee Mills, from which Mother and her sisters had been driven to school each morning in the limousine. As far back as I can remember, they lived on a working farm in Tucker, outside Atlanta. Granddaddy Carroll had retired from business, bought the farm and much of the surrounding countryside.

There was an enormous one-story white frame house fronted by a verandah and hundreds of feet of lawn; another porch ran along one side of the house, which was organized around a long central hall off which branched broad, high-ceilinged rooms heated by huge fireplaces. Even the beds, the tall four-posters with their double mattresses, seemed extra high—hard for a six-year-old to climb onto. Spending the night, I was afraid to try the climb down, the trip to the bathroom far down the dark corridor, no matter how badly I had to go, and would lie numbly till morning, hoping not to wet my pajamas in my proper grandparents' house.

Out the back door, beyond the main house and the brief yard, was a red-dirt area through which wandered chickens, cats, turkeys, peacocks, dogs; it was bordered by the buildings of household management and farm production—storehouse, chicken house, washroom, curing room, tool shed, barns, and miscellaneous buildings. Behind the buildings began the vegetable gardens, the black people's houses, the cornfields, the railroad tracks, the peach orchard, the creek, and the endless sloping pastures.

Though I feared the snotty peacocks and the mean-eyed gobblers, I loved—in the beginning of an obsession with egg shapes —collecting the shit-smeared eggs from beneath the hens and —until one defecated on my Sunday dress, and the sickening lurch of conscience began—poking the genitals of the endless mewing kittens with twigs. Until I learned it was also full of fleas, I loved the long, cool milking barn with its fat red-and-white cows. When there was a new colt or calf, my cousins and I would chase and try to lasso it as it ran around the barnyard. Beside the barn proper was the hog pen, full of creatures who snorted vociferously as the slops from the kitchen were

28

splashed over the fence; when a sow gave birth, the piglets sliding from her hugely distended vagina looked like toys despite their coating of blood and slime.

I watched as my older, more courageous cousins jumped from the hayloft—which later became a fine place to smooch with my eleven-year-old cousin Bubba. In the storehouse, already in love with family history, I pored through musty boxes of love letters to Mother's half sister, Aunt Billie, from her boyfriend. One afternoon, I hung screaming to the neck of a horse as it galloped undirected up a path; on another, a cow galloped toward me full speed from a distance in the pasture: I barely made it beneath the barbed-wire fence, my new pink angora sweater shredded.

But until adolescence, the farm seemed to me a heaven more vivid, more appealing, than the silly singing, the streets of gold described by the Baptist preacher. Still, during the counterculture sixties, I was immune to the mystique of soap making, the romance of rural communes: unconsciously, I must have observed what the farm meant to Grandmother Lee. Those who have been farm wives rarely wish to go back to the "good old days." Today Lee enjoys her electric sewing machine, washing machine, convenience foods; but then the farm must have formed a kind of prison—inevitably, the sensuality of her chores was lost in their volume.

Spring was the time to plant the vast garden in which she grew the food for the main house. Summer meant canning—tomatoes, beans, field peas, okra, corn. I remember watching her pop the kernels off the cob in three sweet milky layers, her knife moving round and down, almost faster than my eyes could follow. Several vegetables were combined for "soup mix." She made peach preserves, blackberry jam, crab-apple jelly, and the pickles—bread-and-butter, sweet, dill.

Almost every day butter was churned—and churned and churned: a pound of butter could cost an hour of time and energy. Every day there were cows to be milked, hogs to be slopped, milk to be separated, eggs to be collected, chickens to be fed, chicken corpses to be scalded, plucked, eviscerated.

Daily, large meals were to be served: breakfasts included homemade "biscuit" (always referred to in the singular), fried fatback or pork brains, cream gravy, and grits. (When *she* was a girl, she told me, breakfasts meant fried chicken, too.) Promptly at noon on weekdays, Lee dished out "dinner"— chicken and dumplings, country ham or meat loaf, squash soufflé, pole beans, probably collard greens boiled with ham hock, more biscuit and corn sticks, and for dessert, perhaps blackberry cobbler or banana pudding (my first husband's grandmother made it in washtubs).

Sunday lunch—"dinner" again—was at one instead of twelve to allow for church, and was fancier: roast or fried chicken, cream gravy, white rice, canned English peas, perhaps a "salad" —red Jell-O in which hung black cherries, fruit cocktail, chunks of cream cheese, sliced bananas, or pecan halves—plus the ubiquitous dessert of cake or pie. As a child, I loved Sunday dinners at Grandmother Lee's—to stuff myself, then fall asleep on a high bed, until I woke at sunset, with cheeks drool-damp, imprinted by ridges of chenille, ready to chase lightning bugs or my cousins. But for Lee, the dinner had meant rising early—in summer, even on Sundays, the vegetables for the midday meal were to be picked each morning from the garden; the meal must be near-cooked before she could dress herself and the younger children for Sunday school and church.

In late fall, Lee worked overtime. As Thanksgiving and Christmas neared, she seemed continuously to bake: first the fruit cakes, from family recipes—white and dark (which, because of the family's commitment to Christian temperance, were kept wrapped in rags soaked in orange juice rather than the traditional bourbon). Then the layer cakes: Lane cake, thick with raisins and pecans; hickory nut, made from nutmeats laboriously excised from hardwood shells; coconut, made with tediously grated fresh coconut—sometimes her knuckles would abrade and bleed from the effort; lemon cheese, with its tart apple-thickened filling, its snowy-white boiled frosting; and my favorite, caramel, heavy with brown-sugar icing through which marched row after row of handshelled pecan halves. Besides the Bible and her Sunday-school text, Mrs. S. R. Dull's *Southern Cooking*, published in 1928, was the most important book in Grandmother Lee's life; it was her gift to me when I married the first time.

When the great days finally came, with the whole family—aunts, uncles, cousins, grandparents—collected, the feasts commenced with roast turkey (I always hoped it was the one that had rushed, beak aimed, at my bare legs in the yard); dressing (the Southern form of stuffing: not baked within the bird, but in large flat pans, like a savory bread); giblet gravy; sweet potatoes souffléed and stuffed into orange halves, the edges of which had been trimmed into Halloween teeth, and topped with a toasted marshmallow; freshly risen yeast rolls; and for an exotic touch, store-bought stuffed olives and canned jellied cranberry sauce. (When everything fresh was homegrown, what was canned, store-bought, was "fancy.") Besides the cakes and pies, by then decorously arranged on the sideboard, there was ambrosia, a juicy compote of oranges, cherries, coconut, pecans; and maybe a concoction called heavenly hash—a mixture of whipped cream, pineapple, cherries, pecans, and melted marshmallows. It was a cuisine that couldn't have been more carbohydrate-laden. (Years later, in New York, I was taken to dinner in Chinatown by a Chinese artist who hoped to please me with a special dessert: he had found a small watermelon stand and assumed that because I was from Georgia, such an end to our meal would make me feel at home, unaware that in the South, the melon is a snack, not to be confused with "dessert," which contains at least a half pound of white sugar, or "why-at-death," as a displaced Southerner in L.A. put it.)

Besides the production and cooking of food, there was the house to be cleaned, and clothes to be sewn—in addition to her own and her daughters' clothes, Lee made men's shirts and suits. Clothes were still scrubbed by hand on a washboard in a deep black pot heated over an open fire in the red-dirt-floored washroom, then dipped in tubs of thick boiled starch, hung out, and ironed. While Pearl, who lived "on the place," was there from seven to seven, along with occasional "outside" help (black women were often paid less than a dollar a day), the running of the household, with its rituals and necessities, was a seven-day-a-week, fifty-two-week-a-year job that held Lee—and more so, her black servants, who had to do the same jobs at home for their own families—captive.

It was a job that formed her character and attitudes, and her daughters' and granddaughters' idea of what it was to be a Southern woman of a certain class—that was, a woman of physical stamina and endless Christian stoicism. Grandmother Lee *was* the long-suffering Melanie, the Mrs. O'Hara who silently gave birth so as not to disturb a household that Mr. O'Hara instantly disrupted with bellows of pain at a splinter in his finger.

Like Mr. O'Hara and other good patriarchs, Granddaddy Carroll was responsible, paid the bills, but demanded that everything be done just so—the buttermilk into which he liked to dip his cornbread chilled to exactly the right temperature, the "pot likker," a greasy green soup left from the boiling of turnip greens, saved just for him; and as he grew older, the cases of "Co-Cola" to which he had become addicted kept at ready on the "back porch" (a kind of anterior entrance hall common to Southern farmhouses). Most of all, the children and grandchildren were to be kept out of his way as he read the Atlanta papers, or later, when cataracts had developed on his eyes, listened beside the radio for news of World War II. Their mutual young were Lee's responsibility, "to be seen and not heard," the ideal of child behavior. Like Mrs. O'Hara in *Gone with the Wind,* Lee referred to her husband as *Mr.* Carroll.

That her initial passion for him had not survived the years of caretaking was revealed in remarks about the diminishing sexual desire of women as they grow older. "The older you get, the more of a chore it is!" she said, shelling peas as she contradicted an article a daughter had just mentioned from *Good Housekeeping* (the nitty-gritty details of the "chore" were unmentionable, even among the initiated—or married—women). After the long years of her husband's senility and finally his death, she had no desire to remarry: "What? And have another old man to take care of?"

Otherwise, she only obliquely revealed to her daughters her ambivalence about her role. "I never let Melissa or the others help in the kitchen," she says; "they would have just been in the way. Besides, they would have plenty of *that* later. . . ." When her youngest daughter, Billie, married, the young couple, following a common Southern custom, lived in the parental house. When Billie became pregnant, Lee carried trays to her in bed —stewed chicken, scraped beefsteak, chicken broth, milk toast. It was as though Lee's aversion to the implications of motherhood had surfaced in the nine-month-long nausea of the daughter who had seen her work hardest.

Lee's daughters, in their beautiful handmade clothes, enjoying the benefits of a prosperous, if provincial, household, were the rural princesses she had never been. Yet it was she who knew and encouraged the importance of beauty and mystique as measures of feminine worth. As pragmatically, as consistently, as a Chinese mother who knows the value of bound feet in the marriage marketplace, she presented an image of self-restraint that neared self-immolation.

Her values—ladylike passivity, conservative good looks, and the ability to cook—were those she knew with a realistic cynicism to be those sought by the men who could give her daughters the most position and ease. Men who were "good husband material" had their own standards; and though she wouldn't have put it that way, Lee knew that they liked to fuck and eat and didn't want any flack.

If she was rigid in her delineation of proper behavior for her female young, it was a rigidity that seemed as necessary and contradictory as the voluntary infliction of pain by the Chinese mothers on their daughters; and her motivation was the same: she wanted safety for them. All her simplified instructions for the manipulation of men—"Don't let him kiss you until you're engaged. . . . Don't tell him too much about yourself. . . ."— were directed toward the enhancement of one's value as a marriageable object.

Today she wears blue pantsuits and pale-blue turtleneck sweaters that complement her silver-blue hair; but when she wouldn't let my cousins and me into her house with "those

33

pants" (blue jeans) on, she was trying to protect us from what she was sure was destructive behavior.

Though she had never been a princess, Lee seemed to me a queen. Granddaddy Carroll was the owner of most of the ramshackle houses in the local "nigger town." At eight or nine, I stood beside my grandparents on the back steps as the blacks came to pay their rent and ask advice. The obsequious way in which they spoke—"Yes'm, Miz Carroll; yesser, Maser Carroll" —made me feel my grandparents were royalty of sorts, instead of the country equivalent of slumlords.

My view was reinforced by my visits to the small unpainted frame house perched on stilts down in the far pasture. There Pearl and her husband, Homer, lived with their five young. Despite the coziness of the two rooms with their fireplace heat, Pearl's rich voice belting out gospel songs as she washed her own children's clothes, and the well out on the back porch into which I liked to let down the old tin bucket to magically raise cool, clear water and sometimes a tiny frog or two, I realized that the simplicity and warmth of Pearl's way of life, especially her outhouse, implied inferiority. From my perspective, it was as though she and her husband were children who had children. To be a *real* Southern woman was to be as responsible, as impenetrable, as unsmiling as Grandmother Lee.

That Mother worshiped, rather than merely loved or admired, her mother, Lee, was made clear to me at seven or eight. As Mother and I walked out to the pen in our backyard in Atlanta to feed our own chickens, she carried a pie pan of cornbread crumbs. She seemed preoccupied, as she often did when we were alone. I tugged her arm to get her attention—I had a wonderful insight, a gift: "Don't you think that Grandmother Lee looks just like a cow in a pasture?" I asked. I had made what I considered a flattering comparison, equating my grandmother's stoicism with the quiet eyes, the cud-chewing placidity of the cows in her pasture.

I looked at Mother hopefully, then pulled away, surprised:

34

her lower lip had already curled into the downward curve I knew preceded violence. Too late! I felt the stinging *whop* of her open palm against my cheek, heard the clatter of the corn-bread pan hitting the gravel. "Don't you evah talk about your grand-pay-rents that way!" she commanded, drawling out the long *a* she habitually inserted into certain words. Retrieving the half-spilled pan, she looked away—as though she had already forgotten my presence—and threw the rest of the crumbs over the fence into the chicken yard.

Neither Anne nor I ever heard our mother question her mother's values, criticize her, or behave any way but submissively toward her. Clearly, Mother considered Lee a model of perfection; within a perfectly patriarchal society, she was indeed the perfect matriarch—subservient, self-denying, self-controlled.

It was a model that for her lifetime, Mother would alternately attempt to evade and embrace. Through her "modern" marriage to Daddy, their urban early married life, and her small family, she sought to remain the little girl, the belle—to escape the pressures with which she had seen her mother deal.

In the last years of her life, remarried to a farmer as patriarchal as Granddaddy Carroll had been, she tried—reluctantly—to fulfill his expectations of summers spent canning beans and corn, hot biscuits for meals as extensive as those cooked by Grandmother Lee, and, most importantly, the consistent exhibition of the stoic temperament proper to a farm wife. In contrast to *her* mother's success, she must have been miserably aware of her own failure.

For Mother, her dream of writing must have meant transcendence of both roles—little girl and matriarch—but here she failed, too. Her fear of her own intelligence, her possible power —and what would surely be the subsequent loss of "love"—was too great. Wary of revealing her repressed rage, the conflicts that were a constant part of her inner life, she confined her writing to self-denigrating stories of struggles with home canning or reverential pieces about visiting male missionaries;

even in writing these, she worried obsessively about the response to them of her husband, her mother, the ladies in her garden club.

During the last years of her life, Mother became more and more girlish, whiny, childlike, until, as though her dependency had reached a depth of no return, she turned for a few weeks resigned, as transcendent as Lee had ever been—and killed herself.

When Mother was a small child, there was not much time—or precedent—for the nurturing of females. With her responsibilities, Lee could not have had much energy, even if she had had the desire, for cuddling or coddling. (Though later, when her only son was born, it did seem, magically, to appear.) "Melissa was always hanging on to my skirts," she said, "but I didn't have time to give her any special attention." Wistfully, she added, "I wish I had known how important it was. . . ." Mother told me how she had feared the entrance of John Carroll into a room, his great booming voice, the *shushing* of the little girls by Lee. She wanted, painfully, to cling to her mother. It was as though the sense of isolation we all share was experienced by her earlier, and continued more pronounced.

After Mother's death, Lee mentioned to me that around eleven or twelve, Mother had had a religious crisis: "Melissa had read in the Bible—you know, where it says you cain't be saved if you believe or think a certain thing—I forget what verse it is—" She fumbled in her failing memory, searching for the troublesome commandment. "Well, whatever it was, she thought she had done somethin' wrong in her thoughts. Of course she hadn't, a chile that age, but she thought she had, and worried and worried 'bout it, thought she would surely burn in hell and so on"—I shuddered, recalling my own teenage fears of literal hellfire—"till finely I sent her off to Billy's house in Macon. He was the Baptist preacher, you know, a *fine* man. Well, she stayed a week or two, 'n' when she came back, didn't say eny more about it."

36

Two pictures of Mother around that time—before she had become the giggling belle, the butterfly—capture on film her frustration. In one, the photographer appears to have snapped her unaware as she meanders down a dirt road in dirndl skirt and white anklets; her brooding sullen gaze focuses unseeingly on the earth near her feet. In the other, a dramatically petulant face is framed by masses of kudzu leaves.

It is the same gaze of cold rage and betrayal that I felt engraved on my own face until beyond adolescence—one borne out by pictures of myself. "Don't stick your lip out at me!" Mother would sneer while curling her own back angrily. "You're the stubbornest chile I evah saw!"

Had she been thinking of her girlhood self? Was I really her replica, as sullen and moody as she had been? Looking at the pictures and at Mother's resentful gaze, I recall the rehearsal of my seventh-grade play: I had been dismissed from the auditorium because of such an expression on my face.

By the time she was fourteen, Mother's roundly indented figure, her natural jet curls and eyes, her creamy magnolia-shaped face, became a picture of full-blown sulky or laughing beauty. She was a girl so pretty that an Atlanta photographer used her image in his shop window as advertisement of his craft.

Lee must have been relieved, certain at last that her erratic older daughter, with her hysterical giggles, her sobs that seemed suddenly to jet from some endless chasm, would be able to find a good man to take care of her; drawn by her lusciousness, held fast by his lust, he would agree to materially care for —with luck, even soothe and pamper—her for a proper Southern lifetime.

Melissa was a product with maximum potential; it made sense to groom her to the hilt. Her clothes, paid for by Granddaddy Carroll, were handmade by Lee and a local seamstress. Dressmaker coats echoed her tiny waist, her full hips. Soft crepe dresses flowed languorously across her plump breasts; scarves, pinned in place by cloth flowers, dripped from her collarbone.

Off-the-shoulder evening growns, bodices held by tiny straps, deep ruffles of ecru lace, clung to her creamy shoulders. Photographs reveal the kind of elegant details called "feminine"—stitched satin lapels, tiny covered buttons, ruching, ruffles, tucks. Dark silk hose, kid slippers that looked like high-heeled Mary Janes—voluptuously curved of heel, fastened by a single silk-covered sphere—emphasized her curvaceous calves, her size-five feet.

Despite her impression of plumpness, she was still smaller than Anne or me. A few months after her death, we each tried on her black velvet evening dress with its fitted bodice and slightly gathered skirt. Neither of us could zip it; nor could we fasten the curved Art Nouveau buckle, the wide mesh belt of sterling silver, circa Mother's sixteenth year. Only my daughter Darcy, with her own "close to the ground" figure, her natural dark curls so like Mother's, could fit into them, creating for a moment a dizzying likeness to the pictures we had spent the morning dividing. It was a likeness to her suicided grandmother that made Darcy quickly pull off the dress, run from the room; months later, I found her silently staring at the picture of Mother that stood framed on the top of my chest of drawers, then into the antique shaving mirror beside it.

In the photograph in which Mother wore these romantically seductive clothes, her complexion is a perfect, if papery, magnolia cream; her cheeks and lips an unnatural Tangee pink, echoing the pink roses she inevitably holds in her arms. Dressed for a dinner or tea dance, she sits still, suspended in time. But even dressed in her school clothes—chemises, middy blouses, pleated skirts—animated and laughing, she is as sexily juicy, a perfect peach, a vamp. "The prettiest girl at Fulton High School," we were told over and over.

Fulton High School was the central-Atlanta school to which students commuted from all over the city and outlying communities. "She could have had any boy she wanted," our aunts told us, emphasizing her choice of our dissolute, if handsome, daddy. Each day Mother and her sisters rode the River car to classes. In Atlanta streetcars of the 1930s, the wicker seats could be slid forward to face the seats behind them. Did the boys jostle and show off, struggling for the seats near her? I can see her holding court among the "popular" boys and girls who were her friends, hear again the giggle that grew more pronounced, more foolish, as she grew older and more disconnected: the giggle of a pretty vivacious girl who thoughtlessly gossiped—with an occasional curl, even then, of her lip—behind a small hand on which the nails were already tinted pink and filed to the points she liked. As the yearbook stated, she was "pretty, popular, and good-natured"—and undoubtedly accepted her good fortune as her due.

At sixteen, she was swamped with young men, more than she could handle. She claimed to have had six dates each weekend. "I had a date on Friday night, then one on Saturday afternoon for tennis or a movie, and a date on Saturday night. Then on Sunday, one boy would take me to church, another for a drive in his daddy's automobile in the afternoon, and I would get home just in time for my date for church that night." At fifty, she still craved the kind of excitement she must have had then. It was as though an addiction to a certain kind of male attention had begun an inevitable course. For the rest of her life, in whatever group or situation she found herself, she would defer to the men around her. Yet there was no reason during that time for her to believe that any of her fantasies—the handsome blond lawyer, the house with columns, the life of self-indulgence—would fail to come true. She had no way of knowing that she was one of those women whose life would peak in the blaze of high school popularity, that her reign held within it the very seeds of her exile, her eventual self-destruction.

Yet within a year after high school graduation, Mother was back home from Georgia State College for Women in Milledgeville. A hundred and twenty long country miles away, cut off from her sisters, her girl friends, her beaus, she had suffered her first long-term depression. In spite of the beauty of the town of Milledgeville, with its Spanish moss–draped live oaks, magnolia-lit avenues, antebellum mansions, and air of a past century—the giggling girls from small towns all over the state, and the forbid-

39

den glimpses of the boys from the military school across the way —she had spent most of her year eating and crying. Even plumper from the institutional food, her taste for costume frustrated by the required school uniform, she had had only one social visitor during the year. Boys were not allowed to visit, even for a Sunday afternoon, without written parental permission; after Lee had transcribed the proper note, Calvin, a high school beau, had driven the two hours to Milledgeville in his newly acquired Ford automobile. For an hour, they sat in the stiff parlor with other girls and their visitors. But Mother must not have given him much encouragement, or else he may have decided the trip was too long to be worthwhile; back in Atlanta, he was soon engaged to Mother's freckle-faced younger sister Grace.

During that year, she cried so much from homesickness that Lee agreed that she didn't have to go back after summer vacation. But back at home, she was a belle out of her element; her high school court had dissipated; she was a useless component in a well-run household of younger children, busy mother, uninterested stepfather.

By leaving college, she had given up her chance at the respectable profession of teaching. It was a move she always regretted. After years as a clerk-typist—when I had already been married three times, had had three children, and had begun to publish poems and magazine articles—she begged me, if she died, to take whatever money she might leave me to go to the University of Georgia to get a B.A. in journalism. Her regard for credentials was a part of the passivity with which she had early been inculcated. "Being a Southern belle is like being popcorn with no salt, a pizza waiting to be taken home . . . ," wrote one of my students. She might have been describing Mother, who, intimidated by the professors and "smart" girls, had never dared voice her ambition of becoming a writer. (Writer Flannery O'Connor, at the same school, had not been the beauty Mother had been, yet had had more motivation toward achievement. Not allowed to graduate till she had completed her white home-ec. apron, she had made the apron—but, also, aprons for six baby ducks that followed her around the campus. Today the college has a room dedicated to her manuscripts.)

Sensibly, Mother had taken shorthand and typing; but a nine-to-five job must have seemed a dreary alternative to marriage. The clothes, the parties, and her mother's dictum that "you are who you marry" had become imperatives for the immediate future. It was time to look seriously for the man who could replace the gentle father she had lost.

In 1934, Mother was the Sweetheart of Sigma Nu at the University of Georgia in Athens. The rotogravure supplement of *The Red and Black* shows her smiling in a dress that looks as though it has a white lace fichu; on the same page are Miss Dixie Dunbar of Chi Theta and Atlanta, and Miss Margaret Mitchell of Sigma Chi and Griffin, Georgia. Sigma Nu was Daddy's fraternity, and it was because she was *his* sweetheart that she had been so named.

When Mother and Daddy met, they were ready for "love"— the kind of love described in the songs played by their favorite band leader, Guy Lombardo. Though they had long known of one another—Daddy, an "older man," was the brother of a high school classmate—the combustion didn't take place until Mother was eighteen, Daddy, twenty-four, and they met again on Atlanta tennis courts.

I see Daddy leaping over the net, agile in his tennis whites; over this, an image in which he stands before a bandstand: as he mouths his saxophone, his black eyes close in sensuous pleasure. It is 1934, the midst of the Depression, not long past the time of *The Sheik*—he is dark, Valentino-handsome. (Years later, when I bought a crumbling copy of the romance from a Woolworth's sale counter, I wondered why—until I realized with a wrench that the dashing Arab of the cover, flicking his whip at the haunches of his rearing white horse, brought back my father's early voluptuous beauty.)

Charismatic, ambitious, he has worked his way through the University of Georgia by selling magazine subscriptions, has his

41

own band, and belongs to the same fraternity as Herman Talmadge. And though he isn't blond, a lawyer, doctor, or minister, he plays on his saxophone Mother's favorite dance tunes; his best friend, Claude, has had privately printed a small blue volume of verse; and he has a fine Scotch-Irish, even aristocratic, name—Parker McDonald Hughes. Too, he has a sense of humor—when he invites Mother to a dance, he addresses the envelope to "Mr. Bukowski's Former Girl Friend." Best of all, he has declared her the most beautiful girl he has ever seen, the girl of his dreams—that he wants nothing more in life than to care for her forever!

In a picture taken outside his fraternity house, Daddy wears a dashing felt hat, brim turned jauntily back from his face; his full-lipped mouth seems slightly to tremble. Mother, in her dressmaker coat and satin-faced cloche, has her arm possessively through the elbow that he juts forward. His gaze toward the camera is proud, solemn; hers is pensively radiant; each is triumphant. "Being a Southern boy is like having a dream," wrote another of my students; "a Southern girl is like someone in a Southern boy's dream." Daddy has the belle he has dreamed of; Mother, the promising, appreciative husband-to-be.

Her dreams, garnered from the romantic novels she favored —and not so different from mine fifteen years later—seemed destined for fulfillment. Gone would be the dark moods, the alienation, the tears of longing for the father she had never known. Life with "Donald," as his friends called him, would be one long dance, tennis game, fraternity party, diffusing gradually into the soft focus of babies, cozy meals, the perfect house —the two motifs unified by perpetual kisses and laughter.

How could she foresee that his charisma verged on that of the con man, that the achievements of his college days would become staples, along with boasts of the men he could buy and sell, of dinner-hour ravings that would end only when his face fell into the fried chicken or country steak and gravy she had prepared after her forty-minute bus ride home from her job as a typist in Atlanta. (When they finally separated, after my first marriage at sixteen, Daddy visited a psychiatrist *once*—a visit that concluded with the therapist buying a set of tires from him, then giving him the couch in his office.)

Indeed, how could either know, at the moment in which the tremulous picture was made, that the other was already consumed, eaten away from within, by deficiencies that would keep each forever from giving the total love and nurturing the other needed for survival. Mother didn't know—and probably wouldn't have believed—that Daddy, noticeably sharing his mother Annie's Cherokee blood, was the literal black sheep of his family. Annie profoundly preferred his blond and dimpled younger brother, Bud; the passive, soon-to-pass-away postmaster who was his father had been so depleted by the demands of his imperious wife, the material needs of his family, that he had little to pass on, either materially or emotionally, to his older son.

In certain parts of the Deep South, whole trees, houses, acres are occasionally swallowed by a geological weakness just beneath the earth's surface known as a limestone sinkhole. It is a phenomenon I sometimes think of when I recall my parents' early naïveté. Mother was unaware that Daddy, like herself, was a physically beautiful and intelligent person of sturdy background who, ironically, was as emotionally bankrupt as the eroded red dirt of South Georgia farm country, that each of them ultimately embodied the self-romanticized and self-deluded Southerners described in the works of Faulkner, personified in the life of Zelda Fitzgerald. Neither dreamed that the skeins of their idealized passion would rapidly weave them into a net of mutual self-destruction. Instead, theirs was the courtship of two handsome and promising young people who were made for each other.

It was an illusion of perfect happiness that for a time was maintained. After their elopement, they moved into a garage apartment on Lucille Avenue in West End, a then-fine-old section of Atlanta. Despite the mid-Depression, Daddy had a good job—twenty-five dollars a week at Campbell's Coal Company. In nine months or less, I was born, and named Rosemary after the heroine in the trashy romance Mother was currently reading. My first memories were of the black-and-white puppies in our backyard, and the family of black children who lived beyond the back fence; my parents seemed always to be laughing.

Carried to the terrace or garage apartments of other young married couples, or bachelors from Daddy's fraternity days, I felt glamorous and grown-up in my sunsuits and white high-topped shoes. At neighborhood movies, I sat securely wedged between them—baby-sitters were unknown. At Peacock Alley, their favorite drive-in eating spot, they shared with me a concoction called Hot Fudge Shortcake. At home, too, we enjoyed high-calorie dishes; besides fried chicken and baked sweet potatoes bathed in a pool of margarine, we had sautéed bananas and Spanish pork chops. For a provincial belle, Mother was an imaginative cook who favored the use of oleo and Crisco.

By the time Anne was born when I was five, pictures showed my parents to be two overly nourished, though still-handsome, young people with plump cheeks; it was a plumpness that foreshadowed the puffiness of later years. Six weeks after Anne was born, a friend asked Mother, "Haven't yew had thet baby yet?" She still weighed 186 pounds, 60 pounds above her normal weight, though Anne had weighed only 5. It was an anecdote she told in later years, equating her fullness, her weight, with that brief period of fullness of spirit.

Despite my early memories of the three of us caught in euphoric tableaus, Mother later told me that she had known something was wrong on their honeymoon. As she had listened to a Sunday-night revival meeting on the car radio, Daddy had abruptly snapped it off. The intensity of his response had seemed out of proportion to the ordinary stimulus of a preacher's voice ranting of hellfire and damnation. Indeed, it had been a puzzling reaction in a young man who, like herself, had been brought up in a devout Bible Belt family—though his adamant refusal to discuss his reasons for it was the usual Southern male response to any question raised by an uppity woman.

It was its implications that made the event significant. What if the new husband Mother had thought so ideal did not *believe*? That flaw alone would indicate a Pandora's box out of which could catapult a dozen others, thrusting her not into the life of the pampered Southern wife, but that of one married to a "no good" man, a woman who must make up through prayer and piousness for the sins of her dissolute spouse. It was a role that prescribed that she *never* give up on his salvation, that a bad man can and should be saved by a good woman. At some point—possibly during her crisis of guilt at eleven or twelve—she had decided that alienation from God the Father (or was it patriarchy?) was a psychic separation too painful to again be risked. Yet as a married woman, half of one flesh, her husband's faith was as essential as her own; and she was responsible for that of both. It was a view that would sap her energies for the rest of her life: if she had been good enough, she was convinced until she died, Daddy would have been better.

Ted Hackett, an Atlanta psychotherapist who also practices in rural areas outside the city, observes that Southerners tend to determine behavior by a fixed set of ethics rather than by feeling or relationship. ("Why did you shoot your neighbor's dog?" "Because he peed on mah bushes." "You were angry because he peed on your bushes?" "Nope, just shot 'em 'cause he peed on mah bushes.") Like most Southerners, Mother had rigid ideas about the way things *ought to be*; yet if her fantasy of perfection had been realized and maintained, would she have retained her fragile sanity?

My picture of her life, of my parents' life together is one of extremes of happiness or degradation, placidity or hysteria. At times, reality met the standards set by her fantasies: Mother laughed, the sun shone. When reality failed, the sky opened, hysteria deluged, as though it had been waiting just beneath the sunny surface. For a long time, I felt that her craziness, their misery together, had begun the moment of my birth.

Why else would my beautiful young mother want to kill me?

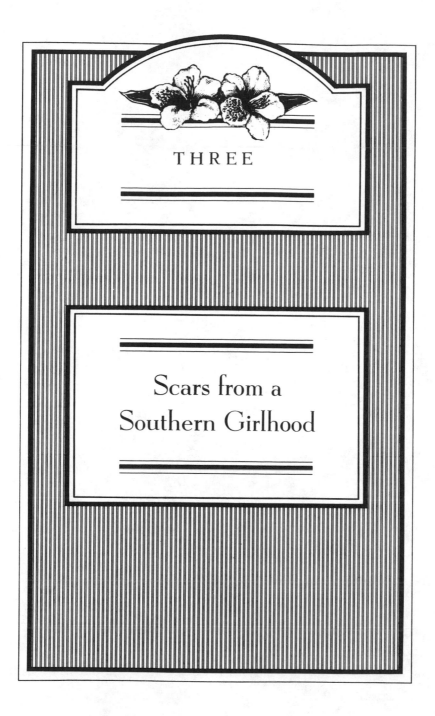

THREE

Scars from a
Southern Girlhood

We now live in a garage apartment on Oak Street. I'm three years old, lying on my back in the big bed in Mother and Daddy's room. Mother has just removed my panties, my last protection; my wrists are tied with something thin, gauzy, yet strong—Mother's precious nylons?—to the headboard of the bed.

My fat thighs burn, forced, knees bent into the air; my ankles are held viselike by Mother's best friend, Virginia, who looks, to my humiliation, at my most private parts, who now smiles as Mother approaches holding high some strange device—red rubber, metal, hose, tube—as Mother thrusts the blunt black end of it toward my exposed bottom, as, though I writhe, thrash, scream, beg her not to kill me, she pushes it into my recoiling flesh.

Yet worse than the invasion of my body is the look on Mother's face: there is no softening at my fear, rather a smirk of pleasure; her upper lip curls above a strange smile, a grimace. As my whole lower body cramps around some strange hot invasion, some animal loss of control, as I scream, "Mama, Mama, don't!" she and Virginia laugh.

Now, in this moment, I understand: never in my life will my mother be moved by my pain or fear, no matter how great it might be, that she is not only willing to watch me tortured in any way, but if necessary, to do it herself.

Even during the years of the Hot Fudge Shortcakes, the black-and-white puppies, the walks to Peachtree Street to buy the chocolate marshmallow hearts that only cost a penny, there was something dark, erratic beneath Mother's sunniness. The plump and pretty housewife, holding me on her lap as she sat in a lawn chair and gossiped with a girl friend, the round-faced young mother, laughing with me at the cartoons at the local picture show, gave hints of being another less friendly being.

49

I had been given a book of Victorian verses, complete with illustrations designed to make children behave. Mother read and reread to me a particularly scary one of a girl burning to death while playing with matches: on the opposite page, an etching showed a skinny girl in a long dress going up in flames. As I sobbed, she giggled. At other times, precedents of the slap in the chicken yard, her upper lip would suddenly curl downward into the snarl that would later become so familiar, yet was always so like seeing a cockroach emerge from the center of a perfect magnolia, and her palm—for reasons my toddler mind couldn't fathom—would crash against my cheek or thigh or ass in an explosion that was followed by a time when her face became vacant, as though she was no longer there with me at all.

I did not know, as a child, that my mother was crazy, or, as I now understand, mad with her own contradictions; like Florence King's Southern belle, she was supposed to be "frigid, passionate, sweet, bitchy, and scatterbrained—all at the same time." Worse, it was imperative that she be as stoic as *her* mother, Lee, and at the same time deal with a husband as crazy as she was. It was simply that, at moments, she became a person I feared. The first and most painfully recalled of these was the one on the bed; it may have been the instant when my image of the embedded penis, of something within me that needed to be routed, was born.

For the next five or six years, or until I began to run screaming from the house when I saw her approach with her hands held behind her back, the enema look on her face, her perineal assaults, or what seemed her assaults, continued. My fear of them never abated, and this seemed to add to her determination; when force was needed, Daddy, looking as though he wished he was elsewhere, was called in.

Once, walking along the sidewalk in my white high-top shoes —I must have been four or five—I heard a younger child screaming from a nearby house. I wondered if she was undergoing the same torture, if this was something all mothers—no matter how nice, how kind they seemed—did to their children in secret or in collaboration with one another. If this was the case, it was truly an invasion against which there could be no protection.

When I was eight, this theory seemed borne out. At Lee's farm, I ate too many green apples. The local doctor was called in, and as my grandmother, my visiting aunts and uncles, and my parents stood around the high bed, I was given what amounted to a public enema. To me, it felt like public rape, the ultimate humiliation, the full cooperation of other adults in a form of torture I had still half hoped was private to Mother. The doctor, I recall, gave me a stick of spearmint gum in an effort to stop my screams; he must have been puzzled at the extremity of my response.

Through my terror and shame, I was most conscious of Mother's eyes: did she enjoy seeing this happen to me in front of others? She in no way appeared disturbed—yes, there was that faint smirk playing about her lips. She looked at me as though she alone knew the secret of my inner malignancy.

A year later, Mother, Daddy, Anne, and I visited the Cancer Victim. Aunt Mary was the wife of one of Mother's stepbrothers; as young, almost as pretty as Mother, she lay dying.

Like many Southern women, Mother had a morbid enthusiasm for the details of physical mutilation (particularly those related to "female trouble"); a straightforward interest in sexuality, which was taboo, was displaced in favor of a fascination with bizarre conditions and surgical details (and sometimes crime and murder: my first mother-in-law kept hidden beneath her mattress a collection of detective magazines, the covers of which inevitably depicted a woman in underwear, bound, and perhaps bloody).

Mother didn't hesitate to describe these conditions in graphic detail. I had recently heard her tell Daddy at the supper table about a man who had fallen backward on a " 'Co-Cola' bottle— it went right up his rectum!" Now, on the way to Aunt Mary's, I heard her say brightly, "They had to cut out the wall between her vagina and rectum."

Playing with Anne's curls in the backseat, wrapping and rewrapping them between my fingertips, I imagined my aunt's—and Mother's, Anne's, my own—lower body as a gruesome cavity, a cloaca, less clean than the single opening in the corpses of chickens into which I liked to stick my fist.

When I was in high school, a classmate, dressed in a matronly bed jacket thick with cheap lace, lay dying of cancer; my girl friends and I, dumb with the enormity of her situation, our first sense of our own mortality, took her an orchid corsage. As though she were going to a prom with Jesus instead of to her death, she weakly pinned it on the shoulder of the bed jacket and thanked us.

Now, as we arrived at Aunt Mary's house, we found her propped up in bed with a white nightgown that would have befitted a bride. But my once round-faced aunt had become a caricature of herself, as skeletal as the survivors of Dachau I had seen in a newsreel at the picture show. Though she was as smiling and ladylike as a hostess at a tea (I think now how trying the Southern insistence on appearances must have been for her), she barely resembled the pretty woman I recalled. As mother complimented her on her gown, as she declared "How Rows-may-ree and Anne have grown!" I glimpsed the loathed enema bag hanging in the bathroom. On the way home, I heard Mother saying to Daddy that she thought the cancer had developed because Aunt Mary had been in the habit of taking enemas.

Something dreadful clicked in my head: my aunt lay dying because of enemas like those Mother had forced on me. *She really had been trying to kill me!*

I was learning that she wished to kill other parts of me, too. Walking down the street with her at nine, I confided my secret ambition of fulfilling my passion for cats, horses, most mute creatures by becoming a veterinarian. Quickly, the lip curled: "What? And spend the rest of your life giving enemas to dogs?" Dogs, she knew, were *not* my favorite animals, being the natural enemy of the cats I loved; and enemas had become the symbol of her intimidation and control of me.

I never again considered becoming a vet—the fantasy had died, writhing nauseously, in the moment of her comment. The acceptable dreams were of becoming like her, a housewife and mother, and maybe a writer—*her* frustrated ambition—for the society pages of the *Atlanta Journal* or *Constitution.* She had guessed my thrust toward autonomy, my wish for another kind of life, and sought to rout it. Yet somehow—like slave to her mistress, victim to her torturer—I had been magnetized, her lover and ally.

Daddy, as Mother obliquely and continually indicated, was too weak to warrant my infatuation or respect. After a brief and flashy success, with his picture in the business section of the *Atlanta Journal-Constitution,* he was failing in his job as sales manager for the Atlanta tire company. It was a career that demanded competitiveness and charm; at home, there was little sign of the charismatic salesman, the romantic lover, the practical joker; though he was, if not too drunk, a Southern gentleman. He insisted Anne and I call Mother *Mother* instead of *Mama,* wouldn't let us use words like *kids*—"baby goats?" he would snort—and prided himself on never saying *damn.*

By 1941 or 1942, he had been turned down by the navy because of hemorrhoids. Working in his Victory garden, hitting a few golf balls around the miniature course he had built in the backyard, he seemed impotent, powerless. Double-chinned on Mother's cooking and booze, he was an overripe gigolo, a Valentino gone wrong. Through Mother's accusations, I learned that he was gambling away most of the money he made or borrowed. Using the traditional Southern woman's means to change, she nagged, whined, and had increasingly shrill hysterics. Daddy, in turn, emerged more and more often from the garage or bathroom with Calvert's Reserve on his breath, a weave to his step.

He had become my and Mother's mutual enemy; the family had divided into two camps—Mother and me, Daddy and Anne. I had learned to expect Mother's aggressive, if often brutal, attentions; Daddy's passivity, agitated by his drinking, felt like rejection. That *he* might read my alliance with Mother as rejection of *him* was a connection I was not yet equipped to make. In the second grade, I went without lunch to buy candy animals to decorate his birthday cake; when he came home drunk and failed to notice my gift, love hardened. When I realized he preferred my sister, Anne, it turned to rigor mortis.

Five years and a month after my birth, I was out on the sidewalk learning to roller-skate; it was the day after Christmas, and I was holding the arm of the uniformed young nursemaid who had mysteriously appeared a few hours earlier. An ambulance turned off Peachtree onto our street, then into the drive of our terrace apartment. Within minutes, I saw Mother—white beneath a white sheet—carried by stretcher into the rear of the vehicle.

Two weeks later, she reappeared with the screaming five-pound creature who, I was told, was my sister, Anne. The ambulance and the long hospital stay, I learned later, were because the birth had been placenta previa, and Mother had hemorrhaged.

I was numb with betrayal when I learned that Mother would share my room with the ugly thing, while I would sleep in the big bed with Daddy. She had had Daddy place the white painted crib—the heirloom from Lee's house that had first been mine—beside my narrow bed. There was also a small new table, covered with strange utensils—among them, a similar but smaller device with which to penetrate the baby's body in the same place where she had so often penetrated mine. Like me, the baby screamed as she did so; but this time, *I* watched, a collaborator, horrified, humiliated for the baby's sake—yet strangely jealous that this time it wasn't me.

My parents were typical Southerners of a certain type—feelings, impulses were paramount, motivations were rarely questioned, introspection and intellectualization did not exist. As I lay in bed with Daddy each night, I felt nauseous, anxious, as he pulled my small body toward him, spoon-fashion. Was this the way he held Mother? I had seen him put his hand between Mother's legs, beneath her housedress, as she cooked in the kitchen; she had slapped it away, but had laughed a funny laugh. "Donald!" she had said, as though she wanted him to stop, but really didn't. Now he put his big brown hand between my thighs, fondled me in a way that I felt must be my fault somehow, just as Mother's enemas surely were.

During a therapy session years later, I bounced my hips on the floor of a carpeted room in a bioenergetics exercise designed to release, along with sounds, the images of the unconscious; suddenly, I heard my own voice—as though outside me, yet coming from some place deep within—crying, "Daddy, Daddy, don't!" Simultaneously, I flashed waking in the middle of one of those nights: a sharp sting, then some kind of blackened screen. Had all my genital orifices been penetrated by my impulsive and frustrated parents by the age of five?

In Cabbagetown, a section of Atlanta settled by Appalachians who came down from the hills to work in the cotton mill in the 1930s, I recently spoke with a blonde girl of nineteen or twenty who sat on her daddy's lap while her pale baby played on the dirty floor. Incest, in the rural South, as elsewhere, is not unknown. Yet, clearly, such caresses by Daddy were invasion, overstimulation. After all, as he so often told us, he *was* a college graduate.

And what of Mother's enemas? As her daughter, I was dependent on her—so dependent that I was in the habit of telling her everything I planned to do, from going to the bathroom to eating all the grits on my plate. She *was* my mother, and I had grown to love her; yet because of the sexual nature of her attentions, there seemed something shameful in that love.

Long into adulthood, in a reaction to my own incestuous feelings, Mother's body seemed to me rotten, unclean; the sight of it revolted me. Because our house was small, and neither she nor Daddy put much stock in modesty, it was hard to avoid seeing her undressed. I was repulsed at the sight of her vulva, which hung too open—a wound. Regardless of how slender she was, her belly had an independence of protuberance that reminded me too much of my origins; her breasts, drooping softly, unassertively toward it, clearly recalled her impotence. (Anne

55

says she felt the same way. Do daughters who find their mothers' lives too excruciating to view as a role model find physical identification as uncomfortable?)

Yet, like the victim of rape, *I* felt guilty; I tried to tell myself, as Mother told me, that what she did to me was for my own good, "a normal part of growing up." But the shame I feel years later indicates that the enemas were indeed traumas. After three decades I would experience a reactivation of my original humiliation when a patriarchal male therapist would accuse me before a marathon therapy group of having solicited, as a three-year-old, such attentions from my parents. His assertions would be my first realization of how blame is placed on the victim as a means of keeping her from recognizing her victimization.

Anne, a victim to a lesser degree of the same treatment, became a nurse as an adult; though it may have been a conventional treatment of children during that time, she could see no medical reason for our forced bowel movements. In any case, my experience of them was subjective, as is that of all children who experience any form of physical aggression or brutality beyond their understanding. An Atlanta man of my age told me of having been given daily massive doses of castor oil; he had been as confused as a child as I had, given to masturbating at his desk at grammar school; at ten, fucking his sister in an overstuffed chair as they listened together to "The Lone Ranger" on the radio. Ironically, our mothers—who had known one another at Fulton High School—had both been "belles." Yet at sixty, one had ended up in prison on a manslaughter charge of killing a child on a sidewalk with her Cadillac while drunk; the other, at the same age, a suicide.

Were Anne, my man friend, and I simply victims of frustration turned outward, an overprotectiveness that rapidly became aggression? In the South, verbal confrontation is to be avoided at all costs; the sensuality of the landscape easily turns anger into sexual acting out.

Yet when I was older, and had become interested in literature, Mother became indignant at the mention of authors who had portrayed the South as unhealthy or deviant. She found the

56

works of Erskine Caldwell, William Faulkner, and Flannery O'Connor, with their allusions to incest and strange sexual alliances, insulting to our region. Yet inconsistency and ambiguity are natural to the Southern mind; for both Anne and me, the enemas—forced upon me, endured more passively by her— continued until I was nine or so. Sometimes even Daddy was given them. As a child, I felt sick as I heard them talking: Mother's suggestion, Daddy's acquiescence, their going into the bathroom together, the closing of the door. Our house was small; we could hear sounds that were sexual rather than medicinal—or that at least sounded the same. I felt humiliated, yet my genitals tingled strangely. It was a feeling of shame that, for years, was activated in me by any allusion to the sexual—a shame that during my teens, agitated by normal sexual awakening and Bible Belt guilt, would cause me the same kind and degree of obsessive anxiety Mother had experienced during her pubescent "religious crisis."

Anne says that at eight or nine, she found an enormous red rubber dildo in the vegetable bin in our kitchen. For me, discovering a picture postcard of a little boy with a huge projecting penis in the top drawer of Daddy's dresser, coming upon Daddy's Trojans or Mother's diaphragm (what part of the body could it fit!?), or having Daddy tell me, as I put cream onto my hands from a strange new tube in the bathroom, "Don't use that —it's for something else," hinted of an unseen, yet spreading, decay.

It was a rot that seemed to be eating out all parts of family life. Mother's once-lovely trousseau lingerie—satin step-ins, slips, gowns deep in ecru lace—had become a mess of spreading holes, ripped lace, stretched elastic, held together as often as not by one or more safety pins. Worse, she couldn't or wouldn't buy new. Money was disappearing: Calvert's Reserve and Virginia Gentlemen bottles seemed to be reproducing themselves in the clothes hamper, the tool box, between the newspapers stacked on the back porch. When Mother tearfully grilled Daddy, he answered as evasively as he had about the revival meeting they had heard on the radio during their honeymoon.

More and more often, I heard their voices deep into the night —hers teary, his slurred. When certain subjects arose—money, religion, Mother's parents—Daddy's passivity exploded momentarily into what seemed like programmed anger.

By the time I was seven, my image of my parents as beautiful, laughing—if often cruel—people was changing. A picture of the four of us—Daddy in a lawn chair with baby Anne on his lap, Mother adrift on a chaise longue, me standing beside her, thin, straight, solemn in my sunsuit—shows a young man puffy with advancing alcoholism, a plump, uncertainly smiling young housewife. It is as though their edges, along with their assets, were dissolving.

I hold myself straight, solemn, apart from the others, already aware that our small family, our unit, is marked from within by something dark, fetid, unhealthy. The holes in Mother's once-luxurious lingerie, her tears at night, Daddy's hidden whiskey bottles indicate and symbolize it, whatever "it" is—a family dis-ease that surely is the reason for the enemas and all the rest, which later in life I would come to think of as being as typically Southern as the smell of a paper mill, or the chickens that hopped headless and bloody in Grandmother Lee's yard.

I'm standing at the top of the stairs at E. Rivers Grammar School with Gail Brown. We're both in the fifth grade; our mothers have known one another since high school. Gail is elegant, slender, with long brown braids; her mother is calm, wears a French twist, and plays the piano. Like most girls at E. Rivers, Gail is a snob: whenever I go to her house, she asks me whether I think the dormer makes it look two-story. Now she is asking me to go home with her after school. I suddenly remember my torn cotton panties, held up at the gaping waist by a giant safety pin. What if we go into the bathroom together, or she wants to play doctor? I can't today, I answer reluctantly.

A belle brought up to be beyond such things, Mother paid little heed to the advice that one should "always wear nice underwear in case of an accident." (Years later, trudging home from her second bus, her seventh year as a government typist, she was hit from behind by a car, her pelvis broken, and was rushed to the hospital in what I imagine to be her usual torn undergarments.) When she was a girl, her handmade clothes had been taken care of by the ubiquitous colored help. Now, because of her nightly harangues with Daddy, her new job as clerk-typist, and her everlasting job as cook and housewife, she had little time or energy for seeing to my clothes and Anne's. As the first day of school, Christmas, or Easter neared, we might be bussed downtown for a new dress from the basement of Davison's department store, or a new pair of oxfords or Mary Janes from Butler's shoe store. Otherwise we, like Mother, wore homemades, hand-me-downs, and underwear full of spreading holes. It was as though we had inherited from her a fungus that caused them to disintegrate from within.

At ten, I was sure that the condition of my underwear was obvious through the X-ray vision of my more prosperous classmates. After Anne was born, Lee and Granddaddy Carroll had loaned Mother and Daddy money for the down payment on a house. A home of her own had long been Mother's dream. But instead of the columned antebellum house she had imagined as a girl, they bought what they could afford—a five-room frame, set, ironically, as far back from the road as the mansion she had fantasized. Peachtree Street divides Atlanta north to south, with the more prestigious addresses clustering toward the northwest end; our house was in an upwardly mobile neighborhood on the northwest side of Peachtree. Though on a street of relatively modest homes, it was not a mile from Peachtree Battle Avenue, site of many of the most elegant houses in the city.

I was to attend E. Rivers Grammar School, on the corner of Peachtree Battle and Peachtree streets. It was a central school for the affluent side of the Coca-Cola–dominated town. Years later I met other alumni—James Dickey, poet and novelist, and Venable Herndon, screenwriter and biographer of James Dean —and was amazed to find them relatively unscathed. Brent, a beautiful postdebutante and mother of four, whom I met two decades later, had grown up in a columned manse down the street. It was one of the houses I resentfully passed as I walked home on the frequent days when I missed the bus.

My classmates at E. Rivers lived in the fancy houses Mother had dreamed of—sprawling two- and three-story mansions, and sometimes modernistic monsters. They had butlers and maids in starched gray uniforms, kept horses in the country, and had parents who belonged to the Piedmont Driving Club, the prestigious WASP club across the street from Margaret Mitchell's house. *Their* mothers *led* the life Mother had dreamed of. Brent told me that she had never seen her mother, a Southern princess who was said never to have made a negative statement, cook a meal, though she *had* occasionally seen her warm leftovers on the maid's day off. (It was through Brent that I learned that growing up rich and pretty doesn't save one: at thirty-five, she hadn't been able to find the courage, even after several years of therapy, to leave the brutal real-estate tycoon who often blacked her eyes. "I just can't do it," she whimpered to me, drained by continual attacks of colitis; "I can't get angry enough." Later, Anne, nursing in an Atlanta hospital, had Brent as a patient; she had developed breast cancer and had had a radical mastectomy.)

A picture of me taken during fifth grade shows a face as angry and hostile as Mother's amid the kudzu. And my classmates are aware of my feelings: since second grade, when I wet my pants in class and had to wear boy's underwear for the rest of the day, I have been declassé. Now on the second day of school, I'm wearing again my one new dress, a brown cotton plaid with white collar and cuffs; I had thought it pretty when Mother and I bought it. "Who has on the same dress she wore yesterday?" pipes one of the rich girls. My cheeks burn long after the moment when the conversation has turned to a discussion of where in Florida each had vacationed.

I fantasize I can read minds in order to know in advance the hateful thoughts the other girls were surely thinking of me. I never can make cat's cradles with a string wound through my fingers; somehow this seems connected to my social worthlessness. I hate to be invited to spend-the-nights on Blackland or

Habersham Road, held by girls who live on estates and have their own horses—especially since Daddy, picking me up in the morning in his Ford, might already be a little drunk. I envy their multiples of Capezios, of cotton dresses with slim patent-leather belts, piping, ruchings, off the racks of J. P. Allen's and Regensteins, Atlanta's two fancy department stores.

And I abhor my provincial roots. At Gail Brown's tenth birthday party at the end of the summer, my classmates and I run through the spray hose in her backyard. As I speed hysterically through the sparkling drops, I pass close to the fence of the next yard where two old ladies sit in white lawn chairs. "Look at that little girl," I hear one say to the other; "she looks like a country girl!" Though years later I realized they may have been charmed by my freckles, my red-brown hair, my chubby thighs, the words ran through me knifelike, spoiling an already self-conscious afternoon.

I was even jealous of my classmates' school lunches—sliced chicken or steak sandwiches, perfect red apples, chocolates in fluted gold or silver foil, carried in fancy metal lunch boxes or new uncreased brown sacks. As I released my own peanut butter and Ritz crackers from the old bread wrappers Mother saved for economy, I imagined uniformed maids trimming crusts from white-bread sandwiches, wrapping each carefully in fresh crisp waxed paper, then securing them with new red rubber bands.

I could see that my richer classmates suffered: Brooke, a pale blonde who blushed easily, wet her pants at her desk every week or so; as she tried to absorb the pool beneath her feet with piles of tablet paper, her vanilla face flamed. Veronica, a voluptuous brunette who I knew had horses and who modeled on Saturdays in the girl's department at J. P. Allen's, often burst into sobs so uncontrollable that her maid was sent for. Yet walking home past their huge houses, the manicured zoysia lawns tended by resident yardmen, I found it hard to believe in their pain. In any case, my recurrent fantasy—that Mother and Daddy, too, were rich, that *we* lived in a white-columned mansion, most of all that we were happy and laughing—was always set on Peachtree Battle Avenue, down the street from E. Rivers School.

A mile away in Springlake Park, our own small neighborhood, Mother had come to hate the "sophistication" of our neighbors —to blame it, along with the competitiveness of Daddy's work as a tire salesman, for his drinking. As a pious Southern wife with a strayed husband, she was able to convince him, for a while, to go with us each Sunday morning to the Second Ponce de Leon Baptist Church on Peachtree. (Since it was an *Atlanta* church, the Baptist was in this case as elite, in her estimation, as the Methodist.) But even there, decadence reigned; brought up to equate abstinence with salvation, she was shocked when members of their adult Bible class wanted to go out for "highballs" after services, even more than she had been by the young parents on our street who got drunk on Saturday nights and slept in on Sunday mornings, making no pretense of churchgoing.

After a while—under their influence, Mother was sure— Daddy (undoubtedly anticipating a few hours alone for heavy boozing) refused to go at all. Since Mother didn't drive, she stoically pulled Anne and me—dressed in freshly ironed puffsleeved dresses and Mary Janes—up the hill to the bus stop each Sunday morning. As though she suspected my impulse to run back down—the Sunday school seemed to me another bunch of rich kids dressed up in fancy clothes—she grasped our small gloved hands tightly. Yet it was an act I imitated a decade later, when, living in a little town in Texas, I dressed myself and my baby each Sunday morning and, leaving my hung-over young husband asleep in our scorpion-infested apartment, walked down the red-dirt road to the Baptist church.

Before she began working away from home, Mother occasionally took us downtown by bus on weekdays. Again dressed in hats, gloves, and coats if it was cool, we would visit the Carnegie Library, peruse Davison's basement, then have lunch at the S & W Cafeteria on Peachtree Street. Mother always chose deviled crab in tinfoil shaped to simulate the shells, an exotic food we never had at home, and ordered for us English peas, creamed potatoes, and bowls of red Jell-O diced into jewels that shimmered beneath their puffy hat of fake whipped cream. We would spoon the peas into the center of our potatoes, creating a dish we called "bird's nest," and hold the red Jell-O cubes within our mouths until they melted and slid effortlessly down our throats. Gurgling through our straws at the bottom of a near-empty glass of milk or "Co-Cola" was forbidden; Mother said it was unladylike, just as Daddy wouldn't let us say "gosh."

It was during such "shopping" trips that Mother taught us the rudiments of proper behavior—that ladies never eat, chew gum, or smoke on the street. Even though we were *nouveau* poor, we were still genteel, and we were not to forget it. After lunch, we would gawk restlessly—"It's not polite to stare!" Mother would say—at the other bored dressed-up housewives, the rouged and elaborately hatted old ladies. As we finally walked blinking into the Southern sunlight, our picture might be taken by one of the sidewalk photographers who roamed Peachtree charging a dollar for pictures of passing shoppers. In one, Mother, dressed in a spring dress and flowered hat, walks smiling, arm in arm, with *her* mother, Lee; she was doing what she loved more than almost anything, shopping, with the woman she most adored.

In another photograph, Mother, this time dressed in a dark fitted coat with a white collar, a dark straw pillbox atop her thick dark curls, pulls along a solemn-faced Anne. A gentle breeze appears to be blowing; my sister looks as she often did at four or five—serious, intent upon the business of holding on to her sailor hat with one small gloved hand. Mother is pretty, round-faced, smiling, giving no hint of her self-destructing core.

Like most belles, Mother wasn't "mechanical." This meant that she could barely operate a toaster, much less drive, which suited Daddy fine, for he considered his automobile an extension of his body, and would have vehemently resisted having it driven by a woman. But this also meant that he had to be recruited for family errands. Each Saturday, the whole family went together to Tenth and Peachtree streets, where there was an A&P, a Woolworth's, a Waffle House, the Ole King Cole Bakery, and an ice-cream stand that sold double-dip cones for a nickel. While Mother and Daddy shopped, Anne and I would gorge ourselves on lemon-custard ice-cream cones, or Lady Locks (French horns) and eclairs from the bakery. When things were going well, Daddy's treat for us was supper at the Waffle House, where, despite our early gluttonizing, we ordered waffles heavy with melted bright-yellow margarine and Log Cabin syrup.

Yet no matter how wonderful, the Saturdays ended in a certain way—with Daddy, already half drunk (where had he hidden the bottle?), driving us too rapidly toward home, with Mother sobbing incoherently about not being able to drive, not being able to go anywhere—"Cain't we jes' go to the Techwood to see a show?" she would sob as we passed the theater in question—about Daddy's drinking, his driving while drinking, what he had done with last month's paycheck, what would become of us generally. . . . In the backseat I played with Anne's long hair, coil after coil, or ran my fingers between her sandaled toes to make her beg me to stop. Sometimes we would fight during their "fight."

Still, as we passed the Atlanta waterworks, my panic would rise: once the front wheels of our car had actually stopped— amid Mother's, Anne's, and my screams—over the edge of a swimming pool. Now I had begun to dream at night of the dark, irregularly shaped pools. As our Ford rounded the curve, I would hold my breath, praying Daddy wouldn't swerve, plunging us over the curb into what I was sure were waters black, endless, monster filled. I didn't yet realize that the waterworks, the pools in which I feared drowning, were Mother's endless Saturday-night tears.

By the time I was eight or so, Mother was as disappointed by her dreams as I would be by suspiciously similar ones twenty years later. Instead of the fulfillment she had dreamed to be her right, she found herself the dependent of a young husband who was going down fast. She was learning, though not gracefully or well, about broken promises, precocious decline. She was over-whelmed, and nagging, pleading, hysteria were the only responses within her repertoire. Yet for a lifetime for her—for decades for me—the dreams themselves were never questioned. She was twenty-seven years old, tried new recipes, and religiously read "Can This Marriage Be Saved?" Daddy had his garden, his miniature golf course, and spent his evenings, however drunken, at home. The term "togetherness" had not yet been coined, but already our family caricatured it.

The only person I had ever seen who appeared as alienated as either of my beautiful young parents was an escaped German prisoner of war. When my six-year-old buddy Richard and I had been playing in the woods behind my house, we had seen his back, imprinted with the block letters P.O.W., desperately re-treating (too late: the police had already been called and were waiting for him as he emerged on the street opposite). I thought of that man—fugitive, speaking a foreign tongue—as the em-bodiment of loneliness; just as my parents, in spite of their good beginnings, appeared lonely, out of place in our neighborhood, at Daddy's company picnics, at gatherings of both their families.

Compared with the other mothers on our block, Mother seemed too prim, proper; at the barbecues given by Daddy's firm, she wore sundresses and clutched her pocketbook, while other wives, wearing shorts, did the jitterbug; as Daddy, already more than slightly drunk, sang along with the other salesmen, "She's got freckles on her—butt she's beautiful . . ." she looked away embarrassed.

At Christmas dinners at Lee's house, Daddy was the only husband and father who was inebriated, who gave rolls of toilet paper imprinted with jokes on every sheet, who went off to lift weights with Mother's half brother while the other men talked business. In true Southern fashion, Daddy's irresponsibility called forth Mother's self-conscious propriety.

Yet somehow, it all seemed foreordained. Daddy was *supposed* to drink. So he did. "I'm the bes' tire salesman in Atlanta,

in Georgia, in the South . . ." he would slur, going on to enumer-
ate all the men he could buy and sell. Mother was supposed to
plead, "If only you had been content to work in a grocery store,
anything . . ." And she did. The perfect modern young couple,
à la 1940s movie plots. Daddy drank and Mother whined.
Daddy raved invective and Mother begged. Daddy, oblivious,
read the newspaper, Mother slapped us.

In real life, the ugly, the violent, is almost always shot through
a cloth woven as much from pleasure as pain. Despite Daddy's
drinking, Mother's nagging—the underlying sense of accelerat-
ing decay—our everyday lives held satisfactions.

Mother's belief that Southern belles should be round, not
angular, was convenient, since she liked eating better than her
figure. A woman was always in good shape, she thought, as long
as her calves, however curvy, were less than hamlike. "But she
has such pretty legs!" she would exclaim of an acquaintance,
corseted and rotund, who weighed in at two hundred pounds.
Conversely, a good man was one who thought fat women
pretty. Daddy passed this test admirably; he liked "a little somethin' I can git hold of." As in Latin countries, the provincial
tradition in which Mother had been brought up decreed that
marriage and motherhood made fat acceptable; indeed, she
associated fat with happiness, thinness with misery (as her life
became harsher, she *did* become thinner). Thus we had hot
breads, grits, cream gravies, fried fatback and pork chops, plus
layer cakes and pies after every meal, just as she had had growing up at Lee's house.

But Mother, more urbanized, more inventive than her
mother, tried new recipes from *Good Housekeeping,* new foods
from the A&P. It was exciting to see what new items would spill
from the brown paper sacks on Saturday nights—fish sticks,
pizzas, hot-dog chili. Anne and I fought over who would get to
work the yellow capsule of color into the margarine that came
in a large fat lump. Daddy liked exotica: pickled eggs, olive
butter, guava jelly became staples of our diet. He liked strange

cheeses with strange names; when, one Christmas, he gave Mother a gigantic wooden bowl filled with cheeses of all shapes, sizes, names, sheathed in cellophane, she laughed: the gift was clearly for himself.

Later, when he and Mother had been separated for several years, and I was married for the second time, I carried brown paper sacks of his favorite cheeses and other foods to the sleazy West End boardinghouse where he lived with a woman he called his housekeeper. He was perpetually out of work by that time; but instead of noticing my gifts, he would lurch toward Darcy, three, who would cling to my calves, screaming at the sight of this strange man who was her grandfather. (With her dark curls, did she remind him of baby Anne, of whom an assortment of pictures were set out on top of his cheap chest of drawers?)

Not long after Mother's death, and a couple of months before his death from cancer that had spread to his brain, I visited him with a gift of the guava jelly he had loved. But he didn't understand my gift—couldn't recall that he had ever liked or eaten it. Despite his illness, I felt again a twinge of what I had at seven when he had ignored the candy animals I had bought for the top of his birthday cake.

At nine, I had accidentally discovered a means to punish my parents for what I felt to be their cruelty, coldness, and general inferiority. One night as we rode home from a visit to Grandmother Annie's house, I began sobbing—involuntarily at first, without apparent reason, out of some deep unseen grief. It was the first I recall of the crying jags that would later, for a long time, become as much a part of my tempestuous emotional life as they were of Mother's.

I continued sobbing until my impotent young parents begged me to tell them what was wrong. I realized in that moment my power: Daddy, not passive for once, held me in his arms and promised jeweled playhouses, bride dolls, horses, if only I would stop. It was my first experience of the possibilities inherent in parent-child guilt, or what I now think of as the Elvis Syndrome. (Elvis's parents bought him his first guitar because they couldn't afford a pony; until he was twelve, Gladys Presley walked her son to school each day; in return, the singer died almost exactly on the anniversary of his mother's death.) "Keepin' the young-uns happy" is important in the South, where the relationship between parent and child—especially mother and son—is senti-mentalized in an attitude reflected in the lyrics of country music. (In high school, one boyfriend with whom I parked could be brought so near tears by the strains of "The Mom and Dad Waltz" on the car radio that he would momentarily forget about sticking his hand beneath my skirt.)

It is an attitude that I later indulged with my own son, David. At seven, he sobbed that more than anything in the world he wanted, indeed must have to live, a *swan*: he had seen the illustration of the Hans Christian Andersen fairy tale, and since he had already had two insanely quacking ducks, assumed such a beautiful creature would be the next of his pets. Thinking he would forget, or at least that he would stop crying, I prom-ised that, at ten, if he still wanted a swan, he would have it. But ten came, he still wanted a swan, and he didn't forget or forgive my broken promise any more than I forgot or forgave the broken pledges implicit in my parents'—particularly Mother's —romantic dreams.

I could pay Mother back, I learned, by complaining of the size of our house or my clothes, comparing them to those of my richer classmates. I was ashamed, I told her, to have a spend-the-night party at *my* house, and enjoyed the hurt in her eyes. I pretended not to enjoy the simple pleasures she provided, and concealed from her my private ones. I didn't tell her that other mothers, more concerned with germs and cat-scratch fever, wouldn't let my friends own tribes of them, as I did. Mother, in her sloppiness, was permissive: I had cats in my bed at night, cats gave birth on the bedspreads, mewed at our back door, surged in as it opened—until, distempered by the Georgia heat, they died of a diarrhea that dripped over the front steps, or else were smushed by the cars that passed in front of our house, then

68

scooped up on shirt cardboards for a proper burial in the cat graveyard, complete with mounds of earth and upright tombstones, I kept in the backyard. Mother didn't object when, after each cat death, each cat funeral—conducted with the hymns and prayers of the other kids in the neighborhood—I stayed out of school for days to mourn and cry, a time when the grief from other parts of my life poured out pleasurably. She didn't know that none of my girl friends were allowed to ride the bus downtown alone on Saturdays as I was, or how satisfied and adventurous I felt, settling down in a big stuffed chair in the basement of the Carnegie Library with *Old-Fashioned Girl* or *The Secret Garden.* I didn't let her suspect that I enjoyed coming home from school after she had begun working because I could freely mess up the kitchen, broiling open-faced sugar-and-butter sandwiches—that without her there, I was conducting experiments in cooking. After poring through her *White House Cookbook,* I decided to make candied orange peel, then coerced the fourteen-year-old black girl Mother had hired to look after Anne and me to spend the afternoon eating a dozen oranges so that I could cook the peels. Whatever I cooked, Anne, the maid, and I gobbled up before our parents returned home each evening. Exhausted by Daddy, the house, us, her job, Mother was only vaguely aware of the disappearance of the foodstuffs she had so carefully purchased the Saturday before.

My parents may have been naïve, shallow, narcissistic, but I was that phenomenon "worse than a serpent's tooth," an ungrateful child. Because they couldn't afford baby-sitters at night, Anne and I were taken with them to occasional picture shows. Though I hated Daddy's ritual joke of standing up to leave just as the cartoon began, and the newsreels of Dachau and Auschwitz gave me nightmares, I was moved by the World War II romances. The plights of Jennifer Jones, Robert Walker, Claudette Colbert, the plots of *Since You Went Away* and *The Purple Heart* raised a sympathy I found hard to feel for those closer to home. Maliciously, I wondered why my own parents weren't so gallant. I learned of the death of Franklin Roosevelt when I went into the drugstore after school to buy bubble gum, and found everyone gone silent, stunned; it was a scene that affected me, causing me to feel, for the first time, part of a larger history—a relief from the narrow convolutions, the assaults upon the ego, of home and school life.

On our block, I felt comfortable: our neighborhood was crammed with a misery that by now seemed familiar—I was comforted by the tragedies of my peers. Except for certain unspeakable experiences that I had already forced out of consciousness, the worst thing that had happened to me to date had been stepping on a rusty nail, which had gone through the top of my foot; it had been pulled out by an uncle at Grandmother Lee's house as Daddy held me screaming; I had been taken to a doctor who stuck a stick dipped in alcohol through the wound, then gave me a sucker shaped like a broom for being so "good" (i.e., shrieking and struggling hysterically).

Another time, Mother placed the coffee percolator one morning so that its cord stretched across one of the two doorways into our tiny kitchen. "Don't come in that way," she warned as I dressed for first grade. But I had, and as the boiling coffee penetrated the cheap porous cotton of my robe, the skin of my back melted quickly, like wax. As I sat on the toilet in shock, the doctor plucked embedded coffee grounds out of my hardening flesh with a large pair of tweezers.

When the scabs came off a month later—big brown crusts as big as my shoulder or half my back, leaving only fresh pink skin —I didn't realize my luck, or what the doctor meant when he called the lack of scarring "a miracle!" Only my fear, when, on my first day back at school, the meanest boy in class said, "Don't think we're not going to tease you anymore just because you got burned!"

Yet these accidents—even my parents' aggressive misery— seemed less tragic than Honey's mother's suicide. Honey, an old-looking seventh-grader, lived alone with her father and liked to take us into the room where her mother's blood and

70

bone had been splattered, where she said she still found bits of shattered skull.

Or Neil's fall off his bicycle, rebreaking his arm in the same place in which he had broken it three months before: as I watched him wring it loosely, screaming, his fat face contorted with pain and fear, I thought of his once-fat mother who everyone said was dying of cancer in the bedroom of their house. "Her side had to be drained again today," I had heard Mother tell Daddy conversationally at the supper table, and wondered, if you broke your arm, and your mother was dying of cancer, who would you run to tell?

Harriet's family was the only Jewish one on our street, and because of the black hair that began to grow beneath her arms, on her legs, during fifth grade, we callously nicknamed her "Hairy"—and were amazed, scornful, when she cried. Her dark bearlike father ran a small grocery and meat market; when he came home each day, he wore a once-white apron smeared with blood, making Harriet even more declassé.

It was a time when fantasies of romantic sufferings, à la 1940s movie plots, abounded. Jeanne Crain and William Holden somehow suffered more elegantly than the adults who surrounded my friends and me.

My two best girl friends and I called ourselves "The Three Musketeers." Aside from our age—nine—and the street on which we lived, our common denominator was that we each had less-than-happy families.

Dayle's snow-white complexion, tinged faintly with pink, her white-blonde hair as fine and floaty as cotton, made her look ethereal, a fairy princess. But it was the fine-pored look ("You've got that *fine*-pored skin," a Southern man will tell a woman in bed) that sometimes distinguishes young girls in the rural South. Her father, Ralph, sometimes got loudly drunk, her skinny brother, Ronald, had asthma and cussed, and her stout, gum-chewing mother wore feedsack dresses that betrayed her Appalachian origins.

71

Louise, or "Shrimp," looked, at ten, already wizened, stunted. Even her mouse-colored hair refused to grow longer than ear length; her legs and thighs, exposed by the short shorts we wore all summer, were covered in large purple spots; she had accidentally been shot by an uncle with his shotgun when he went out to kill a rabid dog. Shrimp's older sister, Sissy, was snotty and oversized; it was their mother who was the beauty; she had divorced their quiet, balding father, and several nights a week was visited by a handsome War Hero. Mother didn't approve of her—even after she married him. (Shrimp and her sister were then moved into a bigger house on a better street; when I visited, I saw that they, too, now had rows of Capezio ballet slippers in their closets. Twenty years later, I read in the obituaries of the *Atlanta Journal* that Sissy had died of cancer at thirty-three.)

Of this crew, I was skinny-turning-plump, freckled, with straight red-brown hair I hated, and wore a perpetual sullen look that was compounded by the natural downward turn of my full lips within my round face. I was angry with my parents, my classmates at E. Rivers, and the world at large.

But with the Musketeers, I could pretend. Together, we sucked the honey from the stamen of honeysuckle, crushed crepe myrtle buds between our fingertips, fantasizing they were fat pink ice-cream cones, and made shoes out of poplar leaves wrapped around our feet and held with twigs. We shat on the big rocks in the woods behind my house, wiping ourselves with oak leaves, and roasted crayfish—live and squealing —over a campfire.

We walked around the block, our mouths crammed with bicarbonate of soda to make them foam, hoping people would think we were mad. We hid behind the couch as Shrimp's mother sat with her lover, listening for sexual innuendos; once, we ate a tin of sherried pecans, hoping to become drunk. While we waited for the school bus, we sucked our upper arms to make hickeys. We talked about sex, played doctor with yellow school pencils (focusing more on anuses than vaginas, which we couldn't seem to find), and rolled the buckshot still within Shrimp's thighs and calves between our fingertips.

I had the Musketeers—and my baby sister, Anne. At first I had hated having to walk her after supper, her diapers falling around her ankles, as the other kids in the neighborhood exclaimed at her long black curls. Was that why Daddy loved her best, I wondered, because she had inherited his Cherokee-dark looks? A picture taken when she was four and I was nine makes my head—because I am standing just behind her—appear to be growing from the top of hers. I cringed at my freckled sullen face, framed by its limp brown hair, atop her impishly pensive one, her full dark pageboy. I paid her back for being born by turning on the vacuum cleaner when Mother was away from home. I loved her screams of terror, her fear of being sucked up.

But I had begun to love her baby-fat body, her silky hair, her air of puzzled seriousness, and after a while, nicknamed her "Cinnamon Roll," because I thought she was so sweet. She was my new pet. Bathing together each night, we pretended we were fish or tadpoles; our washcloths became swimsuits à la Esther Williams, as I taught her to swim within the narrow porcelain walls. At night in our bed together, we stuck our bubble gum on the headboard; years later, she told me she had thought I could make the bed levitate, probably because when I plunged selfishly into its center, the sides rose. Shaken by Daddy's ravings, the eruptions of Mother's sobs, we clung to one another. In our love was the seeds of the empathy I would later feel first for my own daughters, then for my Southern sisters. Indeed, sleeping with my first woman lover at forty would be like sleeping with my little sister again: they had the same tawny skin, the same slim-hipped bodies.

Though Anne and I were close at home, I was still jealous on the block. She played Melanie to my Scarlett, sweetness to my bossiness, and also the group games—cops and robbers, cowboys and Indians—that I scorned. She was popular; I got into fistfights, with the kids in the neighborhood yelling and taking sides. Already, the unladylike aggressiveness that I would try to deny or suppress for the next twenty years was beginning to surface.

I suspected, yet resisted knowing, that I would never be able to live up to the standards of "sloppin' sugah all ovah each othah, buttah wouldn't melt in her mouth" behavior espoused by Mother, Grandmother Lee, Grandmother Annie, my aunts, my teachers, and all the other Southern women with whom I came into contact. (I had not yet begun to question the discrepancy between Mother's literal and emotional slovenliness and her other-directed insistence on correct public behavior.) There was the anger I almost always felt—certainly, an inappropriate emotion for a Southern girl, who properly should be "sweet and nice."

Southern girls are also supposed to take good care of their "thangs"—as in "she takes such good keer of her thangs." But when Anne and I received ice-skating dolls at Christmas, she preserved hers in the box—full skirt perfect, hair smoothly coiffed, lashes laid down over unscratched blue eyes; I felt driven to undress and redress mine, to comb and recomb the hair until it was matted and tangled, to pluck at arms and legs until the rubbers holding them inevitably broke.

Like Scarlett, I was too interested in commerce: at seven, I had sold pictures of Donald Duck, traced from comic books, to passersby on Peachtree. Now I begged or confiscated household items, and coerced the Musketeers to do the same, until we had inventory for our sidewalk store; late Saturday afternoons, we would squat on the sidewalk to divide our profits. Yet I also lacked a feminine frugality: while Anne carefully hoarded any pennies she might acquire, I quickly spent mine on black-market bubble gum, Baby Ruths, and Butterfingers.

But worst was my obsessive and aggressive interest in boys and sex. When I was in the fifth grade, I had a second-grade boyfriend, Kenny, whom I took into the hallway of our house, closing the doors to create darkness, then made him "kiss me like they do in the movies." Because he was smaller than I, he had to do it. He had two sets of boxing gloves, but when we boxed, I always won. (Later, my third husband, Ben, would cite this relationship as an early example of my desire to dominate men.) When I met Daddy's boss's son at a tire-company picnic, I called him on the telephone. When we met again at a company dinner, he pointed at me and exclaimed, "That's the one, Daddy—that's the girl who called me up!" All the way home, Mother and Daddy worried: would my "forwardness" go against Daddy's possible promotion, or even make him lose his already precarious position?

Yet guilt was no deterrent: I smooched with my cousin Bubba, son of the Cancer Victim, in the hayloft at Grandmother Lee's, and pursued him by postcard when he was sent away to military school. On Saturdays, risking the scorn of my older playmates, I took Kenny into the woods behind my house to force him to kiss me and verbalize his love.

On one of these days, a Saturday, I heard Mother calling me from the house. When I went inside, I saw she had been doing what Southern women feel called upon to do after lunch whenever possible—"lying down." When I entered her room, she had again reclined—her face had her *après* nap look. As she continued to lie there, looking out the window, I could tell something serious was coming: did she know what I had been doing?

"There's something girls need to know about," she began ominously. I flushed, my notion of her omnipotence confirmed. "Something that happens every month. . . ." As she described the process that would initiate me into woman- and possibly motherhood, she spoke with the same disgust with which she had responded to my desire to become a veterinarian.

Obviously, kissing and menstruation were connected in some revolting way. I already knew vaguely about what she was describing in details that were making something inside me shrivel, my stomach turn. I had seen the puddles of sticky red left on the hardwood floor when Mother had stood at the front door talking to the Fuller Brush man, the pools she had hastily told the maid to "mop up before Rows-may-ree 'n' A-nne see it." I knew that the bathroom wastebasket was often filled with fat cotton pads, brown and drying. (As with her underwear—indeed, whenever any small economy was involved—Mother was less than fastidious; I had had to learn that women dried themselves with toilet tissue after urinating by watching the

75

other girls at school.) In our small bathroom, artifacts of the perineum, from the loathed enema bag to a giant syringe with a large and puzzling bulb to the bloody or boxed Kotex, were ubiquitous.

To be feminine, I was beginning to believe, was to be penetrated, blood-stained, bloody forever. Shrimp's mother had married her handsome War Hero and had had a baby; Shrimp described the bed, before she left for the hospital, as "dripping with blood." A vampirelike infant, gnawing outward with sharp teeth, flashed through my mind: would what was growing wrongly within me eat me out from within, causing me to bleed and bleed?

Dayle had confided authoritatively that once menstruation began, we would bleed continuously for the rest of our lives. "Think of never being able to go swimming or roller-skating again!" we commiserated, referring to what we already knew were taboos during bleeding (and ignoring the obvious fact that grown women rode bicycles: hadn't Patty's mother, drunk, rode hers into a telephone pole the week before?). Now, as Mother tiredly reiterated cause and effect, I stood suffused with guilt—for forcing Kenny to kiss me, for *wanting* to do that and other things, indeed, for all my aggressive thoughts and feelings. Yet what did the things she was saying really have to do with my desire to have Kenny, my surrogate Van Johnson, hold me and tell me he loved me? The images that flitted through my mind during those moments had more to do with Jennifer Jones and Jeanne Crain and June Allyson, with being grown up and wearing slinky calf-length dresses and shoulder waves, than with gaping bottoms and blood.

Yet sex, real sex, I knew meant penetration. Did it feel like what we did beneath the covers with our yellow school pencils at spend-the-night parties? Was it like the enemas Mother had, until recently, insisted on giving me? I had eagerly gone to see Jane Russell in *The Outlaw,* and though I pretended to Dayle and Shrimp to have understood it, I had not. All the movie had shown was Jane Russell's breasts as she leaned over the cowboy's bed. I was still more interested in romantic love scenes and kisses than in torsos or nakedness, especially as the latter would reveal one's shameful protrusions, one's ugly body hair.

I had learned, since seeing Aunt Billie change into her crotchless girdle, that pubic hair was not a deformity specific to our family. Still, I felt ambivalent about my own swelling breasts and softly sprouting pubis; my ideal female body was the dismembered torso of my Madame Alexander ice-skating doll.

At Gail Brown's birthday party, I had been nervous as I had gone into Gail's bedroom with my fourth-grade classmates from the year before. We were to change into our swimsuits, and I felt shamefully conscious of my changing body. But as we peeled off shirts and shorts, I was relieved. Though the chests of the other girls' were still as flat as nippled boards, their vulvas like smooth hairless Parker House rolls, Gail wore the same growths. Her pretty mother hovered beside her protectively, handing her her swimsuit, folding her clothes—tenderly, as though her daughter's body were precious. But as my own mother talked, I felt shame for my curiosity, my desires, my aggressiveness, for my own physical destiny as a Southern woman.

It was a destiny that seemed most compelling during visits to Grandmother Lee's, especially when Mother's sisters and my girl cousins were there. A woman friend brought up in Chicago, schooled at Sarah Lawrence, later said to me, "I never imagined being admired for anything but my mind." As a Southern girl and woman, I never imagined—until I was well over thirty—being admired for anything but my body and/or its coverings. And the female body, imperfect, was made to be covered, and how it was covered mattered. After Sunday services at the Methodist or Baptist church, the clothes of the other women—Miz Blalock's new hat, Junie's baby-doll shoes—were discussed extensively. Competition was fierce: "church clothes" were the most important part of a Southern girl's or woman's wardrobe. Perfection in every detail—gloves, hat, collar, cuffs, hemline—was the goal.

In whatever room the women of Mother's family gathered, the talk was never of religion, politics, or sex, but of the latest styles in Butterick, McCall's, or the misses' department at Davison's. "I don't know *why* the women in our family have always been so interested in clothes," Grandmother Lee said to me years later in a room strewn with Baptist Sunday-school pamphlets, pattern books, and fashion magazines (at seventy-five, she still read *Seventeen*).

Though Anne says she recalls talk of "female trouble" ("Her womb was 'bout down 'tween 'er knees!") and new recipes for Apple Dapple cake, I remember mostly conversations about the newest looks, or what "they" were wearing. (For years, I couldn't figure out who "they" were; finally, I realized it meant every woman outside Tucker, Georgia—especially those up North, and on the fashion pages of the *Ladies' Home Journal*.) Thrown into the discussion of dress might be a little giggled advice on how to handle men ("Jes' remember they're like little boys or puppy dogs. . . .").

As a twice-married woman and a devout Baptist, Grandmother Lee was an expert on both men and church clothes, especially what I now think of as the Rosalynn Carter look—innocuous and ladylike, rather than chic or, heaven forbid, sexy. "Tacky" was the key word; it was a state to be avoided at all costs. "It doesn't matter what you *do* in the South," says an Atlanta sociologist, "just as long as you don't look *tacky* doing it."

"Light stockings with light shoes . . . don't wear white shoes before Easter . . . always wear gloves when you go out in hose . . . never go out of the house without a girdle . . ." Teenagers were to wear Scotch-plaid pleated skirts, circle pins on Peter Pan collars; though I was still in ruffled white ankle socks and puffed-sleeved dresses, I was learning the rules, but reluctantly and not well. As a grown-up, my style was labeled by a Northeastern woman friend as Puerto Rican Princess, or a cross between *Screw* and *Harper's Bazaar*. I inherited Mother's love of flamboyance; while Anne—typical of her ability to conciliate and adjust—has become the complete Southern WASP: slim-hipped, tan, she looks right in tennis whites, perfect skirts, and silk shirts.

Apparently, Mother had not learned the rules well either. She sometimes carried a white pocketbook and wore black shoes. She was plump, but loved tomato red, azalea pink. Her slip—one of the ripped ones from her trousseau—inevitably dripped lace beneath her hemline. She was one of those women who, like Marilyn Monroe, could look either dumpy or voluptuously gorgeous. With her irrepressible black curls, her short curvaceous figure, she looked too much like an overblown magnolia blossom for propriety.

And as though petals were falling from her, her body seemed involuntarily to spill itself over *things*: she blotted her bright vermilion or fuchsia lipstick on magazine covers, matchbooks, bills; we never lived in a house that wasn't littered with bits of paper covered with smeary red lip prints, just as her tangled costume jewelry spread itself from room to room, bits and pieces dangling from bedposts and coffee tables. Every dresser drawer reflected the chaos of her psyche. Broken lipsticks, empty compacts, beads spilled from broken necklaces mingled with the powder drifting from round pink Pond's boxes, overdue bills, curling family photographs, recipes clipped from *Good Housekeeping,* imprinted repeatedly by her lips.

When I was fourteen, Mother screamed that she had found a mouse nursing her young in one of the drawers; as we gathered around to look at the pink flesh fingertips, the cringing gray mother, it only seemed that Mother's mess had finally spawned life. Everywhere, her hysteria made literal metaphors.

As though it were her safety, Mother clutched her pocketbook. "Do you think there's a sale up there?" my husband Ben teased her as we started the climb up a mountain behind her second husband's farmhouse in North Carolina. Her unquestioning acceptance of her family's standards of appearance and her (and later my) failure to meet them must have added to her insecurity.

Yet they were standards about which she must have been ambivalent: she refused to conform to them even after a more prosperous second marriage should have provided the opportunity for doing so. Her slovenliness and her aggressive bad taste were her rebellion, as was her schizophrenic choice of dress. After her death, I found her closet crammed with new, unworn clothes—Lady Manhattan shirts, Leslie Fay dresses—and coral- and lemon-colored negligees of syrupy nylon tricot, metallic-gold bedroom slippers with harem toes.

Though the Chanel No. 5 that her husband always gave her for birthdays and Christmas sat on the dresser top, the top two drawers, leatherette cases, even shoe boxes, were filled with cheap ten-cent store scents, a gypsy array of jewelry made to simulate oversized pearls, jade, coral, even butter beans! It was as though she had remained not only a girl, but a child who still reveled in fake and glitter.

After her funeral, I crammed as much of the gaudy stuff into the leatherette jewelry boxes, the shoe boxes, as I could, and took them back to Atlanta; later, I would sift through these remnants of my suicided mother, and guiltily laugh. (The writer Alice Walker, looking at them with me, suggested that I sell them to Andy Warhol.) I was unaware that I was responding to her underground stream of joy and creativity that—had it not been distorted by her unmet needs—could have saved her life.

As though I were an extension of herself—more *her* than herself—it was always important (and a goal never fulfilled, in her estimation) that *my* appearance be correct. In the end, clothes were the last remaining metaphor for her power over me.

A year before she died, she called after me in the carport as I left a family Christmas at Anne's house. The event had been nostalgically painful, at least for me. Both my parents—Mother, crippled by a spinal condition, hair grayed and lines engraved by electroshock; and Daddy, a dried-out drunk with sad eyes and a mute addiction to television—had each come with their respective second spouses, their *caretakers* was the way I thought of them, and had met again for the first time in twenty years.

80

As I walked to my car with Darcy and Laura, I felt weighed down by the passivity and defeat of my once-beautiful and passionate parents. At the sound of Mother's voice I turned, still half expecting her to say something that would magically wipe away the defeat of years, giving meaning to her pain; instead, she spoke in her whiniest, little-girl voice: "I thought you might wont these—" What she thrust into my hands, recalling clearly my once-total dependence on her, was my white high-topped baby shoes!

The last words Mother said to me in person had to do with dress. Ben and I had stopped in North Carolina on our way to New York City, where I would have a publishing party, and we would visit the Northeast for most of the summer. I wore a new cotton dress, a French copy, for which I had paid seventy dollars —more than I ever would have dreamed possible at fourteen in Georgia. Pale blue, with a low neck and ruffled skirt, it reminded me of the hand-me-down cotton eyelet, made by Lee, in which I had gotten laid for the first time.

I had thought Mother might approve of its provincial look, so reminiscent of our common background. Instead, she shrilled as I walked into the house, "Rows-may-ree! Take that rag off you!" When I mentioned how much it had cost, she declared I "must have been crazy—it looks like it's made out of an old feedsack!"

She wanted us to go through our ritual: going back to her bedroom to try on her new clothes. Ostensibly trying to find something "appropriate" for me, she insisted that I model each of her recent acquisitions, from a nauseatingly chartreuse sundress to a brown cotton wraparound church dress.

After I tried on the sundress, she changed into it. The sallow color of the cloth made her once-cream-colored skin yellowish; the fabric stretched more tautly around her thickening waist than it had about mine. "See how good this looks on *me*?" she preened. To our husbands, watching the Atlanta Falcons on TV in the den, she simpered, "Don't you thank this suits me bettah than Rows-may-ree?"

Satisfied with their response—they knew by now the proper one—she decided that the dark-brown church dress would be better for me in New York: "A hundrud times more 'phisticated than that ole rag you came in ..." She wanted me to wear my hair in a French twist—a long-standing argument: I hadn't worn it that way in twenty years! I felt myself grow docile, powerless, as I often did in the face of her vehemence. For a moment, I shared her fantasy—me, walking down Fifth Avenue in the brown dress, my flyaway hair caught in a proper twist, looking for once, "ladylike."

Especially for our visit, Mother had prepared a dessert for which she had crushed and boiled fresh blueberries, mixed them with Dream Whip, layered them with homemade cake and Jell-O. I pinned up my hair and, through the two kinds of meat, vegetables, pickles, hot rolls, and dessert, wore the brown dress.

To please her, I decided, I would wear it when I left. While Mother stood in the driveway watching Ben and me get into the car, I noticed the two hats—a pink felt cloche and a dark-brown straw—I had placed in the backseat. Still hoping—at forty—to please my mother, I thrust the pink one on my head. "Rows-may-ree!" she yelled at me from the driveway. "That doesn't look right—put on the brown one!"

It was the last time, outside the intensive-care ward of the hospital, that I would see Mother alive.

In retrospect, I see how the sterility and rigidity of the expectations of appearance must have limited my aunts and cousins, as well as my mother and myself. Yet what I know now was a provincial materialism, I felt at nine was the world. Our extended family was Society, and if I was marked there, as I was at E. Rivers School, I would be elsewhere, forever and ever. My stringy hair, my hand-me-down dresses, my torn underwear, concealed a congenital stain. Mother and Daddy's messy beauty seemed sexual, and their sexuality was connected with failure; like August in Georgia, they were lush, rotting, and inevitably skidding toward disintegration.

In some inner recognition of the envy of her siblings, Mother behaved as humbly around her sisters as Cinderella. Within her family, she seemed to me the victim that every Southern family requires, just as Daddy did in his—proof of her, and thus my, inferiority.

I was ashamed: my uncles mingled bodiless in three-piece suits, smoking fat cigars and talking business; my aunts, who belonged to them, seemed controlled, asexual, in their bubble hairdos, Nelly Don dresses, and dark pumps. Their dresser drawers, I knew from visiting their big houses, were neat. It was out of this standard that Florance called Gloria Steinem's hair "too long" and exclaimed of my teenage daughter Laura's red honky Afro that "I go to the beauty parlor so my hair *won't* look like that!" In 1975, her ideal hairdo was still a short bouffant, carefully teased so as not to touch either her collar or forehead. The aim wasn't flash, but a supreme ordinariness.

"I know I've lost a few pounds, Grace, but thyah's nothin'— nothin'!—I kin do about these ankles."

"Florance, I jes' luv-v-v your new outfit! Did Mother Lee make it, or did you buy it at Davison's?"

" 'Lissa, Rows-may-ree looks so cute in that ole dress of Billie's. . . ."

The dress Florance is talking about is an ugly pale-green faille moiré, jutting from a thick waistband in thick self-pleats—a far cry from the svelte beige rayon linen with red piping on the collar and cuffs, a narrow red plastic belt, that I had seen the week before in the girls' department at Davison's; it had cost an impossible $8.98. Yet dreaming of it, my arms full of books from the Carnegie Library, I had floated down the escalator to catch the bus home. This moment, though, is different: chunky with new baby fat, my hair in sausage curls Mother had made by tying up my mane in old school socks, I shrivel back into the parlor couch at Grandmother Lee's house, feeling the petulant look for which I am becoming known creeping involuntarily over my face. I look angry, sullen, but what I feel is a now-familiar numbness, a sinking of the heart, that must be blocked. Anne, beside me, wears a big bow in her hair, a hopeful expression. Beside her sit two girl cousins of near my age. Vehicle of

Mother's repressed competitiveness (she tallied carefully the compliments Anne and I received, and would quote slights to us bitterly twenty years later), I hate them.

We have just had the rites of the Christmas tree. As usual, Grandmother Lee and Granddaddy Carroll have given each grandchild a new one-dollar bill in a crisp white envelope inked with our given names. They had been arranged among the branches of the huge Georgia pine, and handed out to us after the piles and piles of gifts to our grandparents had been opened.

Now we have our dollars in hand, and sit tensely awaiting our turns: after the tree, each grandchild is required to sing a song, recite a verse, or do a dance. "Mi-nah-gra Nic-ah-rah-gwa is a won-der-ful place . . ." I sing, hearing my voice crack. The aunts and uncles laugh indulgently, but as I sit down, my face flaming, my cousin Bubba, two years older, snickers: "You should stick to poems!" I poke my tongue out at him, not knowing that a year later, he'll be sticking his into my mouth in the hayloft over the barn.

Of all my cousins, it was Bubba in whom I was most interested. He was an embryonic good ole boy: instinctively, I weakened before his budding machoism. In a high school classroom in Savannah last year, almost every student confessed to having what's known in the South as a "kissing cousin"; Bubba was mine. Though when we met years later—he, a prosperous businessman, as bodiless as my uncles had once seemed; I, a woman uppity and literary, undoubtedly the type he liked least—I wondered and doubted if he recalled our hayloft kisses. Yet at that time, in my first flicker of empathy for a man—always easier for Southern women than the same feeling toward their gender— I dreamed that his loneliness, when he had been sent away to the Georgia Military Academy, was much like mine at E. Rivers School, and in my own family.

For his mother had been the Cancer Victim. And because of the method in what I had perceived as my own mother's desire to kill me, or parts of me, I had identified with her. Paradoxically, she also represented to me my opposite, the image I would spend half a lifetime resisting: that of a literally hollowed-out woman, filled only by her own emptiness, who though perfectly, properly passive, is still punished by death.

Intuitively, I knew that her fate had to do with her sweetness and lack of assertion; Mother was also considered to be sweet, girlish, pretty. I was learning that I would be damned by self-expression *or* passivity—in one case, with the loss of love, in the other, with the loss of self.

Not yet understanding the conflict that gnawed at me, the teeth of my embedded aggression, I only knew that I desperately feared both the death of self my aunt represented, and what seemed to me the living death of Mother's life.

The following fall, when Mother and Daddy told us—or we deduced from a thousand tearful supper-table conversations about the money Daddy had gambled away, borrowed, and reborrowed—that our little house would be sold and the four of us would move in with Grandmother Annie in her big brick house in Bolton, outside Atlanta, I was glad. We would be farther from the scrutiny of my supercilious aunts and cousins, the demanding standards of Grandmother Lee and Granddaddy Carroll. Best, I would be leaving behind the girls in the fifth grade at E. Rivers School who, the week before, had pointed at me and laughed as I walked into the classroom with my shoulder-length red-brown hair pinned across my forehead in mock bangs I had dreamed would make me look like Claudette Colbert. No longer would I have to listen as they talked about their evening dresses and horses.

My view of our situation was narcissistic: I could no longer afford sympathy for my young parents, particularly Mother. With genitals like my genitals, any identification—in view of her smudged life—would cause me too much pain. At five, lost from her in the sewing-machine department at Davison's department store, I had become hysterical, imagining the varnished sides of huge treadle and electric Singers closing in on me like sleek monsters. But now I allowed spontaneous love and anger to flow freely only toward my Cinnamon Roll, Anne; she would remain its focus until, in recognition of their power, I would go "boy crazy." With Mother and Daddy, I saved myself by holding myself aloof.

For weeks prior to the decision to move, they had been sick in bed together with a mutual case of the flu that kept both from their jobs. Seeing my already impotent young parents simultaneously horizontal, hearing them weakly argue or fuck, confirmed my ever-hardening contempt. It was as though the disease that afflicted our family was manifesting itself everywhere: Anne had impetigo again—huge scabs crusted her buttocks; all my cats had diarrhea. Our family was becoming more and more like the body after one of Mother's enemas—involuntarily shitty. I longed for another environment in which to keep myself as separate as possible from what seemed like a lack of control, a rotting from within.

My perceptions of Daddy's passivity, Mother's hysteria, even what felt like sexual assaults, might be chalked up to any oversensitivity, a supersubjectivity. As a rationally oriented friend points out, what one feels is not necessarily objective truth; rather, one's experiences are inevitably distorted by one's own internalized crazy-house mirror. Yet at ten I felt permanently marked—as surely as by the faint pink map outlining half my back, the mark on the top of my left foot where the nail had emerged. With her knowledge and invasion of it, I felt that Mother, her very madness, though I couldn't have named it then, had penetrated my body.

At a marathon group-therapy session two decades later, a man would tell me, "You make me think of Snow White or Sleeping Beauty, waiting for the Prince to come along and wake you up." As surely as Mother ever had, despite any achievements I had made in the meantime, I felt that my real power would come from a man. At ten, though I felt I was holding myself apart from it, I was already imprinted by a pattern I would alternately attempt to escape and duplicate for the next thirty years of my life.

At that time, I only knew that I was glad of our coming move. Though I couldn't have known it then, it was a motion that would be pleasantly downwardly mobile. For the first time, I would taste the comforting, if confining, flavor of small-town Southern life.

It was as though Mother and Daddy had had a brief affair with the urban, with upward mobility, and it had failed—indeed, had permanently wounded them. Their provincial psyches, their family histories, had already made them too fragile, too porous, for the rigors of an environment that didn't instantly reward them for their beauty and charm. Never again would they truly have either; never again would they try.

As for me, I had begun to learn, in a superbly effective sub-liminal lesson, that in a Southern climate, open wounds—even scar tissue—can fester for decades.

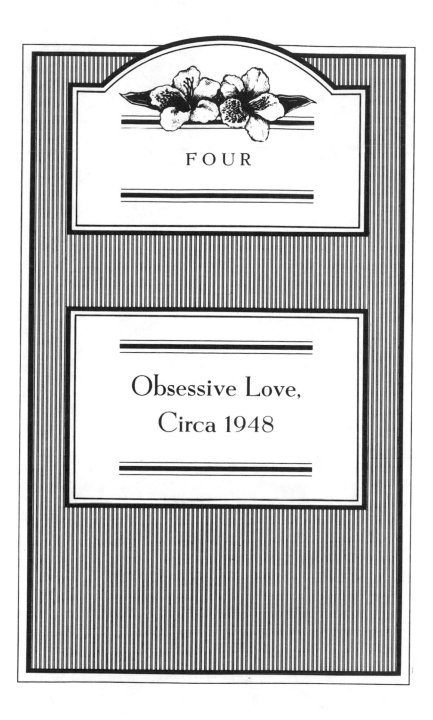

FOUR

Obsessive Love,
Circa 1948

"I just moved to Bolton, Georgia, from Atlanta," I scrawled in number-two pencil across the first pale-blue lines of my new black leatherette five-year diary, with its own brass lock and key. "I hope I like it." That date was January 1, 1947.

On my first day at Bolton Grammar School, introduced by my teacher to the single sixth-grade classroom, I superciliously looked out over my new classmates. It was hard to tell whether the boys, with their varying degrees of hulk, were eleven, like me, or twelve or fourteen: they stared back with a rurally precocious gleam that I recognized from Daddy, Cousin Bubba, and the movies.

The girls, with their peroxided hair, Tangeed lips, their careless assortment of matronly blouses, cardigan sweaters, bobby socks, and scuffed saddle shoes, looked as though they ranged from ten to thirty; they gazed at me with expressions changing from curiosity to dismay. Few of them, I was sure, read *Seventeen* magazine, or even knew about Capezios, much less had closetfuls. None, I was certain, had parents who attended movie premieres or were members of the Piedmont Driving Club. And if they rode horses, they would be like the workhorses or mules on Grandmother Lee's farm!

Yes, here—the New Girl from the Big City, prettier than many, and for once, better dressed—*I* could be the snob. Living in Grandmother Annie's sprawling brick house encrusted with verandahs, on the main road, I was already, I knew, imbued with the status of my dead grandfather, long the community postmaster, and my great-uncle Paul, the snotty local doctor.

At that moment in the little country schoolroom awash with Georgia January sunlight, I stood suffused with conscious feminine power for the first time. I suddenly felt bright red-gold highlights leap within the hair I had thought lank brown.

Breathing deeply, I expanded the bodice of my new green-and-white-checked cotton dress, with the dropped waistline I thought so sexy, and thrust forward my new breasts, needlessly held in place by my new white starter bra with a tiny blue ribbon at its center. I was, I knew instantly, *popular.*

Soon, I would consider myself an expert: "I have found the secrets of being popular," I wrote on the blank back page of my diary: "1. Thinking of others as human beings with their own problems and forgetting yourself. 2. Being attentive and appreciative. 3. Not gossiping, using profanity, telling risque jokes, or being sarcastic. 4. Being gracious. 5. Making others feel important."

"Popularity" brightened that year and the next. It was a period during which everything that was a part of my imprint as a Southern woman—family, community, sexuality, nature, religion—fused easily with my fantasies, inherited from Mother, of becoming a writer and a woman of achievement.

Years later, I would draw a picture of myself for a therapist —sitting on a rock in the woods, daydreaming in the green gingham dress: "pregnant with possibility," I explained to him. At eleven, my fantasies coincided with my burgeoning sexuality in a way that I didn't yet realize wasn't "ladylike." I thought there need be no conflict between my desires for love and recognition. I didn't understand that the Southern culture with which I was beginning a lifelong love-hate affair—which would seem at times the very source of my creativity—would view my ambitions as freakish, a malformation, and that soon I would share its view.

For a while, life held a radiance that was untainted by Daddy's, or even Mother's, despair. Around his mother, Daddy was meeker, a humbled dog; Mother seemed more girlish, less powerful. One Sunday morning, she slid into the front seat of our Ford beside Daddy—who, in his imperious mother's house, could no longer refuse church attendance—for the short drive up Bolton Road to Collins Memorial Methodist Church. Smiling, slender—no longer fat at all—in a beige dress with matching jacket, a cream-colored cloche closely fitted to her thick black curls, her round creamy face, she suddenly looked like the pictures I had seen of her taken before I was born. Freed from the pressures that distorted her pretty features into bitter, even cruel, expressions, she was struck by the light that was beginning to surround everything. It was as though I were glimpsing the vivacious teenager she had been, rather than my hysterical, unhappy mother. Instead of the mother of the slaps, the enemas, this mother was beautiful; I *could* love her. It was a picture that, as an adult, I recalled with a mixture of pleasure and pain, the one to which I wished I could cling, discarding all the rest.

If Mother and Daddy, reduced to dependency, seemed more childlike, less powerful, I was relieved. In the house with her mother-in-law Annie, and Reggie Lou, the virgin schoolteacher-boarder of twenty years, in a community where folks continually "dropped in," there could be no more screeches, sudden slaps, or loudly tearful quarrels. Discipline, which before had consisted of her sarcastic threats of enemas, her suddenly curled lip, the sting of her open palm on my cheek or ass, ceased. I was reprimanded primarily on matters of propriety; the same people who judged one's dress might, at closer range, judge one's behavior: "Don't sing at thuh table ... stan' up when your grandmother comes into the room ... always say 'yes *ma'am.*' ..."

While husbands and children, as extensions of oneself, can be subjected to nervous and physical collapse, hysteria, even violence, a primary tenet of Southern feminine behavior is that of presenting even—*especially*—under duress a controlled and subdued public demeanor. The messier Mother's life became, the less control she had over her destiny, the more she clung to the idea of correct form, of herself as a Southern lady. Blanche DuBois, in *A Streetcar Named Desire,* is barely a caricature of the conflicts, the sense of personal and familial failure, that were eating out Mother's insides.

Was it separation that made my good feelings possible? I

never saw Mother naked anymore and rarely heard the words to her and Daddy's quarrels. They lived in a bedroom in the far rear of the big house; Anne's and my room—wonderful refuge! —was at the very front. A former parlor, it opened off the living room, full of overstuffed furniture, through wide French doors and was shot with light from floor to high ceiling from the tall windows lining two sides of the room. Beyond was the front verandah, which wrapped the corner of the house, becoming the side porch. Boxwoods and white-rose bushes shaded the side yard; live oaks dripping Spanish moss were gigantic presences in the front, muffling the whiz of cars that rose from the main road.

On one wall was a wide fireplace, on another stood a gigantic oak chifforobe, a combination chest of drawers and free-standing closet with double doors that, opening outward, revealed double full-length mirrors. Anne's and my school dresses and scout uniforms hung on one side; on the other were drawers and shelves of all sizes, with plenty of spaces for my new white cotton bras, my new five-year diary, the multicolored pen from Japan, the stories I had secretly begun writing, and later, my toothbrush holder for secret masturbation.

On the high four-poster bed—in spring or summer, the breeze lifting the white rayon curtains, wafting the scent of white roses—I wrote in my diary and clipped the love poems from Mother's *Ladies' Home Journal*s, or devoured the adventure novels I had just discovered at the Carnegie Library. Lying on my back, staring at the old-fashioned round glass light fixture in the center of the high ceiling, I watched picture shows of myself in the arms of Jesus—or was it a brutal blond pirate? In subsequent scenes I was surrounded by my children-to-be, holding in my hand the book I had just written. "I want to get married in a baby-blue wedding dress with six bridesmaids in blue net dresses, have six children, and write novels while cakes bake in the oven," I confided to my diary. On blue-lined notebook paper, I designed trousseaus for the WASP-waisted teenager I had traced from a *True Love* comic book—strapless bathing suits, evening and wedding dresses—and drew plans

94

for the house where I would live with Troy, my seventh-grade sweetheart, when we were married and inevitably prosperous.

When the stories I had sent to *Calling All Girls* were returned with printed rejection slips, I was undiscouraged. I had just read a book about Captain Perseverance, who persistently steered his boat through difficult waters, and was certain that such diligence was all that was required. After all, hadn't I just won the school-wide spelling bee?

While I floated in this amnios, Anne dutifully banged out "Chopsticks" on the old black upright piano outside our bedroom door. Daddy's family, like Mother's, had pretensions: Bud, Daddy's spoiled younger brother, sang in musical comedies and operettas, as did his wife, Vera; Thelma, his older sister, played the piano and sang in the church choir; and everyone said that her son, Jack—a year older than me, who stayed inside practicing whenever he visited—would become a famous pianist.

Probably because Anne had inherited Daddy's Cherokee-dark looks and resembled more his side of the family, Mother had decided that Anne was "musical," I, "artistic." Each Saturday morning, I took the River car downtown to the High Museum of Art on Peachtree Street to charcoal nudes, which I used to scandalize Jack and Anne, who thought them done from life rather than statuary. Greedily, I added their ambitions to my own. Determined to become a concert pianist, or even an opera singer, I repeated Anne's scales and pieces till my lack of success made me turn back to listening to neighbors on the party line of the tall black telephone in the hall, or boiling wildflowers on Annie's black potbellied cookstove in attempts to make perfume that always—no matter what flower I used—ended up smelling like turnip greens.

I had picked the flowers—honeysuckle or stink flowers or laurel—in the woods behind the chicken yard, which was behind the garage and swept-dirt area where Annie swung the chickens by their necks till they staggered bloody and headless, bumping into stumps and rusty car parts. At the edge of the pine woods were the stobs we used for Sunday-afternoon games of horseshoe, and sometimes little plants called pigs, which popped fatly through the mossy ground in fall and spring. Beyond the woods, in a low place near the sinkhole at the edge of the next road, was the town dump.

Pushing aside the clinging blackberry briars, ignoring the beggar lice—the sticky and grasping seeds of a Southern weed —that clung to my bobby socks, kicking away Pabst cans and Southern Comfort bottles, I meandered among blackberry vines, old truck tires, and couches spewing damp stuffing. As I walked, I thrilled to a delicious fear: the brush around me, I knew, was thick with darting snake heads. I had read in the Red Cross first-aid manual a description of the emergency treatment for snakebite—an X razored through one's flesh, then sucked free of poison. As though picking at a scab, I tested in my mind whether I would be able to slash my own calf or ankle.

I knew nothing of rape, or its connection to the shapes of copperheads or water moccasins, and failed to associate my fear with dirty men who sometimes jumped from the boxcars of the trains that passed on nearby tracks. It was only that as I wandered in the dump, which I had come to think of as my own special place, I was suffused with images of Jesus that mixed with a vague sense of arms around me, of flesh rising warmly toward mine. When I finally jumped over the creek to buy a double-dip lemon-custard ice-cream cone from the stand beside the next road, I felt as though something had happened, but I didn't know what.

An erotic mysticism had begun to color all of life. As I walked up Bolton Road to the combination corner grocery and post office, or down it to Bolton School, I floated inches above the street, encapsulated in the glow that now seemed to touch everything.

Across the road lived my best friend, Barbara, a voluptuous blonde seventh-grader with whom I discussed boys, sex, boys, love, boys, clothes, boys, and menstruation. ("I can't go roller-skating today," I told her over the phone in an immediately understood coded message on the day my first period started in sixth grade.) Next door to Barbara lived the millworkers, or "poor people"; in an unswept dirt yard grimy children played with broken-down tricycles or old hubcaps. Beyond the "poor people's" house was the three-room structure where Mabel shrieked at Ruby, her nineteen-year-old daughter who had left home two years before. Periodically, Ruby would reappear, mysteriously dressed in slinky red or black satin, stiletto heels, a dark fur jacket. From inside the house, we would hear Mabel's shrill voice yelling for hours, until finally Ruby would stalk out, slamming the screen door behind her.

A vacant lot stood between Mabel's place and the ivy-covered front porch of the house where Cudden (or Cousin) Lily lay. She had taken to her bed when her father refused to let her marry the man she loved, and had never gotten up. At eleven, I was required to visit her, the family invalid. I hated to go, to feel her moist kiss on my cheek, for by that time she had been in bed for twenty years; her voice was quavery, strange, and her room smelled of sickness. Her father long dead, she and her "no good" brother, Grover, who went fishing every day and had "never worked a day in his life," were supported by their maiden sister, Cudden Myrtie; each day for forty years, Cudden Myrtie rode into Atlanta on the River car to her job as a bank clerk, then hurried home to cook, clean, and care for Cudden Lily.

Down the hill stood the shack where Ba-ma and Pa-pa, Annie's parents and my great-grandparents, had lived almost until they had died within a month of each other in their nineties. Next door was Dessie and Monroe's house, second cousins whose "no good" son, Roosevelt, liked to get drunk and go fishing with Daddy. Past the creek and the dip in the road was the small grocery behind which Billy New, the boy in the seventh grade who had asked me to marry him when I became fourteen, lived with his father, mother, and six brothers and sisters. Below Annie's house, a similar sprawling brick belonged to Reggie Lou's sister, Auntie Sue, and her husband, Madison, with whom, it was said, she had not shared a bed since the first week of their marriage forty years before.

On the other side of Annie's house was the Holy Roller, or Hard Shell, Baptist church, where I was forbidden to go because of its pagan activities, but where, whenever I could, I pressed my face to the windows to watch folks swaying in the ecstasy of speaking in tongues. Once, I looked through the glass as a Wednesday-night wedding took place. The bride was a girl of fourteen or fifteen whom I had seen at the post office and corner store. Dressed in a dark-gray crepe dress, a dark-gray pillbox atop her frizzy hair, dark-blue beads around her neck, she looked sad as she walked down the aisle toward her groom, who was balding and thirtyish. The next Sunday morning, as I passed the churchyard on my way to the more elite Methodist church, I saw her again, a knot of girls around her, and managed to mix with the fringes of her group. As I suspected, she was describing her honeymoon: "It looks like it's a foot long, and feels like it's ten . . ."

Later, as I sat white-gloved, my baby-doll-shod feet crossed at the ankles beneath the blue glow of the stained glass of the Collins Memorial Methodist Church, the shock of physical invasion, the thrilling brutalization of flesh leapt repeatedly through my mind. What did such acts have to do with me, or twelve-year-old Troy, whose blond curls swam in my vision two rows ahead, with whom I was even more in love than with Christ, and whose hand holding mine I always imagined as surrounded by a phosphorescent spiritual glow? Though I had read with excitement Mother and Daddy's hidden book on sex, this seemed different, a violence. Was this why Mother was so sad, my grandmothers so respectively stoic and bitter?

It was a question that did little to deter my interest in boys or love. As I passed—or escaped—Cudden Lily's house on my way up the hill to Carlton's store and post office, I saw my boyfriend Troy's dwarfed brother, Saxon, at the filling station where he worked. Saxon was gnarled and short, and his face looked as though it had been smushed in with a brick, but sashaying past him, I slung back my pageboy and stuck out my breasts.

In the store, I talked with Miz Carlton, and tried to avoid eye contact with her eighteen-year-old son, Leo, who had threatened to get me down and kiss me if we ever met alone. Once when Leo had given me a ride in his car, he had told me a dirty joke: "Do you know who wrote the hymn 'Love Lifted Me'?" he asked, referring to a song we sang most every Sunday at Collins Memorial, then answered himself: "The petticoat!" I had flushed when he teased that my boyfriend Troy was "as purty as a girl—fact, he could near 'bout *be* one." "I know when you go to bed at night, you hug your pillow and think on Troy," Leo whispered to me in a suggestion so outrageous that I stomped out of the store speechless.

Though I hated visiting Cudden Lily in her sickroom, and the way my face flushed when I saw Leo, though I felt exposed by everyone's knowledge of me and my business, I also knew I was important, part of a whole. It was as though everyone who lived in Bolton—from the redheaded ninth-grade girl who Barbara whispered was a "slut" (meaning she had had "sexual inner-course"), from the worn-looking men standing around on the porch of the local boardinghouse, to the virgin schoolteacher listening to her radio and correcting fifth-grade papers in her rented room each night, were elements of total organism, each essential to the body that was the community.

"In the South," says a Georgia State University sociologist, "there's an enormous acceptance of eccentricity, of difference —as long as it's part of one's own family or group." When I was visiting poet in a sixth-grade classroom at the far end of Lookout Mountain in Appalachia, a girl proudly raised her shirt to show me the rubber tube, necessitated by kidney disease, running into her side; as I tried to conceal my horror, the other students yawned; "we seen it plenty of times down at the swimmin' hole," a barefooted boy of fourteen explained as he fingered the dried rattlesnake skin on his desk.

At a consolidated school in a small west-Georgia county, I conducted poetry workshops from fifth grade through high school, and was puzzled at the recurrence in the students' poems of the line, "He has pink eyes . . ."—until I met the albino senior in dark glasses and black leather jacket, a tiger painted on its back. His anomaly had become part of the community collective unconscious, had even made him a local folk hero.

It is a unity often puzzling to non-Southerners, this loyalty, even nostalgia, for the ordinary, deprived, deformed, even violent and ugly—though *ugly* is a word with little meaning in the South. When Anne was pregnant with her first child seventeen years ago, she and her husband, Larry, went into a freak show at the Southeastern Fair in Atlanta. She was appalled, and superstitiously averted her eyes, as her husband and the Lobster Man—who had flippers for arms and feet—struck up a conversation about mutual friends and relatives in Sylacauga, Alabama.

Yet they were simply indulging in what Southerners mean when they say—reverently—"roots," meaning not only a longing for gospel music and barbecue, but even the less-pleasant aspects of Southern life, such as saunalike Augusts and the rigid stipulations of a Bible Belt God. One grows up half believing that it is only here that "real life" takes place, that though the earth may be depleted, loyalties run deeper than elsewhere. Unfortunately, the loyalty is too often a package deal: religious ecstasy and community—the whole bonding of *region*—is bound up with racism, sexism, and an acceptance of violence.

But a bonding, a body, a connection it is. In Bolton, the black snake that lay across the front walk, skittering away headless when Annie chopped it with her hoe; my cat, dying for three days on the back porch with a fishbone in her throat; the chickens flapping mutely in the backyard, dark blood spurting from their dumb necks; and the city dump where I sat in decaying armchairs, thinking of Jesus and my seventh-grade boyfriend—all were organic parts of a whole of which I was part, too.

It was as though sitting in the Collins Memorial Methodist Church, bathed in the glow of the Jesus who rose above me in clear stained-glass colors—the lost lamb who was also me held tenderly in his arms—and listening to my cat cough herself to death were somehow the same thing. Though I would later tell my own daughters to turn their heads when my stepfather stomped a mole to death on his farm in North Carolina, the violence of nature and man and the balm of Christ's tender love were, for me at eleven, a congruence.

"Ruby must be a'visitin'." Screeches from across the road; silence of four minutes.

"Sounds like Mabel's fit to be tied...." Silence of five minutes; squeak of wooden rockers resumes.

Ruby, a red hand print on her pancaked cheek, in a fur coat over her red satin dress, bounds through the screen door of the frame house across the road, and jumps into the front seat of a shiny black Buick; the man at the wheel drives off with a squeal.

Silence of three minutes.

"Sho' does burn rubber, don't he?"

It's Sunday afternoon at three. We've had "dinner"—each stuffing down as many carbohydrates as he or she could manage —at one. Now Mother and Daddy have gone off for a "drive"; Anne sits across the front porch playing Chinese checkers with Annie; Dr. Paul, Cudden Grover, and Reggie Lou occupy three of the five oak rockers; and I'm curled up in the porch swing, reading *The Saracen Blade*, imagining myself the high-born lady caught in the spell of the cruel adventurer. Immortality may be simply lack of change: we're doing what we always do on Sunday afternoon, rocking and talking and waiting for something to happen. What will happen is that Mother and Daddy will return: will Mother be smiling, with that strange flush on her face; or will her cheeks be tear stained, Daddy's speech slurred? Visitors will drive up the driveway unannounced, and we'll go out, if it's a fine day, behind the chicken yard to play horseshoes. I haven't yet noticed that women don't play, so I join the guffawing, back-slapping men; as though by a string, Sunday afternoons have become tied to the *clang* of the heavy metal as it circles the stobs.

That Auntie Sue's father died a few years before of ptomaine poisoning after eating unrefrigerated leftovers hasn't interfered with the custom of leaving out the remains of the midday meal. Later, we'll fix ourselves plates from the food on the cookstove—cold chicken and dressing, gravy, butter beans, biscuits, hunks of chocolate cake, or congealed blackberry cobbler —then get ready for Sunday-evening services at Collins Memo-

101

rial Methodist Church. In the white frame house of God, I'll see, as I did that morning, Cudden Myrtie, Cudden Grover, Leo, Carlton, my best friend, Barbara, my sweetheart, Troy, and Rudene and Leona from my class at Bolton School.

On the Sunday when his picture appeared on the front page of the *Atlanta Journal-Constitution* with a caption saying he had been charged with embezzling money from the bank in Atlanta where he worked, Leona's father had donned choir robe as usual to sing beside us in the choir. "Wondered how Leroy afforded takin' his fambly to Flarda last summer," someone said on the front porch that afternoon, just before Leroy showed up to play horseshoes.

As on every other Sunday evening, the preacher's retarded fourteen-year-old son will be wheeled, diapered and bibbed in a huge carriage, into the church aisle, where he will babble and drool during his father's sermon. After the service, Barbara and I will go downstairs to the church basement to Training Union; even "older" men, like Troy's eighteen-year-old brother, Clyde, who has a job in Atlanta, and his best friend, Boy, hang out there, playing Ping-Pong and Monopoly, and drinking "Co-Colas": in Bolton, there's nothing else to do.

Once a month, on my knees on the red carpet at the rail beneath the pulpit, I take communion of grape juice and soda crackers, and repent such sins as imagining kissing Troy, or making Anne—seven and naked but for white cotton panties beneath her white organdy pinafore—play kissing games at my party when we didn't have enough girls.

As I kneel, the gold hair of my sweetheart, his head bent at the end of the church rail, gleams and blends with the glow of the stained-glass Jesus who rises above us. What I feel as I walk in the city dump, what happens when Troy holds my hand as we roller-skate, becomes, as I bow my head, a vision of myself raised high, safe, warm in a blond savior's arms.

"Put all your weight against him. . . ." instructs Ruth Carter Stapleton in *Gift of Inner Healing.* "Lean hard against him and feel that firmness. His love pulls you closer and closer. Let go and sense your body moving into his body. . . . Every part of you has entered into Jesus. . . . You are one body. . . . He will never leave or forsake you." As she suggests, I have let Him replace the Daddy, the Mother, who are not there for me.

It will be years before I begin to see the Christ figure as androgynous, like myself, part woman, part man—each of us wounded and bleeding. For decades I will believe, like Mother and my grandmothers and their grandmothers, that my salvation lies first in a male God, then in a god-man—even a "no good" one.

Once a year, there was a Homecoming Sunday, or dinner on the grounds after Sunday-morning services. Long tables were set up out of doors behind the church in a grove of pines, to groan beneath platters of fried chicken, fried corn, chicken 'n' dumplin's, Jell-O "salits," biscuit and corn sticks, sweet-potato, blackberry, and chess pies. The women competed as though the dishes were new dresses. Because the chickens in our backyard provided an endless supply of eggs, Mother always baked a coconut cream pie made glamorous by canned coconut and a flamboyant, sugar-loaded meringue, which she beat in a shallow bowl with a fork for a half-hour or more.

"Alway beat thuh egg whites in one direction," she would tell me as she whipped, confiding a vital piece of information that made her resemble, for a moment, her mother, Lee. "If you don't, they won't rise up," she explained, implying that such an eventuality would be particularly tragic. Because of her craziness, she imbued the most ordinary acts or experiences with high melodrama; her facial expressions, her gestures, were as unsocialized as a toddler's, ranging from a glittering mania, through the snarl of her anger, to the deeply creased forehead and wrung hands of anxiety. It was an intensity she projected onto others: "Your black eyes were jes' glitterin'!" she would say of me after an improper display of "stubbornness."

This was apparently a condition only of people with "black" eyes. Just as fat women were pretty so long as they had curvaceous calves, fair people, like blue-eyed Grandmother Lee and her dead father, Huelet, were inevitably "good," while dark-eyed people—me, Anne, Daddy—were Satanic, to be suspected of mischief or worse.

Unconsciously, I adopted her notion. In an extension of the fear and attraction Southern women are taught to feel toward black men, I was certain that God was a blond male—preferably with a Sewanee or Baylor accent. For years, out of my rejection of my failed brunette parents, my early imprint of dark as "bad," dirty, inferior, I imagined black men had black saliva, that making love with one would mean exchanging juices with our kisses, and chose blond love objects. The preference began with my seventh-grade sweetheart and ended only after I was thirty with a long affair with a famous—and blond—Southern poet: the pirate of my dreams had turned out to be more cruel than I had hoped.

Once I reached puberty, Mother began to buy things for me. I had a narrow red leatherette belt of the kind I had dreamed about and red perforated "flats" that made me feel—with my newly long and red hair—like Alice in Wonderland. There was my new green Girl Scout dress and a green felt beret, the green-checked gingham that fit to my hips, then exploded in gathers, and the new white cotton bras with blue ribbons in their centers.

Grandmother Lee had made me a gathered skirt with a red-and-white-checked ruffle that lifted at one point to reveal a second ruffle of white cotton lace, plus a matching red-and-white-checked elasticized puff-sleeved blouse; pulling the elastic off my shoulders for school square dances, I was sure I was as glamorous as Rita Hayworth in *Gilda*, yet when I wore it downtown on the River car, pulled as low as it would go, I was indignant when a fortyish man followed me for blocks.

My best friend, Barbara, had shoulder-length strawberry-blonde hair and, at twelve, a thirty-eight-inch bust that was particularly impressive when she wore her white nylon "see-through" blouse with the buttons down the back. The "see-through" was stylish; I had one, too, and we liked to wear them because the boys at school made jokes about our bra straps, which in turn allowed us to hit them with our pocketbooks.

Barbara and I both wore lacy white cotton slips that hung inches beneath our tiered cotton skirts—the latest fashion according to *Seventeen* magazine—and baby-doll shoes: the higher their wedges, the more we looked like foot-bound Chinese women, and the more desirable we felt. Mine had narrow black ankle straps. Walking down Bolton Road after church on Sunday with my sweetheart, Troy, I felt ethereal, delicate, a fairy princess—suspended in an ecstasy that held me even higher above the asphalt than usual.

Besides clothes, Barbara and I talked about menstruation: with my Junior Kotex chafing precariously between my thighs, I sensed a new asset, an acceptable penis; just as in my favorite hymn, there was "power in the blood," and the blood meant we were women at last. As though we were gobbling down a whole box of Whitman's Chocolates, we compared notes on what to do for cramps, on Kotex sizes and sanitary belts, and on embarrassing situations, such as a spot spreading on the back of a new white skirt, or—horror of horrors!—a sanitary napkin dangling unhooked between our legs as we stood talking to a boy in the hall at school. In the South, a woman's sexuality—and the Southern man's fear of and dependency on it—is the source of her power; I loved the red that swirled in the toilet bowl, or lay close to my body, warmly trapped in cotton.

Now we, too, could manipulate through our femininity. The objects of our new power were Johnny—Barbara's skinny thirteen-year-old boyfriend from the wrong side of the streetcar tracks—and Troy, whom I secretly thought—because of his baby face and his Methodism—more refined. Barbara and I were "in love," we decided, and for hours at a time, avidly discussed love and marriage and "doing it." The last was an act we couldn't comprehend or imagine, much less put together with our crushes on our boyfriends. I had found the book *The New Eugenics: Parents Medical Counselor* Daddy had stolen from the Sigma Nu library. The chapter on "The Wedding" made the bridal chamber sound like the site of rape: "She, gentle spirit, after more or less extended or repeated torture, is convinced that it is her great misfortune [to have married] . . . ;" while the groom was extolled, "Young husband! Prove your manhood . . . by [not] yielding to unbridled lust and cruelty . . ."

Yet when the fifteen-year-old girl who sang in the choir with us eloped with her sixteen-year-old boyfriend, we had a hard time imagining him the carrier of such lust. *Our* boyfriends only held our hands or kissed us during the games of spin the bottle or post office; did something happen with the marriage vows? We sat next door in lawn chairs, drinking RC Colas with a millworker's pregnant wife; as she told us that "when you're married, you need nightgowns: they're easier tuh to pull up," our imaginations gyrated.

Modern Marriage, the book Mother and Daddy kept hidden beneath their bed in the back bedroom, made the act sound mechanical, a painless matter of body positioning; the only thing certain was that it had to do with the insertion of the penis into the vagina—preferably from as awkward an angle as possible.

A section in *Modern Marriage* recommended that the future bride stretch her hymen in advance of the wedding night through sitting in hot water, and the insertion into the vagina of increasingly larger objects. Since marriage was my destiny, I felt justified, enlightened, as I sat in the footed tub in the bathroom at the end of the hall forcing the glass toothbrush holder into my reddening vulva. Was this what *The New Eugenics* meant in its chapter on "The Solitary Vice"? "There is a . . . vice, a monster so hideous in mien, so disgusting in feature, altogether so beastly and loathsome, that, in very shame and cowardice, it hides its head by day, and vampirelike sucks the very life blood from its victims . . ." it read. *Modern Marriage,* with its pragmatic descriptions, was newer—circa 1935—and, I was certain, truer. Yet neither book mentioned the small organ of orgasm directly above my vagina, or female orgasm at all. My strange new habit was too intimate to mention even to Barbara,

106

as were the nebulous fantasies that floated through my mind as I lay in the four-poster bed beside Anne. Troy, his buttery hair turned the molten gold of the blond pirate's in the Frank Yerby novels, the whole surface of his body glowing (where were his clothes?) in the midst of vague scenes of medieval torture, duels, fearful escapes, fading into an end-of-the-world scene, the earth exploding into an inevitable, all-destroying flame; yet at that moment, Troy and I melting together, our naked bodies meshing for the first and last time.

Only the end of the world could justify sex before marriage, I knew from Sunday school and church. When the Winecoff Hotel on Peachtree Street burned down in the late forties and more than a hundred people died, many jumping screaming to their deaths, I was certain that they had been fucking. I already knew that sex, even sexual thoughts, could be a major sin, keeping me from God forever. I was like an Atlanta woman who says that the invention of the atomic bomb when she was a teenager had seemed to her only appropriate: she was sure it had been created specifically to punish her by fire for her sinful thoughts. It was probably this firmly imprinted knowledge that kept me, in my bed-and-bathtub fumblings, from finding my own clitoris; had I found it, the emphasis on feminine passivity could have kept me from learning to stimulate myself to orgasm. "I *did* learn to masturbate, though I didn't have a name for it," says a woman from Charleston; "but I was afraid to go to bed at night, because I might talk in my sleep and admit to *it*, whatever *it* was . . ." In spite—perhaps because—of the aggressiveness I hated in myself, I still needed the permission of a male god or author. In my fantasies, I was passive, the ravished maiden or submissive wife, going directly from my Betty Crocker kitchen to a bedroom that was operating-room chaste. That my desires were my own, and not external to me, I had not yet recognized.

Barbara and I talked about the girls who weren't "nice." "Whores!" she indignantly whispered of the two girls who went

107

to the Holy Roller church. "See that redheaded girl? Somebody said they were at a house somewhere, and she went up in the bedroom with a *boy*, and then the bed started squeakin'. . . ." "I'm glad I'm not cheap and common like that," I wrote in my diary, avoiding an actual reference to what I had been told.

Only love, which meant marriage, justified sexual activity. When Carol Raper, who we thought looked just like Susan Hayward, married at fourteen, Barbara and I envied her; when I saw her three years later at a cheap Atlanta department store, the same green coat she'd worn to seventh grade pulled around her thickened waist as she Christmas-shopped for her three children, I still did. We didn't realize that it was adulthood we craved, not children and housework. Yet sexual love, marriage, adulthood seemed inevitably linked, with little variation possible.

While we gossiped about possible love relationships among adults at Collins Memorial Church, we never imagined the possibility of actual adultery. We knew the married choir director who sometimes drove us home from choir practice had once been in love with a woman named Polly, who had married another man; when he parked in the churchyard, the motor running, and asked us to join him in renditions of "I Love You Truly" and "Let Me Call You Sweetheart," we found it sadly romantic. That their love might have been consummated—or that he might have had anything else in mind when he parked the car—was a possibility that never occurred to us.

Was the Pleasure Principle—titillated by religious guilt—covertly enjoyed in Bolton in 1948? Did the pagan images of the Blood of the Lamb, Christ on His Cross, infest the imagination, overstimulate the genitals as they had Mother's and later would mine? Barbara and I suspected that the declassé Holy Rollers at the Hard Shell Baptist church next door were "wild." But our imaginings were as naïve as the clear tints of the stained-glass windows at Collins Memorial Methodist, as gentle as the scenes of Jesus lifting the lost lamb. Sexuality and religiosity melted together within the phosphorescent glow that encapsulated everything. What filled me as I stood in church surrounded by neighbors and classmates, lustily singing a song, counterpointed by the babbling of the preacher's idiot son, of the blood shed and shed by Christ my Savior was an ecstasy part sexual, part sacred.

"I am going to make my life pure and stainless for Jesus," I stated to my diary; " Troy makes me want to be good...." After a party where we had held hands, I wrote, "Dreamed about Jesus last night.... Had a wonderful time at the party. Troy and I fed each other...." That my dreams of a male God and the feeling in my stomach when my sweetheart touched my wrist might be related was a connection I was not prepared to make, even as I added, "Daffodils are blooming and the sunshine is beautiful. They make me think of Troy and God...." Even when we began playing kissing games, I rejected my sexual feelings in favor of virtue: "Troy held my hand and put his arm around me, but didn't try to kiss me.... I'm glad because I want him to respect me...."

Since he was the necessary male link in my future ascent to the arms of Jesus, I was as pious in my concern for his soul as Mother had been for Daddy's: "I made a resolution to give Troy a lecture to make him come to church more regularly," I wrote; "... When I saw Troy today I told him I wouldn't like him anymore unless he went to church 5 Sundays in a row...." Already into the Good Woman syndrome, I felt superciliously correct. And when things went wrong, as in country-music tradition they inevitably would, there was always the Lord: "I'm through with boys, I guess ..." I decided when Troy and I quarreled; "I'm going to dedicate my life to Jesus and try to save the lost...."

My and Barbara's worship of our sweethearts equaled what we felt toward Christ. Yet neither of us imagined that the feelings we associated with them might come from within *us*, instead of God the Father or the boys. I didn't recognize—as I wouldn't many times during the coming years—that I had initiated my and my sweetheart's relationship. Following grammar-school protocol, I co-opted girl friends to ask him on the playground, "Do you like Rosemary?" "Barbara asked Troy if he likes me today," I penned; "He said 'not particularly.' I have a feeling it means yes!" The lesson of Captain Persever- ance, I found, could apply in love as well as work: when Troy carved my initials on his forearm with his pen knife, I wrote, "I hope darling (Troy) doesn't get blood poisoning ..." and added, "I never knew anyone so heavenly, swoonderful, ro- mantic. . . ."

Yet in the seventh grade, acknowledging the force of my fantasies was too threatening. When my teacher told me I was too bright to grow up and only marry, I was furious. "Didn't you notice," she asked after the class roller-rink party, "that even the instructors at the rink asked you to skate? That's because you're *different*—and you'll have more chances in life. Don't sell yourself short with an early marriage!" I turned away re- sentfully. An early marriage was exactly what I wanted *most.* ("I'm going to marry when I'm 17, right after graduation," I confided to my diary; "I'd better work on that hope chest. . . .") Did she really think I would give up what had become my primary ambition, my very success as a Southern woman, to be a shriveled old hag like her?

Besides, I was getting too good at it, this art of being aggres- sive without seeming to be, of telling myself that sexuality and power came only from males. At the roller rink, where more boys had asked me to skate than any other girl, I felt powerful; swirling around the rink on curves of music, hands crossed over sweaty hands with one partner after another, I was, for the moment, beautiful, desirable, superior. What could be better, I wondered, not realizing that as Belle of the Roller Rink, and later, as cheerleader at Tucker High (where Anne complained of having to follow in the footsteps of a sister who had the reputation of "having more dates than anyone who ever went to this school"), that I was simply following in the footsteps, repeating the peak experiences, of Mother, whose choices I thought I had rejected.

Mother, I felt arrogantly sure, was a failure because of her lack of skill at the game. If a woman behaved correctly—that is, in a properly manipulative and feminine way—she would receive the rewards of a doting (and successful) husband, comfortable house, beautiful children, and freedom from the need to work for a living. That this assumption still exists in the South was demonstrated to me recently when, as a guest on an Atlanta radio talk show, I discussed my and other Southern women's experiences. "Ain't you a three-time loser?!" asked a caller, referring to my three marriages; despite the fact that I had just described my Southern background, he added vehemently, "Why don't you jes' go back up North where you come from—we don't need your kind down here!" A woman caller insisted that "if only them women would *act* right, they wouldn't have none of those troubles." According to the myth, there exists, like the diploma at the end of a course, a perfect, or perfectable, man for every woman who has learned her skills.

With the superiority of a twelve-year-old, I knew that had Mother "acted right," Daddy wouldn't drink so much, she wouldn't cry so much, and we would have our own house. On the other hand, Daddy's older sister, Thelma, had apparently behaved correctly. She was married to a colonel in the army and she and my cousin Jack traveled with him to Japan and Germany. Thelma sang in the church choir, talked about Jack's brilliant future as a concert pianist, and made tea sandwiches by tinting cream cheese green and pink, spreading it on white bread from which she had trimmed the crusts, then stacking the slices and cutting them into Christmasy stripes. Intuitively, I knew this was something women learned to do when they were married to important men. It was only appropriate that when they came home on furlough, Anne and I should temporarily give up the front room to sleep on cots in the back bedroom with Mother and Daddy.

When I went back into my old room to rescue my diary from the chifforobe, I saw laid out on the bed two gray-beige cones of foam rubber. Mother, pretty, young, and powerless, endured the open disdain of her homely sister-in-law, yet asked in whispers of Anne and me whether we agreed that Thelma looked "just like Olive Oyl." Now I remembered—Olive Oyl was flat-chested, wasn't she? The cones of rubber lay like symbols on the

111

bedspread, proof that the proper *form* was even more important than beauty, particularly beauty as undisciplined as Mother's. It was the *appearance* of having breasts that mattered, just as proper behavior mattered more than passion.

Uncle Enoch, Thelma's husband, was the head of a whole army post and took her and Jack on trips to places I could barely imagine; but he was bald, mean talking, and wore ugly khakis. Was *this* the romantic reward of propriety? And what of Reggie Lou, our schoolteacher boarder, who was *always* proper, but had neither a husband nor property? Though Anne and I liked to be invited into her room to sit beside the fire as she graded fifth-grade papers, and to eat from a blue Chinese bowl the fat white mints that turned to tingly air in our mouths, we knew somehow that she wasn't important, that, like Mother, she didn't count.

Aunt Vera, Daddy's brother Bud's wife, added to my confusion. An operetta singer, she practiced, entered competitions, and took singing jobs away from home. She and Bud had met when they sang together in a local operetta. Now her picture was sometimes in the *Atlanta Journal-Constitution;* the hallway of her house on the northwest side of Atlanta was lined with signed photographs of people who looked as though they were famous.

Vera was tall, glamorous in a way that was opposite Mother's giggly roundness. Her long jet hair floated above her broad shoulders in a perfect pageboy, her laughter was removed and throaty. Her bearing was different from Annie's bitterness, Thelma's self-righteousness, Mother's obsequiousness, Reggie Lou's passivity; it was as though she was encapsulated within her own certainty. She had been spoiled by *her* mother, Annie, Thelma, and Mother agreed. Vera's mother, Mrs. Varner, had always encouraged her daughter's ambitions, and lived in Vera and Bud's house as a sitter for their children. Such female-to-female nurturing obviously was considered inappropriate. "Annie always cooked Bud's eggs in butter," Mother told Anne and me resentfully, "leavin' your daddy to fend for himself." This improper nurturing of the male, she indicated, was the direct cause of his drinking and gambling.

When there was talk that Bud and Vera would be divorced, no one was surprised. How could a woman have a career, a live-in mother-sitter, and a happy marriage too? It was the beginning of the conservative fifties: family consensus was that Vera was at fault; she had been too active, too assertive of her own desires. And apparently she had done something I had never heard of outside of Hollywood: she had found a second husband before giving up the first. This man, I heard Daddy telling Mother in a lowered voice, had come to Bud's house when he was away and had laid out one-hundred-dollar bills all over Vera's bed (she and Bud slept separately). And the night before she finally left, she had gone into Bud's room and had "kissed him all ovah." I'd never heard of fellatio, and I couldn't imagine anything more dirty than putting one's mouth all *over* someone, yet I sensed from Daddy's tone that this was some especially erotic act. Later, when we heard that Vera had dyed her hair platinum, given up singing, and was living in a house in Macon with a sunken marble tub, I was more puzzled than ever. Apparently it was not romantic love or her work Vera wanted, but something else—*what?*

It was not something I could ask Mother as she hurried, skinnier than ever before, from her job as a clerk-typist to the kitchen to help Annie cook supper; nor could I ask my grandmother as she bitterly presided over the big room at the back of the house. With its treadle sewing machine, black potbellied stove, big white kitchen table, and Frigidaire electric range, the kitchen was the stage for the play of Annie's angry gestures. Flashing the amethyst ring Bud had sent her during his tour of duty in Japan, she stirred the gravy so hastily that it was full of floury lumps, and boiled the collard greens with their coarse leaves still dotted with sand. Her biscuits—unlike Lee's airy pastries—were heavy white lumps with hard brown lids. Her triumph of economy of energy was a dish she called "poor man's pie"—blackberries from the woods behind the house mixed with flour and white sugar, topped with slices of white bread, then baked. "A lot better than rollin' out all that dough!" she declared, although the finished dish was as disgustingly soppy as the milk toast Mother fed Anne and me when we were sick.

That Annie's real life had little to do with family or homemaking, she made clear. She came alive getting ready for day-long shopping trips to Atlanta, or Tuesday nights spent at the picture show with Dr. Paul and his wife, Mabel. Each week, regardless of whether there had been a change of feature, they drove downtown to the Fox Theater, an Atlanta monument built like a Byzantine temple, complete with balconies and silver stars twinkling against a black velvet sky. When Annie came out of her room dressed in her good navy coat, a navy straw hat heavy with silk flowers perched on her pinned-up hair—a cerise or fuchsia scarf or two wound Isadora-fashion around her imperious throat—it was hard to imagine her wringing the neck of a squawking chicken, or impatiently plucking its soggy feathers.

Flashing her amethyst, laughing as throatily as Vera, she seemed as disembodied, unreal, as she had when I had sneaked into her bedroom. Perpetually darkened by closed blinds, filled by overstuffed chairs, the four-poster mahogany bed, the floor covered by stacks of old magazines and *Atlanta Journals*, it was a place I had rarely seen. As my eyes and nose grew used to the musty dimness, I saw on the bed, beside a huge pair of peach teddies, a strange garment of coarse peach cotton, elastic, hooks, laces; it still held my grandmother's shape. I recognized it as the stiff casing that held her flesh in place; bumping into her, I already knew, was like bumping into an ironing board: there was a literal separation, a lack of contact as visceral as that created by her anger. When she died almost twenty years later, I stood alone in a room in the funeral home and tentatively reached out to touch her arm. I had never before touched a dead body, and began giggling hysterically: my grandmother had always seemed stiff and cold, yet in that moment I knew through my fingertips the rage that had so long held her erect.

When Annie and Thelma held tête-à-têtes, I was one of the subjects. "She'll be married by the time she's fourteen," Thelma

114

predicted disapprovingly when she noticed I had shaved my legs. Though I knew that she, not my passionate and improper mother, was the arbiter of what was "proper," I was undaunted. I was twelve, and all the seventh-grade girls at Bolton School shaved. Besides, I was too full of good feelings about myself: wearing a new white waffle-piqué dress, my shoulder-length auburn pageboy held to one side by a new tortoise barrette, I had just graduated from grammar school. On the last blank page of my diary, I listed my gifts:

camisole —	Grandmother Lee
petticoat —	" "
cosmetic case —	" "
pearls —	Aunt Betty
panties —	Reggie Lou
night gown —	Mom & Daddy
lipstick —	Grandmother Annie
rouge —	" "
pocket book —	" "
handkerchief —	" "

"I feel like a bride!" I added at the bottom.

Already, everything pointed in that direction. Knowing how important it was to attract a man, Mother encouraged me to dress sexily. When I was fifteen, she would shop with me for black strippy high-heeled sandals and a black crepe dress much like Ruby's. Throughout his life, Daddy's only gifts to me would be sexual items of lingerie—lacy panties, sheer black hose and nightgowns—that would sickeningly reaffirm my sense that my only value lay in my sexuality.

But at twelve, I had little sense of how I was absorbing the values fed me. Instead, I only had inklings of the end of innocence. One morning I walked into the kitchen to announce to Mother and Grandmother Annie a new bit of scientific knowledge found at the Carnegie Library—that boys had something called "wet dreams" that made sticky stuff called semen come out of their things at night. Annie grunted disgustedly; Mother giggled guiltily, as though someone had just said her slip was showing. To cover my embarrassment, I grabbed a raw oyster from a can in the refrigerator, covered it in catsup, and swallowed it whole. (Was I already making the connection Ben made years later when we sat eating oysters in a bar in New Orleans—that people who can't eat raw oysters can't deal with female sexuality?)

I felt the same thrill of fear I had experienced with Bobby, the hulking fourteen-year-old seventh-grader to whom I had sold the pictures I had drawn of naked women. As he held one of the crayoned Amazons—Wonder Woman and Brenda Starr with pubic hair and nipples—over my head and threatened to expose me if I didn't kiss him, I knew that my boldness had gone out of bounds and that my interest in the sexual was its most disgusting symptom. Grandmother Lee had told me of a girl who had been ruined: "Of course, nobody would have enythang to do with her after that; she couldn't git married, and it followed her daughter, too. . . ." Had I already ruined myself by the reading of romances, my impure thoughts?

When I was in the eighth grade, and Troy in the ninth, my worst fears proved true. Each day we rode the River car—the same streetcar ridden by Mother to and from Fulton High School in Atlanta—from school together, then walked down Bolton Road to my house. At first, we stood around at the end of the driveway, cutting up with Barbara and the other kids. But soon, as though magnetized, we began making excuses, hurrying away from the others to sit together in the white metal love seat in the side yard. The boxwoods on our side obscured the view from our bedroom windows, and on the other side of the yard a bank of white roses bloomed dizzily, concealing the area from Auntie Sue's house next door.

At first, we pretended not to notice our new privacy and only touched hands gingerly and joked. But when I leaned over to mash his blackheads, Troy's blond-fuzzed cheeks turned bright pink. The bushes around us suddenly seemed to be spinning; my insides lurched, spiraling like the white flowers. As though we had been overcome by the scent of roses, we were in each

116

other's arms—kissing in a way we never had during games of post office. In that moment, Troy's white-gold hair, the dazzle of the blossoms, the cool paint of the metal chair turned warm behind my eyelids, became a small white-hot lick in my belly, a wetness in my lower parts. For the next month, afternoon after afternoon, we snuck away from the others and kissed without pretense of restraint. Though I knew my compulsion meant the end of our pure love, of my dreams of our baby-blue wedding, our Betty Crocker kitchen, and six blond children, I was hooked.

Worse, it was proof of what I had feared: that aggression and desire resided within *me*, rather than the outside world; that my grandmother and aunt had been right in their estimation of my worthlessness; that our time in Bolton—soon to end with another move—had only been a respite, a remission in the cancer that was our small family's life; that what had been implied long before by my parents' early misery, Mother's enemas, indeed, my very birth, was true. I was malformed, a vessel of evil—and nothing in my ungentle background could save or make me into a good Southern woman.

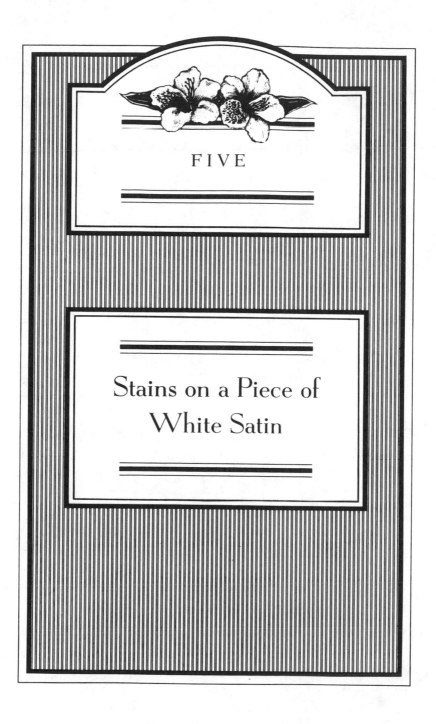

FIVE

Stains on a Piece of
White Satin

"But what if I get pregnant?"

"I'll just count back the months and prove it wasn't me. . . ."

Because I'm in love, that remark slides right by me. David and I are parked on the lower slope of Stone Mountain, the favorite parking place of teenagers all over the county, the place I will later refer to—after fucking both my first and second husbands there for the first time—as the spot where I lost my virginity three times. Like dark beetles, other cars perch all around us on the stone; below, one light rises from the shack that sells Moon Pies and RC Colas.

We've just been to Redan Baptist Church for Wednesday-night prayer meeting, then out on the highway to Jack's Drive-In, which we could see from a mile away because it's lit by a huge pink neon jackstone. Here, we listen to Hank Williams on the jukebox and eat double chili steaks in the car. Sixteen to my fifteen, David is blond, like Troy—a football player at Stone Mountain High School. His cheeks glisten with tiny gold flecks in the quiver of neon, and my heart turns over: I feel the same way I had in Collins Memorial Church, kneeling beside Troy during communion. When he puts his hand on the bodice of my cotton summer dress, I can barely swallow my chocolate shake.

We've dated on and off for months, but the week before as I walked into church in the blue eyelet dress that made my figure look good, in the new white high-heeled sandals Mother had bought me for Easter, I had felt his eyes on the backs of my legs.

Now he's putting his hand down the front of the blue dress, then beneath my skirt, inside my panties—his finger slides into my vagina. I feel wet, faint with excitement and desire.

". . . besides, I've got something . . ." I know what he means; all the boys carry them in their billfolds. He puts my hand on what feels, through cloth, like an enormous lump, a bone thinly

121

veiled in skin. Is this the thing I've dreamed, writhing, inside me so many nights in bed beside Anne? He unzips his pants, putting my fingers again around what feels like dumb flesh; awkwardly tears at foil and unrolls something sticky over the thing—making it seem more foreign, less human than ever.

But there's no turning back now; besides, I don't want to. I want to do this more than I've ever wanted to do anything. As he pushes up my dress, pulls at my panties, shoves me back against the handle of the car door, it's as though my whole life has led up to this point—till I feel the strange lump bump against my belly. "Wait," I gasp, remembering what I had read in Mother and Daddy's hidden book on sex; "there's a better way—let me sit on your lap . . ." He looks irritated—who ever heard of a girl saying how to do it?—but sits back. I try to lower myself slowly onto this thickened flesh, this stob—but he pulls me down abruptly. For moments, the pain amazes me, seems more than I can bear, an invasion more brutal than I have ever imagined during my manipulations with the toothbrush holder.

But in a half minute, it's over; his head is back against the car seat, his eyes closed. He pulls himself out of me—my raked flesh recoils—peels off the rubber, throws it out the window, zips his pants and starts the car. It's as though I'm not there. I pull my dress down gingerly, feeling ashamed. As he drives me home, we don't talk; at the door, he kisses me once.

For the next few weeks, I dream of walking into school basketball games, my old green coat pulled over my stomach— married, loved. But when my period starts and David never calls again, I'm not surprised. My self-hatred balls in my belly, a constant I can only calm by eating more and more chili steaks, chocolate shakes, banana splits—all the things that make my acne run wild, my hips swell wantonly. I did wrong, sinned— what's worse, wanted *to. Everything Mother, Grandmother Lee, and my Baptist Sunday-school teacher said was true: if you let boys have their way, they won't like you anymore: you'll be ruined.*

It was too late. I was.

I had two boyfriends in high school, and married them both.

It was before my loss of virginity, and because of my baking, that I met my first. The dividing line for attendance at the high school in the next county was a half mile down the road from our house. Often, I watched the most handsome boy I had ever seen—a muscular blond, the pirate of my dreams—swagger past. His name, I knew, was Junior (not junior to anyone, just Junior), and he went to the other school. One day as I walked to the end of the driveway on my way to a girl friend's, a pan of fresh brownies in my hand, he decided to stop. As we stood talking, he put his fist into the pan, gouging out the brownies in huge chunks; when he had eaten them all, he said "See yuh latah, alligatah," and walked off.

A few days after, as I sat in the front yard in the white painted lawn chairs, rereading *The Foxes of Harrow* and thinking of Junior's swagger, he reappeared. "Kin yew go out on dates yet?" My heart bounced beneath my Peter Pan blouse. "Are yuh busy Friday night?" he pursued when I nodded. Speechless at my good luck, I shook my head. "Wall, I'm doublin' with my cudden T.J., 'n' he don't have a date. Will yew go with 'im?"

T.J., as muscular and with as much of a swagger, turned out to have a plain round brown face, brown eyes and hair. He was part Cuban, he said ("Yew might not b'leeve this, but T.J. stan's for Tony Juan"); and was known—though I didn't know it yet—for having thrown his high school principal's typewriter through the window in a fit of temper. As we sat in the backseat of Junior's car, driving to I didn't know where, I was afraid: they were older—seniors—and might even drink beer! I smoothed the skirt of my pink waffle-piqué dress across my thighs, thinking how the scallops at the hem matched the shape of my neat pink genitals. "Can I ast yew sumthin'?" T.J. whispered into my ear. I nodded fearfully, waiting for the outrageous sexual suggestion I was sure would follow. He cupped his hand at my ear so the others couldn't hear: "Are yew a Christian?"

Though I didn't see T.J. again for a year, we were married in two.

When I was thirteen, we had moved to Tucker, the small country town outside Atlanta where Grandmother Lee and Granddaddy Carroll lived. On the condition that we live near them, they had loaned Mother and Daddy the down payment for another house, this time a three-room white frame set way back from a winding county artery.

Every Sunday morning, and every Sunday and Wednesday evening, we went to the Tucker First Baptist Church, because that was where Granddaddy Carroll was a deacon. Anne and I shared a rollaway bed, which folded up against the wall during the day, in the kitchen. Our maple chest of drawers stood beside the Frigidaire, and I hid leftover cakes and pies beneath my bras and panties to gobble down when I came in ravenous from dates. On the surface, life was better: Mother grew sweet peas and zinnias in our huge yard, and we had cut flowers on the table every day. We had a cocker spaniel named Prissy, a pet white rabbit, a cat with a broken tail, and to look after Anne and me after school and during the summer, a fat black maid named Precious, who wore a knife in her stocking top. Because Daddy worked for a tire company that also sold appliances, we had one of the first television sets in town and spent Tuesday evenings watching Milton Berle cavort with his Texaco Men. Daddy was given a new company car, and the four of us took our only family vacation—to Jacksonville Beach. I had a new bathing suit with a bare midriff; Mother wore a suit with a flounce skirt and smiled bravely; and Daddy rode the Ferris wheel on the boardwalk over and over with Anne. For my fourteenth birthday, Mother even planned a party with a bakery cake with yellow sugar roses and *Happy Birthday to Rosemary* written on it in green icing.

At Tucker High, as Miz Carroll's granddaughter and Bubba's —the star quarterback's—cousin, I was immediately popular among the two hundred or so students. As I walked down the school halls, my new pink angora sweater seemed to exude electricity. All the cutest boys were my boyfriends, and the most popular girls, my pals. My popularity spilled over outside the school. Besides boys from Tucker, I dated BMOCs from the other county schools. I even had a boyfriend—later to become my second husband—who was in *college*, whose daddy was an architect, a professional man, and who came to pick me up in his daddy's black Buick Riviera when we went to picture shows at the Fox Theater in Atlanta.

When the student body was given IQ tests, a fat, quiet girl and I tied for the highest score. As a result, I was offered a scholarship to the Dale Strebel College of Cosmetology. But Mother, true to her sense of our genteel Methodist superiority, insisted that I refuse. I didn't care: *my* favorite subject was home ec.

Yet this Southern-fried *Seventeen* magazine success story was a thin skin barely covering my true feelings. It was not my popularity, my sewing, and my election to the cheering team that were my reality, but the rot that lay just beneath my giggly surface. And like mildew in August, it popped up everywhere.

Despite my cake with the yellow roses, my one birthday party ended with the ninth-grade boys throwing grapefruits against our living-room wall, and me in tears because the boy I liked liked another girl. Daddy's company car, a Frazier, was not the right kind, a boy I had a crush on told me: its presence in our driveway denoted our inferiority. On the beach in Jacksonville, I cringed in shame at what I was sure was my deformed body; Mother cried every night in our cheap motel room; and Daddy was drunk morning as well as evening. As our shameful car careened down U.S. 95 toward Saint Augustine, where we planned to see the crocodile farm and the country's oldest schoolhouse, Mother sobbed and Anne and I clung to each other again.

Years before, the Atlanta waterworks had become a staple of my nightmares; now, I added the crocodile farm: walking a narrow bridge above a moat full of huge hissing reptiles would become part of my dreams, along with the queasy terror that was beginning to accompany everything. When I read, a couple of years ago, that a child had actually fallen into the moat to be dismembered within seconds before his parents' eyes, the feeling rose in me again, full blown.

I had earlier begun my reputation as a female who didn't take care of her "thangs" by dismembering my dolls, and carving ROSEMARY deeply into the surface of the maple coffee table that was one of Mother's few pieces of good furniture. Now even my pet rabbit, Snowy, became a sign of my lack of control. Hopping around the house, she left permanent bright-orange spots on Mother's hand-crocheted eggshell bedspread; when I left her in a cage overnight with Anne's lavender Easter chicken, she ate off the chick's toes. Her incorrigibility seemed to echo my own, and so did her anxiety: when she met the cat in the hallway of the house, she screamed in the unearthly voice of a mute creature driven to expression by terror.

Later, she disappeared into the cornfield that lay behind our house. In a few days, she dragged her small body—fur matted, dehydrated, as light as a seashell—back to the edge of the yard, where she died in my palm. As she lay in my hand, her once-silky fur stained like the piece of white satin that my body should have been, I knew I was as defiled, and deserved to be as severely punished, as my pet.

That night as I lathered Noxema onto my face, I noticed that the small red pimples that lay just beneath the surface of my skin were gathering strength and color, signs of the pus that must be filling my interior. When Prissy, our whorish cocker spaniel, was in heat, male dogs flew up to hump Anne and me when we walked into the yard. Now I was certain that it was my body that was the source of evil.

I lay on the rug watching Milton Berle and writhed in flames of self-hatred. Like the Brazilian girl who had herself crucified for three days to "free my soul from demons," I was determined to flagellate myself. The next day after school, I chopped my long hair off at ear length with Mother's pinking shears, then poured a bottle of peroxide over it. Within hours, my once-lush locks turned a hacked, brassy orange.

To be feminine in the Southern tradition meant being fragile, pale, Scarlett O'Hara–ish like my best friend, Darlene; my rosy and freckled Scotch-Irish plumpness was, I knew, another sign of my defectiveness. But Mother had taught me only one way to soothe my anxious soul: at ball games, I guzzled "Co-Colas," gobbled Milky Ways and Baby Ruths; at home, I filled up on hot biscuits dripping margarine, and huge chunks of homemade cake. "Pear-shaped!" boys whom I had once French-kissed would tease. My calf-length cheerleading skirt had a heavy gold satin lining; worn with the paper-soled black ballet slippers—$2.98 at Butler's shoe store—which I now wore everywhere with the *de rigueur* thick white bobby socks, it made me look, as Grandmother Lee had said of Mother, *very* "close to the ground."

The pink dress with the scallops at the hem, made early in my home-ec. career, had turned out to be my masterpiece. As my self-esteem plummeted, so did my sewing skills. A gray wool skirt had a raw protruding seam, a gold jersey blouse had an ugly buttonhole that couldn't be fixed, a red polka-dotted skirt and vest matched my pimples too well.

Since my craziness demanded form, I now had a ritual: my clothes were to be thrown into the corner of the room, never hung up at all—the gray skirt, the gold blouse worn only on Mondays and Wednesdays, the polka dots on Tuesdays and Thursdays. I had three equally ugly sweaters: a tent-size white nylon given me by a boyfriend, a two-sizes-too-small dirty white cashmere Mother had found on a sale table in Davison's basement, and my letter sweater, which had a permanent waffle on the back where I had scorched it on the heat register. These I could wear any days, but my pink angora sweater—my one magical garment—was reserved for Friday, the lucky day preceding date night.

Tuesdays and Thursdays were dreaded, especially Thursdays: if I didn't have a date for Friday night by suppertime on Thursday, I knew I would spend the rest of the evening crying in the bathroom or on the front stoop, praying for the phone to ring, a voice to say, "This is Pee Wee . . . Hunky . . . Leroy . . . Do yuh wanna double tuh thuh game tuhmorra night?"

I already realized that I would never be able to achieve the reluctance Grandmother Lee implied was necessary to get a good husband, that I would never "make a wife for a home-lovin' man." When I liked a boy—and I liked many—I could no more resist his tongue in my mouth, or his fingers inside my panties, than I could resist breathing. Since Southern boys were considered "a sissy if you didn't," as a male friend later told me, the pressure—despite the opposite pressure on girls to remain pure—never let up. "Onct yew git ust tuh it, yew have tuh have it," warned Lewie, who sat beside me in study hall; "'n' sum of thuh boys have been sayin' you're already gittin' thet way." I was too guilty to realize he and his buddies were mad because I had moved outside local male bonding by dating boys from high schools with rival ball teams.

My sexual feelings, I was sure, were written across my forehead in letters as clear as those on a billboard. Worse, they could even be read by people like Grandmother Lee. As I sat talking with Aunt Billie's new husband, Lee had come into the room and opened the door, sternly saying, "Leave this doah open!" My face flamed at the implication of her words; I was sure it was me, not male lust, that she mistrusted—that she thought that, at fourteen, no man could be left alone in a room with me.

On the nights when I had been petting, I lay in bed beside Anne, writhing in the eternal hellfire I was now sure would be my only fate. Because we were living in a little house again, we could sometimes hear Mother and Daddy fucking. But now I knew it was me, as well as Mother, in whom a messy, excessive passion thrived, like mildew in a place too moist and dark.

Daddy confirmed my depravity. "Your fans are callin'!" he would sneer when he answered the phone to a boy's voice. As I talked, he might walk by and pour a glass of water down the back of my neck. "Whore!" he would yell when a date was due to arrive. Graphically describing what he expected me to do during the evening, he sometimes tore off his clothes, till Mother would shove him, naked, into the bedroom and lock the door. As she, my date, and I made polite conversation, we would hear him cursing and falling against the thin walls. On the night he raised the butcher knife above my head, Mother held his wrist with both her small hands, tears rolling down her cheeks with the effort, until he fell backward on the dining-room floor.

In our household of women, Daddy had become a negative force, a dark spot to be dealt with. It was now him I hated to see nude: watching him at the bathroom sink, his once-honey-colored skin bruised mauve and green by drunken falls, his penis and testicles hanging like some small animal with its neck broken, I felt nauseous about myself.

"A bad reputation!" Mother cried resignedly. As she lay back on the crocheted bedspread, with its orange spots of rabbit urine, she no longer looked like a belle reclining, the delicate-if-plump beauty of a Fitzgerald novel, but a disheveled, drooling washerwoman. The curly lamb coat, the cream felt cloche, the trousseau nightgowns I remembered from years back were totally gone.

I had already been kicked off the cheerleading team for riding to the games in cars with boys, instead of riding the school bus with the others. When the Baptist preacher, who lived across the road, complained to Mother that I had boys visit during the afternoon while she was at work in Atlanta, I only felt contemptuous. I stood before her with the same sulky expression with which I had listened to her description of menstruation at nine. "Rows-may-ree, don't you know that, as a gurl, your good na-ame," she pleaded, drawing out the long *a*'s she considered a part of refined speech, "is awl you have tuh git a good husband?" Something inside my chest hardened: Mother had had a good name; did she have a good husband?

Now she was speaking of the *True Confessions* and *True Romances* she had found hidden beneath my mattress: my great-grandfather had been a Methodist minister, my uncle was a university president; we came from a "refined" family; we didn't read such things. In the same helpless whine she used with Daddy, she referred back to the week before, when I had come in at three in the morning after a date on a school night: "Rows-may-ree, are you sure nuthin' *happened*?"

As she spoke, I flashed myself beneath Melton, the twenty-three-year-old ex-sailor who was my current boyfriend, my backbone mashed against the raw springs of his old Chevy, his nicotine-stained fingers gouging the lips of my vagina. Mother would die, I thought, if she knew how my life was now dominated by fingers—fingers under my bra, fingers inside my crotch: prodding, prodding, prodding me in much the same way, a way which I now called "love," as she and Daddy had when I was five.

But Mother had other, more imperative, problems than what happened to me in the backseats of cars. Her life had become an unrelieved morass of fatigue, money worries, and draining daily scenes with Daddy, who was now rarely ever sober, and who had lost job after job. "If only you would jes' work in a grocery store, enythang that's not on commission...." she would beg. It was a useless plea. Daddy had rules for himself: he wouldn't leave the sacred tire business, and wouldn't ride buses. What was accepted by Mother—the job as a clerk-typist, the two buses to and from Atlanta each day—was beneath him: he was a man.

Since her small salary was now practically our sole support, we had had to give up Precious. Anne and I each had door keys, and each afternoon, after walking home along the railroad tracks, I was supposed to make the beds, wash the dishes, and start supper. But most days, exhausted by late dates, and a lethargy that seemed to pervade every cell of my body, I lay sprawled across my and Anne's unmade bed till Mother trudged in, too tired to complain. Anne set the table; we floured and fried pork liver or brains or fatback, which, with its streak of lean through its center, reminded me of what Mother called my "streak 'a meanness." We boiled cabbage or collards and made the ubiquitous cornbread or hot biscuit. Mother had long since given up her efforts toward gourmet cooking; economy and nutrition were now her only goals. But supper was still her one daily pleasure, and if we managed to get through it without Daddy's ritual harangue, she liked to linger over the dessert we still always had, imprinting with her fuchsia lipstick cigarette after cigarette, cup after cup of coffee.

Mother, smoking and holding her coffee cup so tensely that its hot handle engraved itself into her small fingers, seemed unhappy in a brittle way that the mothers of my country girl friends did not—but then, none of them had been belles. Crystal's mother was a big-boned dyed-blonde divorcée who worked on the night shift at a factory and left Crystal in charge of their ramshackle duplex, with its linoleum rugs and red-dirt front yard, and five younger brothers and sisters, while she worked or went out on dates. Maudine's daddy was "no good," and beat her when she stayed out too late. The family lived in a three-room shack behind a service station on Main Street; because there was no indoor plumbing, the family had to take baths in a tin tub in the kitchen. But her mother, wearing a white uniform like a nurse's, worked in the produce department of the general store and liked for us to come in after school to share our gossip; her face, already crisscrossed with wrinkles at thirty-five, crinkled as she giggled with us. Gayle's daddy "drank," too. But her mother had bought a white-and-gold-painted "French Provincial" bedroom suite (pronounced *suit*) for Gayle's room in the garage apartment where they lived, and went religiously to the beauty parlor on Main Street to have her hair set in the convoluted upsweep that Gayle confided was held in place each night by sworls of toilet paper. The fancy furniture, the weekly trips to the Tucker Beauty Shoppe, even the hair worn on top of her head, gave Gayle's mother a supercilious air that Gayle emulated.

Darlene's mother was close to the rural Southern feminine ideal. Placid and plump, she kept her pantry filled with home-made blackberry and peach preserves, and the cake plates in her kitchen filled with homemade layer cakes and pies. She never contradicted Darlene's father, a stern, skinny carpenter who yelled, "Naow they're ashowin' big black niggers!" when a *Life* magazine with a black face on its cover came in the mail. The "they," I understood, was New York, and the whole world outside Tucker, Georgia; and with an intuitive awareness of the relationship between racism and sexism, I felt queasy as he ripped the magazine in two and threw it violently into the garbage can. But I was soothed by watching Darlene's mother

131

lay piece goods out on the dining-room table: she weighted the Simplicity pattern pieces with silverware from the kitchen, then cut out the sections of cloth and sewed them together expertly, without basting, on her treadle sewing machine. Darlene had a heart-shaped face, a twenty-inch waist, hip-length brown hair, and, because of her mother's sewing, more circle skirts, blouses with Peter Pan collars, sundresses with jackets, than any other girl at school. The youngest and only child at home, she was the family pet in the Southern tradition of people who have little pleasure except from their young. Whenever I visited, I lapped up the acceptance and affection that slopped over onto me as Darlene's little friend.

After a double date spent mutely necking at the drive-in, my cheeks were chafed red by my date's whiskers; as I walked into the kitchen with Darlene, with whom I was to spend the night, her mother, who had been waiting up for us, exclaimed, "Rowsmay-ree! What's the mattah with your face?" "I must be allergic to grapefruit," I answered inanely, knowing the heat in my loins must be ablaze on my pimply forehead. But she had believed me; and denying that I was too plump, or that I had any acne at all, had plied me with great hunks of her homemade coconut layer cake with milk before I went to bed.

Darlene's mother must be dumb, I thought, not to realize the kind of person I really was. That my girl friends were loved for simply *being,* that their home lives were not some dark shameful secret, like mine, made me feel meaner, more of a misfit. Daddy's drunkenness, Mother's misery, my own desires were unspeakable. It was fine—at meetings of the Secret Seven—to light up Lucky Strikes, strip down to our slips, and wave from the window as the boys passed, honking, in their broken-down Chevies. It was okay to talk about menstrual cramps, clothes, and other girls, but not problems with our parents, or what really happened between us and our boyfriends. We might double-date and dry-hump, finger-fuck—even fuck—in the backseat, our date tossing his used Trojan out the back window while no one was looking; but none of us ever confessed to having "gone all the way," or to wanting anything out of life other than an all-white wedding at Tucker First Baptist Church.

Cataclysmic life events, like the loss of virginity, couldn't be discussed even among best friends: it was too dangerous. When Darlene and I shared a room at a Baptist youth conference, I suddenly longed to tell her what had happened with David, of how he had "done it" to me, then had never called again. "I've got a secret to tell you . . ." I began tremulously as we lay in bed. Together, Darlene and I had operated on a live chicken, cutting open its craw and sewing up the wound; once we had walked blouseless down the railroad track, deliberately exposing our small breasts. But now her long brown hair, her heart-shaped face lay too near. I couldn't begin the words. Besides, I felt uneasy: this closeness, this sweetness, couldn't be right between girls.

When our classmate Cherry had confided her dream of wanting to go to college, Darlene and I had thought she was weird. But now she had done something we admired: at fifteen, she had married sixteen-year-old Frank, one of the cutest boys in the eleventh grade. When she was nine months pregnant, she invited me to "spend the day," a common Southern invitation that means hanging out from morning through suppertime. Frank had quit school, too, and would be at work at his job as a bricklayer; we would entertain ourselves, she said, by making fudge.

As she beat the thickening cocoa and sugar, my eyes were glued to the bulge beneath her chenille housecoat; it seemed funny to see my girl friend from school with her belly poking through her robe. Was she afraid, I wondered? Now that she was married, it was okay to talk obliquely about sex: "On our wedding night, I went out to the outhouse [they had honeymooned in a shack without indoor plumbing] and when I came back in, Frank unbuttoned every button on the back of my blouse. It had a *lot* of buttons. . . ." She seemed as though she wanted to say more, but didn't know how. I was excited at the thought of Frank, with whom I'd flirted in the school halls, unbuttoning her blouse. Words pressed at my own mouth. But without admitting my own experience, I couldn't respond: the culture had tied both our tongues.

A couple of years later, I saw her riding by in a car with an older woman and two toddlers, a cigarette hanging from the corner of her mouth. She must have been seventeen.

Had Cherry wanted to confide in me because she knew I was ruined?

And if *she* knew I was ruined, what about the One Who Knew Everything? When I had been baptized in the pool behind the pulpit, I had only been aware of the way my wet white dress clung to my pink nipples. On dates to church on Sunday and Wednesday nights, I sat in the back row with boys who tried to kiss me during the long prayers, thinking not of Hellfire and Damnation, of being Washed in the Blood, but of what might come later—of tongues, fingers, Trojans, penetration. Was I hopelessly lost? The stained-glass windows I had once loved rose above me accusingly.

Each summer, revival meetings were held every night for two weeks to give the Holy Ghost a chance to penetrate. With the other sinners I walked down the aisle at the end of the service to do what was called "rededicating my life to Christ." As the rest of the congregation softly sang, "Jes' as I am-m-m— with-ou-ut wun plea-ea-ea—but the-ut thy blu-ud wuz she-ed— fuh me-e-e . . ." tears of release gushed down my plump cheeks. But through the melting Kleenex I held to my eyes, I noticed that among those rededicating themselves was the woman os- tracized by the community, who, now pregnant with her fourth out-of-wedlock child, her belly taut beneath her feedsack dress, had been drawn, sobbing, into the arms of two women near her. Later, in the churchyard, I saw her wandering through those hugging, kissing, crying, as invisible, as alone as ever. I knew about the rayon scarves that were kept behind the pulpit to throw over the exposed thighs of the women who fell down in ecstasy. In such an atmosphere, sexual sins were hardly for- givable.

Even the preacher, it turned out, was not exempt. A good- looking foreigner—meaning "not frum aroun' hyah"—he was said to have been seen kissing the old-maid pianist. Darlene's daddy and the other deacons held a meeting to run him out of town; though Granddaddy Carroll had come to his defense, he had been outvoted. The pianist blossomed and got married, but we heard that the preacher had had a nervous breakdown and was having something called shock treatments, that his wife was supporting the family by sewing slipcovers for rich people in Atlanta.

In my usual myopic way, I was disturbed: if a grown man, an agent of God, had been punished for his unseemly desires, what in Jesus' name would happen to a female wretch like me?

A lethargy took hold of me that made me let even boys I didn't like do anything they pleased. Melton, the ex-sailor, worked as a machinist's apprentice. Because of a perpetual leak in his Chevy, his kisses always tasted like brake fluid. His best friend, Al, was covered in more and larger blackheads than I had ever seen on one person. But I responded positively when Melton suggested we become engaged. "David says yuh did it with him," he said at the conclusion of his proposal; "Did yuh?" It didn't occur to me to lie. When I nodded, he added, "Well, if yuh did it with him, yuh should do it with me, too, shouldn't yuh?"

For the next six months, we rode at ninety miles an hour down country roads and fucked in the backseat of his smelly Chevy. "I larned sumthin' in thuh navy: a wo-man out in Californyah taught me ..." When he whispered in my ear that I should kiss his "thang," my lack of shock shocked him. When I suggested that he pull out my tampon during my period so we could "do it," he recoiled. "Sum thangs are jes' goin' too fur!" When he found out I wore falsies under my cheerleading sweater, he suggested we not see one another anymore.

T.J. called a year after our first date, just after I had broken up with Melton. In his car at the end of our driveway, he pried open my vulva with a forefinger with a wart on it, then fucked me without further foreplay, pressing me into the door handle with the full weight of his 225-pound, football-player's frame.

All that spring he picked me up at school each day and took me out to the pine woods, where, twisting me like a rag doll into every possible position, he fucked me on the sperm-stiffened blanket he kept in the backseat of his old car. When he took me to his mother's house while she was at work, shoved me to my stomach on the living-room rug, and fucked me in the ass because it was my period, I knew it was love in spite of the pain.

As I stumbled to the bathroom, I felt satisfied: his treatment of me was much like that of Mother and Daddy; and besides, I deserved to be punished, didn't I? What if he picked at his nicotined warts in church and was known as the wildest boy in the county? When he suggested we get blood tests and elope, I was relieved.

With the twenty dollars Mother had struggled to give me as down payment on a class ring, I skipped school and went downtown with Darlene to buy wedding clothes—a half slip of cheap pink veiling, and a two-piece pink suit from Davison's. Then we met T.J. at the public-health center, where we both filled glass vials with blood. That night I had a long-standing date with my college boyfriend, Paul, whom I now scorned for being too nice. T.J. showed up, too. "Yew'll have tuh choose between us," he growled, his thick forearm possessively around my shoulder. I held out my arm, indicating the Band-Aid within my elbow; "We're gittin' married!" I said proudly.

Paul looked stricken, but Mother smiled grimly, as though she'd known it all along. To keep me from quitting school and marrying at sixteen would take energy she didn't have, an energy that was no match for my stubbornness. The next Saturday she took me to Davison's basement to buy, out of her meager paycheck, a trousseau of pink batiste peignoir and gown, and panties that said *Monday* through *Saturday,* garments that were far from the heavy satin and lace lingerie that had been a part of her going-away clothes. But they meant, for my distracted and ever-more-maddened mother, a great sacrifice—

and besides, the pink gown was embroidered with tiny blue rosebuds.

As I packed for my honeymoon to Jacksonville Beach, Mother came into my room and closed the door. "Use this right aftah you do it," she whispered, handing me a red rubber douche bag. As she graphically told me how, I looked away, my face hot. The bag and its use reminded me too much of her enemas: their relationship to my new sexual life suddenly felt nauseatingly close.

In the rooming house by the ocean, T.J. found the douche bag in my suitcase and held it up, laughing. On our way down U.S. 95, he had stopped twice for a six-pack of Pabst, and as he ripped off my new flowered gown, his breath smelled beery. The next night as we swam on the deserted beach, he threatened to hold my head under till I drowned. On our way back to Atlanta two days later, his Ford broke down and we waited for repairs in a South Georgia café, where T.J. guzzled more Pabsts and I talked with the waitress, a pale girl about my age, who wearily said she was married, too.

T.J. had quit his job as a stock clerk at Sears, Roebuck just before our wedding. When we arrived at his mother's house, where we were to live while he looked for another, my urethra stung, my vagina burned, my ribs ached. I felt feverish, sick, but it was worth it: now I was a married woman, miraculously pure again.

A few weeks after our wedding, T.J. and I wandered among the sideshows at the Southeastern Fair, eating barbecued-pork sandwiches and candied apples. On a stage above the midway, a figure in purple satin, with what looked like a womanish man's face and the cropped black hair of a flapper, lounged against the trailer looking bored.

"Her-uh-map-uh-fro-uh-dite, uh-huh!" shouted the hawker in the style of Bible Belt "suck back" preachers who sharply suck in their breath after each syllable for emphasis; "Come-uh-in-uh-'n' see-uh thuh real-live-uh her-uh-map-uh-fro-dit-ee-uh!

Man-uh-in-wo-man-uh in wun-uh! Thuh stranges'-uh thang-uh yew evah-uh seen-uh!"

I tugged at T.J.'s arm: I wanted to go in, and for once he concurred with what I suggested. We walked through the trailer into a space divided by a curtain with a small platform at its side. The men were to stand on one side of the curtain, the women on the other—"dew to the intimat nachur of this hyah demonstra-tion," explained the hawker in a now-hushed voice. "This hyah is sumpin' made by Gawd, but rarely seen by man or wo-man ..." he went on as the creature in purple ascended the platform, which was visible from both sides of the curtain.

The hawker unrolled a scroll that turned out to be a line drawing of what looked like a nude man with breasts and broad hips: HERMAPHRODITE, read the heavy black letters at the top. "—'n' this hyah"—he indicated the individual on the plat-form—"is IT, the rill thang!" When the person in purple opened his robe, he placed his hands beneath breasts that looked like the ones I had had at twelve, then lifted a small penis, and looking off into the space over his audience's head, separated with his fingers what looked like a vagina.

I chewed my candy apple, staring at this creature who resem-bled my former image of myself, who actually was both man and woman. With my femininity at last assured by my marriage, my brutish husband, I could look at his—or her?—genitals with-out anxiety. But it was an image that would cling long after T.J. and I rode the bumper cars and went home.

I was sixteen. Friday night dating, the cheerleading team, and my bad reputation were all behind me. At last within the fold of female frigidity, it was proper that my friends be other mar-ried women. My best friend was now Caroline, who was mar-ried to Kingdom, one of T.J.'s no-good good-ole-boy pals. Twenty-five-year-old Kingdom "didn't work," like T.J.; instead, he spent his time lounging beside a six-pack or lunging down country roads in his old pickup. Caroline, pregnant for the third time, took her two babies to a day nursery each morning, then left for her job as a file clerk in Atlanta. At home she chain-smoked and did all the cleaning and cooking. While I sat with her in the kitchen, watching her country-fry steaks and boil potatoes—the two men, at more than two hundred pounds each, had big appetites—T.J. and Kingdom sat in the main room, chugalugging more beer and saying things like, "It looks lak it might cloud up and crap, don't it?" When Caroline, skinny and not yet twenty, began bleeding from the hemorrhoids caused by the pressures of her closely spaced pregnancies, Kingdom cursed: "Goddammit, woman! You bleed frum thuh front enuff! " Smoking her fiftieth cigarette for the day, Caroline repeated this to me with satisfaction.

Like Mother and me, Caroline believed in female perfection and male fallibility—in the myth of the saving qualities of a good woman's love and the necessity of martyring oneself for one's man. Five years later, after one of their four children was burned and disfigured when a sitter sat her on a gas stove to tie her shoe, her patience paid off. Kingdom turned around in the 180-degree way only a no-good good ole boy can do: he simultaneously got a job as a milkman and got Saved. Every time the doors to the Stone Mountain Baptist Church opened, he was there.

I was certain that I, too, would succeed where Mother had failed. As soon as we were home from our honeymoon, I began reading to T.J. each night from the Bible. Later, when I had remarried, I went downtown wearing a new fur jacket, given me by my second bridegroom, to have lunch with the still-bleeding Caroline. Through a puff of cigarette smoke, she looked at me disapprovingly. I had deserted; she had stuck it out.

It was a relief when T.J. was drafted. At least we would have an income other than what I made as a sales clerk at Davison's department store. Rather than live with his mother or mine, I followed him to Fort Knox, where in exchange for a basement apartment without running water in the kitchen, I went up-stairs three times a day to wash dishes for a colonel's wife, to

139

iron the colonel's white shirts, or to baby-sit for their two-year-old. I listened to the radio while I ironed, and walked the baby to the PX, where I bought a new *Ladies' Home Journal* or *Good Housekeeping*. Only on weekends did I have to put up with hikes with T.J. around the parade ground, with his gobbling down what I had cooked, then repeatedly fucking me.

On the night I "forgot" to get up and douche, I had just turned seventeen. Six weeks later, I put on my favorite cotton skirt, printed with big flowers with metallic gold centers, and walked to the army clinic. Imagining the baby coiled in my belly like a butter bean, I felt as light, as high off the ground, as I had at eleven. I had never been to a gynecologist; as the doctor brusquely pried, lit, and looked up my vagina, my face turned to liquid heat. But my cunt, which was of such interest to Mother, T.J., and the boys at Tucker High School, seemed to bore him. In a voice stating a faintly disagreeable fact, he confirmed that I was pregnant.

Despite my happiness at the colonel's house, T.J. soon insisted we move to a rented shack on a farm where all the outbuildings were occupied by enlisted men and their wives and everyone shared an outdoor toilet. The outhouse, and the camaraderie between the tenants, made it seem like living in the little house in Grandmother Lee's pasture. Our house had a ceiling of less than six feet: T.J. had to stoop to enter. The stove didn't work; T.J. pissed out the kitchen window; and, newly pregnant, I staggered out into the yard to throw up about five times a day. Because of the heat—it was August, 102 degrees some days—and the outhouse, flies buzzed everywhere. While T.J. was at the post, I lay beneath the low ceiling, beneath the tin roof that seemed like the lid on a pressure cooker, eating Kraft caramels and fighting the urge to vomit. I didn't have any books, a radio, or a sewing machine, and because the stove didn't work, couldn't bake cakes or pies. To break up a depression I couldn't understand—after all, I had a husband and was pregnant—I decided to make a custard pie and bake it in the landlady's oven a quarter mile up the dirt road. With the filling sloshing in the pastry I had rolled, cut out, and crimped, I walked slowly up the road, onto the back porch, and into the farm wife's kitchen. As she held the oven door open, I lowered the pie toward the oven rack—and suddenly, with the tilt of gravity, the heavy filling splashed into the bottom of the oven. "Goddammit!" I cried—the first time in my life I had used profanity. The smell of burning custard filled the hot room. "Naow, no need tuh use *that* kind of language—takin' the Lawd's name in vain—no mattah *whut* happens!" chastised the farmer's wife. Like Grandmother Lee, she was a good Christian woman. Were the signs that I was not beginning to show again?

One day my girl friend Jean and I went into town. She bought a wringer washing machine on time, then we went into a dress shop to "look." There were princess dresses with rayon collars and cuffs, cotton sundresses with fitted waists and circle skirts. I was suddenly awash with the kind of longing I had felt in Davison's department store at ten. The tags read $8.95, $12.95, even $17.95. "Someday I'm goin' to have dresses like that," I vowed to Jean, who looked at me skeptically. Though seventeen like me, she was pragmatic, as a young matron should be, and could see the frivolity of my desires. I was already weird enough, she undoubtedly thought: I sometimes talked about things that happened in books, and on a private's salary, bought *Look* and *Life* as well as *Good Housekeeping.* I was probably snobbish, I could see her thinking, because instead of being just a plain old Pfc., my husband was in Officers' Candidate School; the colonel's wife had talked to the colonel, and he had given T.J. a recommendation. Yes, maybe if he became an officer, I might someday have my own washing machine and dryer—maybe even dresses that cost $17.95!

But when T.J. couldn't take orders because of his temper, he was dropped from Officers' Candidate School and transferred to Fort Hood, Texas, as an army cook. Mother had divorced Daddy after my marriage, and now lived with Anne in a big old apartment in a suburb halfway between Tucker and Atlanta. I was a married woman, my allotment check sent to me each month;

I could even pay board. I went to live with them to await the baby's birth. The apartment, where I slept on my growing stomach beside Anne each night, was peaceful. Just we three women and no men.

A few days before the baby's birth, I waddled into the clinic, where an uninterested doctor stuck his finger up my ass and said labor would soon begin. Mother had told me that when I had been born she had looked up, terrified, into mirrors where she had seen nothing but her own spilled blood. At the hospital, the straps around my wrists, the spreading of my thighs, the exposure of my lower body to a room full of strangers, made me feel as defenseless as I had during Mother's forced enemas. I had read Dick-Read's *Natural Childbirth Primer* as confidently as I had read the *Ladies' Home Journal* and the Bible: when the pain came, I was amazed. The next day, green and blue bruises bloomed between my now-skinny thighs, red streaks etched my once-smooth teenage belly, milk dripped from my breasts or hardened like a bad silicone job. My whole body felt as though it belonged to someone else.

Back at Mother's apartment, T.J.—home on leave for the baby's birth—tried to fuck me despite my stitches, my raw groin; using what little strength I had, I struggled to shove his two hundred pounds off me. As a married woman *and* a mother, I was now sufficiently sanctified not to have to put up with his no-good ways; besides, he was not going to become an officer, and I probably never would—I was beginning to realize —be able to depend on him for the $17.95 dresses.

"If you keep suckin' that baby's head, you're goin' to blow his brains out from the inside," a voice says to me in a dream in which I had first been eating a boiled crayfish (in Louisiana, called "suckin' heads"), which had turned into my baby; my lips were glued to his forehead as though only my mouth could save him from certain death.

Other nights, I dreamed tall buildings crashing, his fragile skull breaking. In the hospital, I had fallen in love with his lick of Cherokee black hair, the dimple that formed in his cheek when he stuck his minute thumb in his mouth. *David*—this crush was more intense than any crush I had had in high school, and this man couldn't disappear from my life, or reject me.

But back home he was far from the obliging teddy bear I had imagined. Trying not to look at the soft spot that beat at the top of his tiny head, or think of the vulnerable brain that pulsed beneath it, I rocked him in the family rocker and fed him warm water from a Coca-Cola bottle capped with a rubber nipple. But the breasts he had rejected throbbed, my bruised thighs ached; he screamed with colic, and I sobbed with frustration. I was skinnier than I had been since eleven. When I walked the mile to the pediatrician's office and back for the six-week checkup recommended by Dr. Spock, David squirmed in my pale arms like a sack of hot, wet bones.

Our peaceful household of women had been disrupted by males—first T.J., home on leave for David's birth, and now by David's crying throughout the night. Mother, puffing a cigarette before catching the streetcar for work each morning, grew crankier and crankier. Rather than straightening the apartment and starting supper as I had before David had been born, I now spent my days scrubbing diapers in the kitchen sink and boiling them, alongside the bottles, on Mother's old cookstove.

It seemed like a good time to join T.J. in Texas. As I walked from the prop plane in Waco, holding David over one damp shoulder, his diaper bag and my purse over the other, the permanently pleated skirt of the beautiful new pink polyester dress, for which I had carefully budgeted $12.95, flew over my head. When the plane had landed, I had seen T.J. standing below; he wore a cowboy hat, and his beer belly was bigger than I had ever seen it.

As I primly stepped up into the pickup he had borrowed from a friend, I tried to hide my dismay at seeing him. Sticking one hand down the front of my new dress, the other beneath my skirt, he roughly kissed me, mashing David, who began to howl. Things would be better, I hoped silently as we ate tamales at a roadside stand, when we arrived at "the beautiful four-room apartment" my husband had promised in his letters. The pink

143

dress stuck wetly to my back, the baby's wet diapers stuck hotly to my thighs. Though David was three months old, my menstrual periods had not yet started again, and I felt puffy. It was 104 degrees, T.J. said proudly, and probably would be for several more days.

As though we were going to a fire, he drove us over bumpy dirt roads for what seemed like a very long time. Through the puffs of dust that rose around us, I could vaguely see a landscape so dizzyingly flat that I expected a tornado to break the grayish horizon at any moment. At last we entered what looked like a little town, and he squealed to a stop in front of a one-story white frame building with a dirt yard in front.

When we walked through the front door, roaches by the hundreds scattered at our feet. A mean-looking insect sat on the kitchen counter, swaying a long tail. "Uh scorpyun," T.J. explained, brushing it away and stomping it with his boot. As I tried the water at the sink, thick rusty drops emerged.

"Whut will we do 'bout money?—the rent's a hunnerd a month ..." T.J. worried as we lay, David hot and cross between us, on the sticky bed sheets. "Why don't we sell the car?" I asked, trying to be a helpful wife. T.J. had driven our '43 Ford to Texas, and now it sat in the sun before the duplex, a broken-down monument to the only money Daddy had ever given me —a loan of fifty dollars—and to relative prosperity.

I should have realized that suggesting a good ole boy do without his automobile was tantamount to suggesting voluntary castration. At my words, his fists began to pound my forehead, body, thighs. When they stopped, I walked numbly past him into the bathroom, with its tiny rusty shower, and looked into the flaking mirror at the bruises developing as fast as the color on Polaroid film. There was one phone in Copperas Cove, Texas, T.J. had told me. The airport was ... thirty?, fifty? ... miles away. And if I called Mother, would she have the seventy-dollar airfare to send me? And if she sent it, how would I get to the plane?

T.J. had followed me into the bathroom. "I won't never do it agin," he sobbed.

144

For the next year, I dodged T.J.'s fists, chased the fat, inch-long roaches with a broom, and learned to kill the hissing scorpions. When a copperhead slid from beneath the kitchen sink where David had just been slithering on his belly across the dingy linoleum, I screamed for T.J.—chopping the snake in two was a duty a good ole boy could relish.

Two or three times a week, I walked David in his stroller to the Laundromat where, in a room thick with ammonia fumes, I and other enlisted men's wives pushed wet diapers through the stiff rollers of wringer washers. (While the wives of junior officers might live next door or shop at the same store, they never spoke; it was as though some invisible but firm line had been drawn. When Anne's husband became a lieutenant in the marines, she followed him to a base in South Carolina: I realized that had I been in the same place at the same time and we had not been sisters, we would have been separated by class.)

Like the other wives, I had a tab at the local grocery, to be paid on payday. But because T.J. was a cook, we also had food —stale rolls, hunks of leftover roasts, tins of evaporated milk— that he had stolen from the base. In order to save money, I drank the milk straight from the cans and poured it over my oatmeal each morning. I was determined to be a good wife; over second and third cups of coffee, I ate up paperbacks like *Woman to Woman* by religious writer Eugenia Price, or *The Power of Love* by Bishop Fulton Sheen.

The unmarried bishop had an uplifting answer to everything. So what if my husband beat me? Feminine martyrdom was obviously the will of God, and a role I had seen played in both ingenue and mature interpretations by Mother and Grandmother Lee. To give myself strength for it, I walked down the dirt road to the Baptist church each Sunday morning while T.J. and David slept. If marriage had purified me, then suffering lifted me higher. I was good again, held in the arms of Jesus, as I had been at eleven.

Almost every night, T.J. drank a six-pack of Pabst or Miller; sometimes his buddies came over, and they drank together. I expected that; after all, they were men. But when the other

145

wives drank Jack Daniel's along with their husbands, I priggishly stuck my nose in the air. One night, as T.J. and I drove down a dark strip of Texas highway, we passed a wooden shack that was lit from within by a bare yellow bulb. Two women in tight red and black satin dresses, like those Ruby had worn, leaned against the doorframe, cigarettes hanging from the corners of their glossy mouths. With a shock, I realized why they were standing there that way at the edge of a barren field in the middle of nowhere. We were on our way to Fort Hood to visit T.J.'s good buddy. When we arrived, the friend introduced us to a faded blonde woman who looked Mother's age, but who obviously lived with him. Her pet raccoon, climbing her arm, perching on her shoulder, made David crow, and its face, pressed to the window as we drove away, reminded me of the woman's loneliness. But I felt as disgusted, as arrogant as I did about Mother's failed life. Though it had already happened to me without my knowing it, I didn't understand that cultural forces could press women into relationships that had little to do with free will.

Indeed, I was determined to better myself. From the back of one of T.J.'s matchbooks, I had answered an ad that began, "Didn't finish high school? . . . Now you can complete your education at home! . . ." When the salesman appeared one hot afternoon, knocking at our door in Copperas Cove, I was ready. As David wiggled in my sticky lap, trying to get down to pull at the laces of the man's shiny black shoes, I listened impatiently as he described the courses, then paid him the down payment of ten dollars I had carefully saved from the grocery money. At Tucker High School I had barely studied at all, but now, filled with vague fantasies of a better life, I pored over biology and civics as avidly as I once had Mother and Daddy's dark book on sex, and passionately pasted the papers that came back to me through the mail, inscribed with a *98* or *99* at the top, in a special notebook.

After T.J.'s discharge, we drove along the Gulf Coast toward Atlanta. When we stopped at a roadhouse in rural Louisiana, I sat in a booth with David and fed him bits of my barbecued-pork sandwich, sips of my RC Cola; T.J. stood in a dim back room, jostling and laughing with a gang of Cajuns. Back in our old Ford, he put his head into his hands, leaning them against the steering wheel: "I jes' gambled it all away—the sev'rance pay." It was our only money. "I'll never do it agin," he moaned, just as he had after each time he beat me up. Self-righteously, I looked out the window at the Spanish moss that swung like unkempt gray hair in the Louisiana dusk. I was used to his apologies; the lack of cash just meant that we would have to live with his mother, Goldie, again instead of getting an apartment right away.

T.J.'s relationship with his divorced secretary mother was as intensely and intimately protective as that between Elvis Presley and his mother, Gladys. Indeed, it was a study in acceptable Southern child rearing: she had nursed him until he was four or five—I could visualize her pendulous breasts dangling perpetually from a cotton print wrapper—and he had slept with her till he was ten or so. "I jes' dot-id on thet boy," she repeated proudly. "Why, I'd ride 'im in thet buggy through the groc'ry store and let 'im buy enythang he won-id!"

Goldie was one of four sisters known as the "Bal-lew Sisters" of Stone Mountain, mothered by "Miz Bal-lew," an old lady so wrinkled, raunchy, and given to saying things in company like, "He don't know his butt from a hole in the groun'," that the sisters were in constant conflict about who would next have the misfortune of having her visit. The brutishly handsome Junior, who had eaten my brownies and introduced me to T.J., was one of the hulking sons that the sisters obviously preferred, along with each other, to their spouses. They spent as many evenings "visitin' " as possible; and each was in the habit, either alone or in the company of one another, of "takin' off fur a spell" for indefinite visits to low-rent motels in Climax or Plains or Waycross, Georgia.

The difference between a good ole boy and white trash, says Billy Carter, is that a good ole boy throws his beer can in a litter container as he goes by in his pickup, while white trash throws it alongside the road. Since I had married T.J., I had often been in the company of folks Mother and Grandmother Lee would have called white trash had they not been too genteel to use such words. When T.J.'s cousin Betty laughed about how she had once "put shit 'tween sum biscuit, 'n' gave 'em tuh sum li'l nigger kids 'n' tole 'em it wuz peanut butter," I recoiled: it was not the kind of story that would have been found amusing in *our* family.

Once in the middle of winter, T.J. took me to the country where he left me for the day in a house with an open hallway —a dog trot—down the middle. As I huddled with the family of thinly clad children beside one of the fireplaces that were the only source of heat, he went hunting for the day with the men. Were these people white trash, I wondered? But as I helped cut up the skinned rabbits for frying, as I patted out biscuit from flour one of the other women had cut with lard, I could see that, for them, the hunting had been essential: there was nothing else in the kitchen.

When he took me to visit the fat middle-aged couple who shared his passion for red hound dogs and wore matching red stretch pajamas, I realized white trash had as much to do with taste as poverty. I had seen the woman before, I realized as she offered us dill pickles after our fruit cake and coffee to "cut the sweet," yelling cuss words at the Tucker football games: she had six huge sons, all of whom had been quarterbacks. Despite their big cars and pretensions to refinement, I could tell, with the certainty of one whose great-grandfather had been a Methodist minister who read Milton and Shakespeare at the table, that she, and all the Ballew Sisters, were hopelessly lower-class. The richest of them, whose husband ran a barbecue-and-hamburger stand in the black part of town, where he mixed the meat half-and-half with corn meal, threw her fur coat on the floor, and beat her children with a can opener, or whatever lay at hand.

T.J.'s father had been no good, like mine, and had long since left home. Indeed, in the process of "protecting" Goldie, T.J. had beaten his father up and thrown him out of the house. When he wanted to marry me, Goldie had been as indulgent as though I was one of the "thangs" in the grocery store. "Why, y'all kin jes' live right hy-uh with me," she had said. "Why, T.J. done said to me, 'Ma-ma, I jes' got to have me thet li'l gurl!' " When T. J. had been kicked out of Officers' Candidate School, she had understood: "Thet life's jes' too hard fur a boy!"

Back in Atlanta, T.J. was faced with the almost-unbearable prospect—to a no-good good ole boy—of getting a job. He was jealous of David and my biology book and didn't like it that, with my slimmer figure and hair grown long again, I was prettier than I had ever been. I no longer bothered to read the Bible to him; he could tell, he said, that I didn't love him anymore. One day when he came home from fishing to find that his cousin Junior had come inside to make a phone call, he held a pillow over my face off and on for over an hour, threatening to smother me if I flirted. He had held the pillow over my face before, and had found this scared me more than anything else. I wasn't surprised that he wanted to kill me—hadn't Mother? —but I had stubbornly decided, because of David and my long hair, that I wanted to live.

As soon as I had gotten back to town, I had visited Mother. As we sat at the kitchen table, I held David on my lap, describing his eating habits and adorable quirks. But instead of beaming at her first grandchild, she clutched her coffee cup and stared beyond me. In a few days, Grandmother Lee called to say that Mother was being taken to Peachtree Hospital for shock treatments; Anne, fourteen, and sounding frightened, got on the line: Mother had come home from work one day, saying she had forgotten how to type, and had started crying and hadn't stopped. She had been dating Mr. Bottoms, the white-haired man upstairs, and had stayed out later and later, until she had started saying she couldn't get to sleep at all. And one time Anne had heard them arguing: Mr. Bottoms had been saying, "Come on, honey, come on . . ." and Mother had been crying, "Not unless we git mar-rid . . ." But Mr. Bottoms hadn't sounded like getting married was what he wanted at all.

At the Peachtree Hospital I held Anne's hand as she, T.J., and I trooped in to see Mother. She had just had the first of the shock

149

treatments and lay on a wheeled table, covered to the neck by a white sheet, sobbing and moaning incoherently. I wasn't unduly concerned; I had been hearing about feminine nervous breakdowns all my life and had heard Mother carrying on in the same way before.

Mother, her forehead screwed in an exaggerated concern that failed to conceal her pleasure, often told stories herself of the breakdowns of other women. After her own breakdowns began, she seemed to enjoy these stories even more. A favorite was the one about the cousin who had overdosed on diet pills: the woman had remained at home with her mother in North Carolina for the first twelve years of her marriage, till finally, at her husband's insistence, she had followed him to his construction job in California. After six weeks, she hadn't been able to stand it anymore and had flown home, her husband following in his old Chevy, lugging her household goods back across the country in a U-Haul trailer. When he arrived, he angrily told her he wouldn't be sending her money anymore, and she had promptly attempted suicide. "She'll have to go to the state hospital," the local psychiatrist had advised her mother, who had retorted, "No membah of *our* fambly will evah be in thyah!" She had simply put her quivering daughter to bed for six weeks, "and I saw her the other day at the garden club," Mother laughed; "She had on a new hat and looked re-el good!"

In a few weeks, she would be giggling, through the vagueness left by the shock treatments, about "that nervous breakdown I had." After years and years of relapses—even the one so severe that the local doctor suggested to Grandmother Lee that she be lobotomized—she still insisted that money was better spent on a new dress than on a psychiatrist, which may have been true, since the therapists she consulted on her meager salary dealt out only electroshock and drugs. Like most Southerners, Mother had little capacity for, even an aversion to, self-analysis; the stories about others' breakdowns served to minimize the seriousness of cracking up. Indeed, there simply seemed to be two types of Southern women, those like Grandmother Lee, who one couldn't imagine breaking down under any circumstances, and those like Mother, who, delicate, perpetually girl-ish, were obviously as fragile as porcelain. To save myself, I was determined to become one of the tough kind. But the first problem was immediate survival.

T.J. and I were eating cornbread crumbled into buttermilk, along with chunks of raw onion, when Goldie came into the kitchen. As she often did, she began berating me for the way David was dressed—too warmly or not warmly enough—or for "not feedin' thet baby right," or something else related to my youthful ignorance. But this time I went beyond my usual sullen look: I talked back—and her long red nails flashed out, through the gaping neck of my robe, gashing the tops of both my breasts. "I've got to get away from your mother," I sobbed to T.J. as she huffed from the room. I would call Grandmother Lee, I told him, and ask to stay there with David until he could find an apartment for us.

In Grandmother Lee's driveway, I tearfully kissed him good-bye. But the moment I was inside, I tore open my blouse to show my blood-and-pus-tinged scabs to Mother, Anne, and Grandmother Lee. "I have to get a divorce," I cried. "But Rows-may-ree—" Mother began shrilly, "mar-ridge is sa-cred!" I had called her from Texas after one of T.J.'s beatings, but she hadn't thought it sufficient cause to leave my scary young hus-band. After all, look what she had endured for the holy state of matrimony.

When Grandmother Lee nodded that yes, she would help me, Anne eagerly took David from my arms, and I collapsed in bed, where tears ran down my cheeks—though I felt no particu-lar emotion—for three full days. "You mus' be allergic to zin-yas," said Grandmother Lee, referring to the red, yellow, and orange flowers that burgeoned all around the house, as she handed me a third cup of hot lemonade to ease my congestion.

Her pragmatism calmed my jerking guts again as T.J. glared at me from across the courtroom. Since the divorce proceedings had begun, he had repeatedly vowed to kill me, and now his eyes were as red as a red-neck intent on homicide. But Grandmother Lee, in white gloves and navy straw hat, sat beside me as calmly as though we were at a Sunday-morning service at the Tucker First Baptist Church.

What did she feel about her broken pretty daughter, the two granddaughters, and the toddler who had unexpectedly become part of her household just when her other children had all left home? There was never any sign that we were an inconvenience. If Grandmother Lee was the long-suffering Melanie, she was also, like Melanie, good: helping to pick up the shards of our crushed lives was what a good woman did.

As for Mother, the electroshock treatments seemed to have broken what little control she had left. David, jabbering continuously and pulling pots and pans from the kitchen cabinets, made her burst into tears. Each day, when she came home from work, she sat on the couch clutching a glass of sweetened iced tea, smoking cigarette after cigarette. Over and over, she told Anne and me about how people at her office were talking behind her back, how a new girl was plotting to take over her job. Every few nights Daddy called to drunkenly tell her he was starving, that he had lost his job again. "If only I hed done God's will—not gotten that awful divorce," she would cry. Listening to her rave, rather than trying to reason with her, made her monologues pass more quickly, Anne and I had learned— though no matter how we responded, she often ended by exploding into deep racking sobs. In the middle of the night, we would often hear her crying again or getting up for more water. Her illness had made her thirsty in a way that could never be sated; for the rest of her life she kept a filled glass beside her bed to drink when she frequently woke.

Mother's face and life were being pulled down as though by invisible inner weights. But in my nineteen-year-old obliviousness, I found her misery a minor irritation. For the first time since Mother, Anne, and I had shared an apartment during my pregnancy, I felt untroubled. Now we lived together again on one side of the big farmhouse; Grandmother Lee and Granddaddy Carroll lived on the other. Anne and I shared a room once more and fought every night over who would get to sleep with David, wet double diapers and all.

When I applied for a job at Emory University, the male interviewer asked if I wore a panty girdle, then whether I had ever had sex with anyone other than my ex-spouse. Flipping my long hair over my shoulder, I answered his questions coolly, as though he were inquiring about my typing skills. After I was given an IQ test, he said that I had done so well that, despite my failure to graduate from high school, I would be given a job as receptionist to the director of student aid at $40.00 a week.

I was ecstatic: I had a job, long hair, a flat stomach, and David. Each morning, I left him with a fifteen-year-old black girl whom I paid $15.00 a week; and just like Mother, hailed down the Greyhound bus as it rushed down the highway in front of the farmhouse. In Decatur, a town halfway between Tucker and Atlanta, I transferred to another bus that took me to my job. It was in Decatur that I spent the bit of money I had left after paying the baby-sitter and board to Mother—on hair barrettes, Tangee lipsticks, even the $17.95 dresses I had dreamed of. I found that through a process called layaway, I could pay the store a few dollars a week until the dream garment was mine.

Every day, despite the walking I had to do, I wore three-inch heels from Butler's shoe store because I knew they made my legs look good. When a handsome boy with freckles came into the student-aid office to apply for a loan, he handed me a note: *You are the most beautiful girl I have ever seen. Will you have lunch with me at my frat house tomorrow?* "No," I giggled emphatically. After all, I was a nineteen-year-old woman with a two-year-old son; and though he was my age, and cute, I knew he wasn't a good prospect. He had two more years of college.

That I might have been one of the students myself, instead of just an employee, never occurred to me. Mother and Grandmother Lee were already nervously wondering who I could marry next; and when I telephoned Paul, the steady serious boy I had rejected in favor of T.J., I could hear in his surprised voice that he still liked me. I remembered his long black lashes, the tender blue eyes behind his glasses. He now had two degrees, he said; he was working in an architect's office and planned to become a registered architect like his father. "Such good husband material!" Mother, Aunt Billie, and Grandmother Lee enthused. Mother wanted me to elope as soon as possible, before he could get away. Grandmother Lee advised me not to let him "go anywhere with the baby till yew're mar-rid!"

On the night of my second wedding at twenty, I sipped my first martini in a restaurant that had once been the Peacock Alley on Peachtree Street, where Mother and Daddy had taken me for Hot Fudge Shortcake at three. My new groom was Presbyterian, a step up, I felt, from the Methodists and Baptists. Before our wedding, the minister had questioned me about my first marriage, and I had felt appropriately guilty. T.J.'s imperfectibility, I knew, must have been my fault. This time, I vowed, I would be a perfect wife.

The wedding in the Decatur First Presbyterian Church had been paid for by Paul's grandmother, who, in view of my nonexistent virginity, thought the more formal the event the better. I had worn a veiled yellow organdy pillbox atop my coiled hair; a tiered yellow organdy dress, fastened down the back by sixty tiny covered buttons; dyed-to-match yellow satin pumps; and a waist cincher and bra with push-up pads to make my now-skinny shape more Scarlettish. As I walked down the aisle on a red satin cloth, I carried yellow roses centered by one perfect green orchid, and held my uncle Son's arm. Grandmother Lee had stated that it was an occasion that would have been inappropriate for Daddy, now living in a run-down boardinghouse in a black section that was Atlanta's skid row, and Mother had tearfully agreed. But there had been a photographer to take pictures on the church steps and a reception with a tall wedding cake, covered with more yellow roses, and topped with a toy bride and groom, in the church hall.

Now, as I sat in the restaurant with my new husband, dizzily sipping gin and vermouth, I wore the "going away" dress made for me by Grandmother Lee. It was a pale-green linen sheath, embroidered all over the bodice with seed pearls; and with my

154

white straw picture hat over my auburn chignon, I felt as much of a belle as Mother had been. Yet that night in the bridal suite at the Atlanta Biltmore, as my bridegroom fucked me ten times (he counted), I experienced nothing but an irritating friction, a numb exhaustion. It would be ten years before I would understand what an orgasm was.

On our honeymoon to the mountains of Tennessee, I burst into inexplicable tears several times a day. Despite having entered the middle class through marriage to a professional man, I felt weak and sad. And back in Atlanta in our apartment with two-year-old David, I found that Grandmother Lee had been right: when David squatted to shit on our back steps in view of our new neighbors, my young husband began to weep, saying he wished he was back home with his parents.

Two weeks later, as I stirred black-eyed peas and cornbread batter, David darted out the front door of the apartment. Though I ran out behind him, he was already in the street. As the car came around the curve, as his head and small body first flew into the air, then hit concrete with a *thud,* a shriek broke like an animal from the top of my own skull.

While Paul and I rode to the hospital, a moaning David on the lap of a doctor who lived nearby, I moaned, too, imagining muscular snakes emerging from my every orifice, wrapping my own skull and squeezing it till it broke. "If only you'll let him live," I promised God, "I'll never do it again. . . ." I knew *it* was everything Mother had tried to kill, my sexual feelings at fifteen, my desire to escape T.J., even my pleasure in my job.

I remembered the dreams I had had the week after David's birth—tall buildings crashing, his head cracked open. Was this, my dream's actualization, to be the price of my new life? Was God's punishment for my dreadful sins beginning? For the next few years, I nursed David with a devotion and indulgence that would have warmed Gladys Presley's heart. I gave birth to two daughters, washed diapers, cooked meals, and tried to please my oblivious young husband. More than anything, I fought to fulfill the promise I had made that night on the way to the hospital.

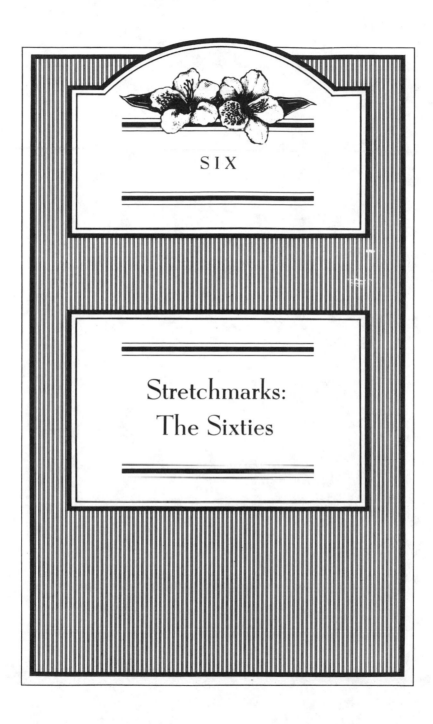

SIX

Stretchmarks:
The Sixties

"Rows-may-ree, those beans are burnin'!"

Mother was sitting on my bed, holding on her lap four-year-old Darcy, whose halo of dark curls and pensive heart-shaped face echoed her own partially regained beauty. She wore a svelte green linen sheath, and her hair—now Claíroled to cover the gray that had sprung into it after the shock treatments—was set in neat finger waves. Her "nervous breakdown" behind her, she had remarried and was a housewife again.

She had just been wondering aloud why I "wasted my time" and "neglected those poor chirren" to do something as insignificant as write. After all, I had a split-level house with built-in pink appliances, a professional husband who also mowed the zoysia grass each Saturday, and could belong, if I chose, to both the bridge and garden clubs. At last I was leading the middle-class life she had always wanted for her daughters and herself.

The man she had married, a farmer and land surveyor from North Carolina, believed as strongly as she that the only proper life for a woman was that of being supported, and dominated, by a strong man. "As Christ is thuh head of His church, so a husband is thuh head of his family," he had told her the day after their little wedding, just before he insisted that she call her office at the U.S. Forestry Department, where for ten years she had worked as first a typist and then a secretary, to resign without notice. Though she told Anne and me that she had felt nervous about losing her seniority at her age—forty-five—she had obeyed: he was her husband, a *good* man, and he wanted to take care of her. It was a marriage she had experienced another near-breakdown to achieve: having sex without the security of commitment, the sanction of the church, had made her beg him—despite his recent widowhood—to marry her and save them both from the sin into which his lust had thrust them.

As a divorcée living in a third-floor walk-up in Atlanta, she had had as neighbors—she shuddered when she spoke of it—single women who drank and slept with men they weren't married to, and even "those sick men who like other men." It was a part of the attitude that made her object to my writing. She revered normalcy, and writing, especially when you had a good husband and didn't have to, wasn't *normal*. She had willingly shelved her own writing ambitions; that I wouldn't was just another sign of my stubbornness.

Yet because of her paternal grandparents, Mother considered herself literary. She liked to make trips to Asheville to visit the boardinghouse where Thomas Wolfe had lived. She bought the picture postcards to send to me. But she didn't approve "the way he talked 'bout those people all over town" in *Look Homeward Angel*. And she avoided the site of the asylum where Zelda, mad Zelda—too much a belle like herself—had died.

Even Faulkner was beyond the pale. "When I lived in Oxford, Mississippi," my new stepfather told me, "Bill Faulkner lived down the road a piece. And the way he kept his yard—full 'a weeds 'n' trash—the way he walked aroun' not talkin' to nobody—made a body *know* he was jes' no good!" Over a table groaning with hot biscuits, cream gravy, and three kinds of boiled vegetables, Mother nodded in proper, if fatigued, wifely agreement. It was their way of letting me know that a married woman's place was behind the stove, not a typewriter. Thinking too much might give me brain fever and interfere with my duties. "But Rows-may-ree!" Mother had gasped after reading a poem I had written, "this sounds like it's about *doin' it*!" If only I would write something "sweet and nice," I could see her thinking, some religious verse that she could read to her Sunday-school class.

How would she feel if she knew that, at twenty-seven, I had already committed the Sin of Adultery?

It had started after the birth of Darcy, my third child. "See you next year!" the nun had said cheerily in the hospital room where I lay like a blanched seashell, washed up on an isolated beach. The birth had been harder, longer than those of David

160

and Laura. Now I saw myself plunging from the third floor to the street below, or dropping my new baby from the high hospital bed to the floor—pictures I could counter only by imagining floating through the window, rising up, up, up in the strong arms of Jesus.

My anxiety must have been caused by Laura eating all my eggs while I was pregnant, I thought. Peach-haired Laura liked eggs, and no matter how many I cooked each morning, she would clamber onto my diminishing lap and eat mine as well as her own. When I got home from the hospital, she, Darcy, and David (who, because of his accident, had been slow in toilet training) were in diapers simultaneously. Wet diapers, wet bed sheets, baby shit, diarrhea, staph, chicken pox, measles, sex turned into a sea of urine, feces, pus, blood, semen—a wave that threatened to bring with it a madness that would outdo Mother's. When I went down into the basement playroom to pick up the moist mountains of laundry I had thrown down from the top of the stairs, as I shook out the crickets who lived and chirped in the damp cloth till wash day, I was flooded by an unnamable fear—an anxiety that grabbed my gut afresh each morning as I walked into my pink kitchen to make breakfast, sending me racing to the bathroom. As I pushed Laura and Darcy in my grocery cart—each clutching the heads of dismembered dolls, and occasionally smashing jars of Gerber's to the supermarket floor—I had dizzy spells that made me certain I had an advanced brain tumor. One morning, as I looked into the bathroom mirror, I noticed for the first time my uvula, hanging at the back of my throat—a metastasis, I was sure; every day I felt the sides of my throat for new growths.

Like Mother, I pored over the new recipes in *Good Housekeeping*. I made more and more lists on how to be a better housekeeper. I dressed the children for Sunday school and church each Sunday, and agreed to teach Bible school in the summer. But nothing seemed to assuage my terror, or the overwhelming disorder of my life. I was so alienated that the fortyish blonde next door, the president of the garden club, bleached hair perfectly swirled above her pink face, like the whipped

161

cream on a strawberry soda, could have been on Mars. The children's guinea pigs, gerbils, parakeets, white mice, Easter ducklings, rabbits, and cats seemed friendlier to me than the clerk at the supermarket, or even my own husband.

When at last I saw the blood in the toilet, it was only what I expected. As the gynecologist shoved what looked like a stainless-steel knitting needle through my cervix, drawing out tiny pieces of my interior, then pushed a broad lighted phallus into my anus, I lay passively. Penetration, the invasion of my body by others, was now my life, and besides, I was certain to die shortly. Hadn't the same doctor, a year earlier when I had been twenty-three and pregnant for the third time, explained out of his male omnipotence that the spidery red threads on my calves were simply "what happens to us as we get old"? "Just nerves," he said this time, writing out a prescription for a tranquilizer to be taken four times a day. "All the young mothers feel that way."

Since I was not to die right away, I had to find something to fill up my life. When I read that a poetry workshop was to be offered at a nearby university, I told my puzzled husband, between sobs that were far too much like Mother's, that I *had* to enroll. At the first class, the Famous Southern Poet read from his poems. I felt a rapture much like that I had known at eleven, sitting beneath the stained-glass windows of Collins Memorial Methodist Church. His oral tides were as thrilling as a preacher's, as sexy as the words to "Washed in the Blood," and his blond hair, which at thirty-nine still adorned his broad skull, was as fair, as angelic, as Troy's had been. When our instructor reverently told us that the great man had agreed, for two dollars a head, since he was living on unemployment payments, to meet each week with our workshop, I felt as though I was in a dream. Though I tossed and turned that night, fearing hellfire, though I filled my journal with new and disturbing doubts about the godhood of Jesus, and the legitimacy of the Ten Commandments, I had already found, without knowing it, a new god to replace the old. Yes, his spirit had grabbed me. Now I would sit at his feet.

It turned out to be the position in which he preferred me. "Keep working with me, baby, and you'll be a great writer," he whispered, putting his hand down the back of my panty girdle as we sat in his dark car after class. I shivered, not because the height of my ambition was to have a poem published in *Cat Fancy* magazine, which, I had read in the veterinarian's office, paid fifty cents a line, but because a totally forbidden idea, one I had never considered to be within the realm of actuality, was fleshing itself out in my mind. *Adultery!* Was it literally possible?

And was this the blond pirate of my dreams? Well, he had been a pilot, he told me, had flown a hundred Black Widow missions over Japan and the Philippines. And how the poor man suffered: his wife, I imagined, even wore her panty girdle to bed. I thought of her cold, impenetrable flesh, her thick back turned against this sensitive poet. My sympathy made me so weak that I stood helplessly at a drunken class party as he unzipped the back of my dress, moving his hand up and down my bare backbone. As Paul watched, stricken, from the kitchen door, he whispered in my ear that he would call me at eight A.M. on Monday, that he had to see me naked. "Are you brave enough for it, woman?" he murmured, implying an act of moral courage.

Yes! yelled the core of will that Mother had tried so hard to rout. But now I didn't have to worry, because I had a new deity —and he was white, he was blond, he was a man. Pointing to the cover of a *Life* magazine, he told me that I looked like a redheaded Marilyn Monroe. Did he recognize our similar passion for self-immolation? I was a zero who knew my place and purpose. When I told him shyly over the phone, "I have my period today—do you still want to meet?" he laughed, pleased at my recognition of what I meant to him.

A long-standing member of a network of adulterous good ole

163

boys, he had borrowed a fraternity brother's bachelor apartment for our rendezvous. He sat back in a stuffed chair and had me serve him a double dry martini, then stripped the green ribbon from my hair and made me kneel at his feet. We would have intercourse without my diaphragm, he instructed, because he liked it better that way, and because he wanted me to have his "chile," which I would raise as my own. Then, after he left for his teaching position in California, I would send him a postcard in code, letting him know whether or not our lovemaking had taken. If I did become pregnant, I was never to tell Paul the true paternity; he would send me a box of candy for the baby each Christmas. He said this with all the solemnity with which Southern men regard "chirren." "Keep 'em barefoot 'n' pregnant" was something I had heard men say all my life. By making me the mother of his child, he would simply be making me worthy of his love. As he fucked me without touching my clitoris—of which I had still not heard—I almost swooned. What if he *had* taken for a poem of his own, soon to be published in *The Atlantic Monthly,* a phrase which had been the title of one of mine? It was 1962, almost seven years before I would hear of the women's movement, or the phrase *male chauvinism.* And abortion was still illegal: I had never known or heard of anyone who had had one.

Now, in the writing workshop, I literally sat at the Famous Southern Poet's feet. When another woman student accused him of favoring my work over hers, I felt glorified: that such a system could later work against me was something I didn't yet recognize. One night we held our class at his house and I met the wife he had so often described. She looked as harsh, as insensitive as I had imagined—the cause, I was sure, of the poor man's infidelities.

She led us into the living room, where my lover sat in the corner, playing his guitar without looking up; the expression on his face was the same one he wore during orgasm. On the coffee table lay a huge pair of fuzzy dice, the kind rednecks hung behind the windshields of their pickups; on one wall was the stockade of weapons—this time bows and razor-tipped arrows

— one expected in a good ole boy's house. That the scene might have been posed, or that I might have better taste, were sacrilegious thoughts I hastily brushed from my mind.

"Beer or 'Co-Cola'?" his wife was asking. "Jes' brang me a bourbon and branch wawter," my lover said without looking at her; instead, he looked at me and winked. "Whut do yuh thank I am? A barmaid?" she snarled in a voice that made me cringe. *I* would never talk to *my* husband like that, and he wasn't even a Famous Southern Poet. Though Mother had whined, begged, and cried, she had never spoken to drunken Father in that manner, and, of course, Grandmother Lee had never been known to speak to Granddaddy Carroll with anything but respect.

I sat with my legs crossed, looking primly down at the floor, feeling little, feminine, superior. "Yew left one of your li'l white gloves," my paramour told me a few days later; "I jes' wanted to keep it, it was teeny as a li'l gurl's!" Yet something nagged: "A man will treat you just the way he treats his mother" had been one of Grandmother Lee's bits of advice on husband hunting; could it be that a lover would treat you as a wife, even—especially—if he was a Famous Southern Poet?

For the next few months, aside from unsuccessfully trying to make sure I would bear one of his "chirren," the Famous Southern Poet told me stories: how he had grown up in the mountains of North Georgia "without a pot to piss in," until his family had come into that famous tonic fortune, and had moved to a mansion in northwest Atlanta; and, implying romantically that his whole life had been lived on borrowed time, how he had been bitten on the sole of his foot by a water moccasin at twelve and had had to carve into his own flesh with his pocketknife and suck the poison out himself. Like many Southern men, he liked to bring mortality—the excuse for everything—into his conversations. Emotionally alluding to his love of family and "the South," he talked about the Jap fighter planes he had shot down, then went on to the Japanese and Filipino women he had fucked, and the sexual excesses of other Famous Writers, which made me feel like a starlet listening to inside gossip about Hollywood.

Which were true and which were stories was hard to tell; when it comes to his macho image, a certain kind of Southern man has, or pretends to have, a hard time separating fact from fantasy. And woe betide the woman who breaks the charm—and *her* charm—by acting skeptical during the telling. The fun comes in the gullibility of the listener, in the widening mascaraed lashes, the open little-girl mouth. Southern men, I was learning, meant Southern lies, especially lies about personal intention, marital status, genealogy, money, and achievement. Sentimentality, about himself, even his fantasies of himself, is the hallmark of the grass-roots Southern-male mind. (Once my skepticism about their stories had taken hold, it barely allowed for fantasy turned truth. When Lester Maddox ran for governor of Georgia, fresh out of the Atlanta restaurant where he had sold ax handles to red-necks to "chase off niggers," I thought it impossible that he would be elected. In 1974, when Jimmy Carter announced that he planned to run for President, I laughed, imagining it another case of good-ole-boy megalomania.)

Any woman who wants to see the term *male bonding* made concrete need only complain of one good ole boy to another, and watch the glaze form, instantaneously, over the eyeballs of her listener. It is a lens through which it is impossible to see any flaw in one's brother: "He's jes' a good ole boy!" is a phrase a Southern man will use to excuse anything from armed robbery to bigamy, especially in male kin. (The double standard, of course, is not crime, only custom; "Did'n yuh know he wuz jes' lyin'?" a man asked incredulously when I marveled at Jimmy Carter's statement in *Playboy* that he had been literally, if not mentally, faithful to Rosalynn.) He speaks certain in the knowledge that they—in the face of an uppity female or an overeducated Yankee—will stand by him. If the unpleasant interrogator persists, he will abruptly change the subject to some inane story about a man and his dog, or "what ole Charlie did over in the county dump last Friday night"—a response designed to make the other party feel foolish, frustrated, and, if a Southern woman, that most uncomfortable of all feelings, *unfeminine*.

By the time Paul found out—by reading my ill-concealed journals—about my affair with the Famous Southern Poet, my lover had long since left Atlanta for California. Paul had been brought up in a family as repressed as mine; he couldn't believe that such a thing had actually happened. When I saw the hurt in his eyes, I thought with relief that I was about to be punished for my congenital evil. But instead of leaving, as I had expected and half hoped, my young husband became totally obsessed with my Sin. As we lay in bed at night, as we sat with the children at the supper table, as we drove back and forth with them to church each Sunday, he talked and I cried; in the backseat, David, Laura, and Darcy tussled and fought, ignoring us in the same way Anne and I had tried to blot out Mother's whine, Daddy's slur, as we careened down Atlanta streets.

The next summer, when the Famous Southern Poet returned to Atlanta, I clung to my vow to Paul not to see him. But when we vacationed at my stepfather's farmhouse in North Carolina, Paul still followed me into the kitchen, the bathroom, the living room, rehashing my defection, extracting fresh promises. As we drove down the mountain road between Franklin and Highlands, North Carolina, passing the exquisitely sheer drop of Cullasagee Gorge, I shook and burst into tears, begging Paul to drive carefully in much the same way Mother had begged Daddy. I had already noticed my impulse to jump from any height, to swallow sewing needles that lay about the house, to cut myself instead of the celery or steak with the kitchen knife.

On the third day of our vacation, I leaned over and something excruciating happened inside my lower back; for the rest of our trip I hobbled on a cane, tears running down my cheeks as they had after I left T.J. I was twenty-eight years old. I stopped painting my toenails. Without even trying, I had managed to make my life a replica of Mother's, my children's a copy of what mine and Anne's had been.

As we say in the South, I was "jes' a martah, honey!"

167

"Bebe, you're drivin' me crazy!" whispers the Famous Southern Poet in his new fake Brando voice, nibbling my earlobe as he presses the elevator button. Wearing an English cap to cover his thinning blond hair, he's in New York for an appearance on the "Today" show. I'm wearing a red leatherette minidress with a motorcycle belt around my hips, red strip high-heeled sandals, gold lamé hose, and a lot of gardenia perfume. It's 1964. We're leaving a party on Riverside Drive.

Mother and Grandmother Lee would have understood had I continued in my feminine inability to cope, even in having a little Southern "nervous breakdown"—after all, as the good doctor had said, "all the young mothers feel that way." But again, my unseemly will had won out: Paul had finally agreed to move from the suburbs to a house in midtown Atlanta, and that I might take a trip alone to visit a woman friend, a painter from New York whom I had met at an Atlanta poetry reading. As soon as I made plans to go to Manhattan, I wrote the Famous Southern Poet (who now lived in Washington), breaking my promise to Paul without hesitation.

I had been to New York once before, with my husband. Still in the throes of hysteria about heights, I had clutched his arm during the champagne flight like a primitive who had never heard of air travel. In the city, the sounds of the subways from beneath the sidewalks had burst in my South-softened brain like bombs in a blitz. That night I had imagined our room on the eighteenth floor of the Barbizon Plaza detaching itself from the building and crashing into Central Park. But this time, riding up, up, up in the red-velour-and-mirror-lined elevator of the Gotham Hotel, I simply admired my thick auburn curls, the effect of my new fake eyelashes. "Elevators lak this are made for wimmen lak yew, bebe!" murmured the Famous Southern Poet, pinching my ass.

Standing on the pedestal of his desire made me feel powerful. (Had Mother, "the prettiest girl in Atlanta," suffered the same delusion?) "I want you to get a divorce and marry *me*," I had whispered to the Famous Southern Poet between our kisses in the yellow cab. He had chuckled, amused at my audacity: "Yew jes' save your pennies, bebe, so yew kin come visit Daddy!" Yet the next night, when I was fifteen minutes late for our assignation, he lurched from the bed and slapped me across the cheek. "Thuh doctor says I'm dyin' of di'bee-tees!"—it was the first I had heard of it—"and hyah yew are, runnin' around with other men!" I burst into tears, grabbing my purse to leave as he pushed me down to the wrinkled sheets—"A li'l spirit, jes' whut I lak!"—struggling with the intricacies of the nude body suit I had put on beneath my princess dress.

I knew how Southern men responded to anything—chemises, garter belts, panty girdles—that formed a slight barrier to male lust; also, how it was essential to maintain the illusion of female reluctance, male pursuit, like the low hurdles in a fox hunt. "Let 'im chase you till you catch 'im" was a motto I had heard since puberty; indeed, it had been the reason for my lack of promptness. But my lover, I was beginning to learn, liked not only reluctance, but humiliation, even fear. I knew his passion for hunting deer in North Georgia with razor-tipped arrows; now I recalled how he had told me in his other, literary voice—that "the deer love to be hunted."

The next morning, we met the television people in the hotel lobby. In the South, it's more desirable that one's mistress, as the Famous Southern Poet called me, be someone else's wife; introducing me as "Mrs. Daniell," he kissed me theatrically. I wore huge dark glasses and thought I looked like a movie star, but I felt like a whore. "Bye, bye, bebe!" my lover waved as he left with his entourage. It was Sunday morning in New York, and I didn't know where I was. Outside on the dog-shit-and-trash-littered sidewalk, without the reinforcement of a man's desire, I felt suddenly empty, as though a plug had been pulled.

But at last I had found a way to separate the warring parts of myself. As all Southerners know, if you do it in New York, you didn't really do it; if I could be in two different places, I could divide my role as a proper Southern housewife from the actions motivated by my wicked, willful self. All the next year I struggled over articles for the *Atlanta* magazine, which I had found was a good way to educate myself—I wrote pieces on adult education, humanistic psychology, the Yerkes Primate Center, any subject that struck my fancy. By the time I told Paul I wanted to visit my girl friend again, I had three hundred dollars of my own.

This time I spent days lunching and shopping with my friend, nights with a Chinese painter whom I had picked up at a gallery opening. Hundreds of Times Square photographs of women in garter belts, negligees, or nothing—all rubbing, sucking, or simply lying back, vaginas spread—littered his studio. He used them, he explained, as inspiration for his passionate acrylics. I lay on a single mattress on a paint-flecked Indian cloth, watching a cockroach crawl across the floor. What looked like a green neon moon flickered across the street. The stranger's shiny jet hair, his silken ocher flesh (was this the same as doing it with a black man?), his voice telling me in pidgin English what he planned to do to my body, made me feel as though I had been catapulted from the red dirt of Georgia—my messy kitchen, the endless laundry—to another, more romantic planet.

My other life, like a grain of sand, began to rub within my brain: I couldn't really get away with this, could I? God would surely strike me down. To make sure that He did, I called Paul from the painter's studio. As he complained to me about Darcy's bad cold, about how selfish I was to make a trip alone, I stared down at a table full of slick pink cunts and burst into tears. I had on brown Italian pumps and a red linen sheath, the same proper outfit I had worn to a garden-club luncheon in Atlanta. Reminded of my real life, I knew I needed more excitement to regain the euphoria I had come for.

At my girl friend's apartment, I packed my bags to leave and walked out to Broadway to hail a cab. It was the one New York thing I had learned to do, a kind of magical transportation system that landed me wherever I wanted to be. But instead of the airport, I asked to be taken to the Chelsea Hotel, where for seven dollars, I took a room with a sink and refrigerator, but no bath. As I walked around the room, I was puzzled by the same thing that had puzzled me at my friend's apartment: did everyone here keep house as badly as Mother? Didn't anyone read *Good Housekeeping,* or "Heloise's Household Hints"? A layer of black soot covered everything, including the phone book, which had a neat, deep rectangle carved from its center—to hide what?

I had checked into a hotel alone for the first time in my life; and also for the first time, I went to a hotel bar alone and ordered a Black Jack straight up. Dressed in the red leatherette motorcycle dress, I took a cab to the East Village and the Electric Circus. As I walked past two men fighting with pocketknives, beneath the awning and up the fluorescent steps, a huge black with a black leather band around one thick wrist reached out to stroke my skirt. I flinched, relieved when a blond man in T-shirt and bandana headband fell in step beside me.

"Isn't this autistic?" I asked as we separately danced through the jelly-colored lights. "Yeh, it's ah-tistic!" he moaned orgasmically. He was a black belt in karate, he told me—he, too, wore a black leather band on his wrist—and was writing a thesis on Marshall McLuhan. I asked if he would like to read an article I had written on the information explosion. "It's back in my room at the Chelsea," I explained. He had a car, he said, and wouldn't insist that the black man, who was his friend, go with us.

In the room, I acted surprised when he put his hands on my breasts, then pushed me backward onto the sleazy gold bedspread. My Southernness wouldn't let me tell myself what I was doing. Just as in high school, I had imagined every boy who had put his finger inside my crotch as my prospective bridegroom, I also had dreamed myself the wife of the Famous Southern Poet, and then of the Chinese painter. Now, as my pickup fucked me, I felt the pimples on his thrusting back; and knew that for the first time, I was having sex without a future—just as for the first time, I had knowingly risked my life to get back a sense of it. But as in high school, I was ruined, and it didn't matter anyway. Besides, it was the only way I had found to deal with the screeching conflict between my own exotic desires, and the roles Mother, Grandmother Lee, and everyone else I knew in the South assumed I, as a female person, would willingly play.

"Why are you doing this?" asked my puzzled one-night stand. He had learned I was a housewife and mother of three from Atlanta; I had found out he was a graduate student just my age, thirty, from a middle-class Jewish family in New Jersey. "It's a circular rug!" he exclaimed, accurately describing my whole life as a Southern woman.

"Please love me!" When I arrived home from New York, I found a note from seven-year-old Darcy on the table beside my bed; she had folded it like a greeting card and illustrated it with a drawing of her Poor Pitiful Pearl doll, who had come dressed in brown burlap, a permanent plastic tear stuck on her styrene cheek.

Already, without knowing it, I had been doing to her what Grandmother Lee had done to Mother, and what Mother had done to me, neglecting to nurture her because of my own driven needs. Yet some kind of tide was coming in, maybe even a tidal wave, and there was nothing I could do to stop it. Indeed, its very hurricane force came from my turbulent center.

Leaving the children behind with Mother, Paul and I went away for a weekend in Savannah. During the five-hour drive past junked cars and ramshackle farmhouses, while we walked the moss-lined brick sidewalks, peering through gates into sealed gardens, over she-crab soup and oysters Bienville, he interrogated me.

In a famous cemetery I read the gravestones of women— *good* women—who, two hundred years before, had died in childbirth, or of malaria, at sixteen, nineteen, twenty-three. Near where two raised graves had recently been moved, I found what looked like a thick chunk of skull. Holding it up to the soft gray light, looking at the lined indentations on its curved underside, I wondered whether it had belonged to one

of the women, who had lived a perfectly selfless life, like Grandmother Lee, then had died. I imagined her to be like a creamy
magnolia blossom, picked before the petals had begun to stain
at all.

Back at the hotel, Paul fucked me with a force that seemed
designed to shake the lust loose from my brainpan. Afterward,
in the mirror that faced the bed, I saw myself reflected in my
new black crepe nightgown. That woman with her white, white
skin, her long dark hair, was just a shell, someone else: I hated
her loveliness, knowing it was just a thin layer, covering putres-
cence, a rot that sickened everyone she touched. I no longer
believed that Jesus or the Famous Southern Poet or New York
would save her. I imagined myself moving toward my pocketbook beside the dresser, taking out my manicure scissors, stabbing her, stabbing her, stabbing her.

When I heard of a new form of salvation—one as harsh, demanding, and male-ruled as the Baptist and Methodist churches
—I immediately became a Believer.

"I imagine myself a courtesan," I coyly answered the handsome blond psychotherapist. I wanted to seduce him, certain his
love would save me where Christ's had not. Because he believed in touch therapy, I was sitting on his lap, my arms around
his neck. Later, he would have me take off my skirt to do
bioenergetics in my panties, then pull me down to the carpet
for some full-length kissing.

Though he liked to kiss, he couldn't be seduced. He had a wife
and eight children, and besides, it wasn't ethical. Frustrated, I
visited another blond therapist, an Elmer Gantry of local psy-
chotherapy who had come into note as the head of the New
Consciousness Growth Group. As I interviewed him for an article for the *Atlanta* magazine, I poured out my life story, liber-
ally lacing it with tears. He would give me free therapy, he said,
as soon as I finished the article to his satisfaction.

At our meetings, I lay on the floor covering and masturbated
at his feet. (I still didn't know *how* yet, but he didn't seem to

notice that.) Then he would join me on the gold acrylic carpet
—essential for proper therapy?—where, without touching or
fucking me, he would have me suck him off. It would help cure
my frigidity and my destructive tendencies toward independence. "If you were married to me," he added, "you would never
write again!"

Was my desire to do anything other than share the car pool
and spread my legs a symptom of my desire to castrate men?
Driving home, my thighs rigid with what I didn't know was
sexual frustration, I felt agitated and ashamed. Yes, I thought,
if I had a good husband like him, I could be relaxed, dominated,
good. That my own gentle spouse couldn't control me was just
another sign that I was choked with evil—an evil of such
tenacity that it couldn't be dealt with by an ordinary man.

Soon I had something new to add to my shame. David,
twelve, had begun to hang out with those frightening new
people called hippies. At home, he locked himself in his room
for hours, listening to music that definitely wasn't Hank Williams, and taking, I suspected, the chemicals I had just begun
to hear of.

His soft brown hair was Beatle length. One morning an "in-
vestigator" came to tell me (my rubber gloves still dripping
greasy Joy suds) that it was disrupting the whole school, that I
must do something about my son. And, true to the Southern
obsession with appearances, Mother and her husband in *Deliverance* country said he could no longer visit them because of his
hair. Not long after, a hippie who rented an area farm was taken
out by locals and brutally beaten and shorn. But David vowed
he would kill himself before he would cut his.

When he was expelled from the seventh grade because of the
length of his hair, I knew the real reason too well: his stubbornness and nonconformity were the direct result of my writing,
my liaison with the Famous Southern Poet, my trips to New
York, indeed, everything I had done because I wanted to,
rather than out of the propriety and self-sacrifice expected of
me as a good Southern woman.

I imagined what the Famous Southern Poet would think, the

slight sneer that would indicate that he, too, held me responsible. I was a woman, wasn't I? And it was the goodness of Southern women that made it possible for Southern men to be both bad and redeemed, just as the frigidity of white women had permitted "fucking aound with black wenches." "And, bebe," his expression would say, "thet's the way it's s'posed to be!"

I had stepped out of line, I was not Mother, Grandmother Lee, or Gladys Presley, and my son was paying the price. It was what I had known would happen when I had dreamed of his head cracking just after his birth, when I had seen his body fly through the air at two. Yes, Mother had been right about my evil core. I was the castrating bitch that both the handsome therapists said I was.

Yet where to go for help but to my new religion?

In family therapy, David sat sullen and angry, smoking Camels, looking beyond me, even spitting on the floor. One of the things the new therapist said was that I should learn to become angry, too. Brought up like Mother to be "sweet and nice," I had never experienced anger directly. Tears, sulkiness, hysteria, even girlish temper tantrums, were expected of me as a Southern woman, but I had never heard a lady, or even a gentleman, express direct anger. Later, during my third marriage to an articulate Yankee, I would find that being verbally attacked was more painful than being struck ever had been.

When a criminologist at Florida State University wrote a paper claiming the South to be no more violent than any other part of the country, a male friend of mine, incensed, said, "Let's go beat 'im up!" Southerners don't like others attacking their myths, even when they themselves suspect them to be inaccurate. But the Southern gentleman lets others express the hostility that he would find inconsistent with breeding and good manners: red-necks do the dirty work on blacks and white trash; and it is their literal—rather than verbal—violence that keeps things soft and gentle for the genteel classes.

When the therapist said to ten-year-old Darcy that she

"didn't look the way he liked little girls to look"—meaning curled hair, white gloves, Mary Janes, instead of pigtails, jeans, boots—a fat tear, like a plastic one on her Pitiful Pearl doll's face, ran down her plump cheek. And something strange rose at the back of my neck: it would be two years before I would recognize it as rage.

During the sixties, my rural Southern past collided with the future. In 1959, I had been embarrassed when Mother had asked my black maid, a mother of nine, whether she thought it was "all right" for Laura and Darcy to sleep in the same room; the woman's children, I was sure, slept far more than two to a room; and I had long sensed the similarities between being black and female.

In 1965, the world seemed more foreign each day. Stirring beef bourguignon or hollandaise sauce, I watched scenes from Selma on the evening news. When I saw blacks and young civil-rights workers shoved by fat sheriffs with billy clubs or cattle prods, I felt that feeling at the back of my neck again. But that similar demonstrations were taking place just two miles away in downtown Atlanta, or that they might have anything to do with me, was a connection I still couldn't quite make.

The children were closer to the real world than I was. "I jes' luv-v-v to feel of his head, Mother!" Darcy said admiringly of Ralph Abernathy, Jr., who sat in front of her in fifth grade, the only black in the class. On a visit to the state capitol, the class stood on the tall curving staircase and sang songs for Governor Lester Maddox. Back home with a picture of Lester and Virginia, their signatures printed at the bottom, Darcy was incensed. "Dear Lester Maddox," she wrote. "You are mean to treat black people that way, and besides, you fuck your wife." It was the worst insult she could imagine, and I was still repressed enough to feel guilty about her language. "Dear Lester," she began again at my request; "I hope you will be nicer to black people. How would you like somebody to treat you that way?" At the bottom of the page of notebook paper, she taped a conciliatory lollipop. When she and Laura heard the seventyish white widow next door repeatedly berate her black yardman, they made a chocolate pie of mud topped with Crazy Foam, and left it on the woman's steps, accusing her of loving to fuck and being "mean to your yardman, too!" In Darcy's sixth-grade class, each student was asked how the school might be improved. "Burn it down!" she enthused.

Inexorably the aggression that I went to such lengths to conceal was coming out in my children, and there seemed to be no way to dam it. Overnight, it seemed, David had become a street person who wore a razor blade in his jacket lining, a knife in his boot—a person who listened to strange music and took pills I didn't understand. At nine, Laura had forced her collection of Barbie and GI Joe dolls into intercourse, cut them with steak knives, painted them with Mercurochrome, hung them by shoelaces. Now she refused to wear dresses and for the next five years would wear nothing but Levis and hiking boots.

When the Bay of Pigs had taken place in 1961, I had rushed out to buy canned water and frantically planned how I would save my young. Indeed, I had feared having three children because I only had two hands with which to grasp them. By the late sixties, I knew I had been right. I couldn't manage my progeny anymore, or even the life of a middle-class housewife. Our new house had crown moldings, but was older, less convenient than our split-level in the suburbs. I spent eight hours a week at the Laundromat, reading trashy novels while the wash swirled and swirled. I began dinner at three-thirty each afternoon and searched out recipes that were more and more complicated. "Why don't we ever have anything *twice*?" Paul asked. Now an associate with an Atlanta architectural firm, he drank double martinis every night and complained that I didn't wear enough makeup, that I wore dresses that only cost $17.95. Though Davison's department store was only minutes away, and I could afford to buy the dresses I once dreamed of, I ordered my and the children's clothes from the Sears, Roebuck catalog.

Every night after dinner we talked about (a) David, (b) my infidelities, and (c) divorce, which Paul said I couldn't manage because I couldn't make money. Remembering my forty-dollar-a-week job as a receptionist, I was frightened. The money I made writing for the *Atlanta* magazine was pin money, escape money, a couple of hundred dollars every few months if I was lucky. The year before, Coretta King and I had met at a mothers' meeting at our children's school. Now it was 1966, the height of her husband's glory; despite her spouse's power, my attempts at middle-class conformity, we were both still frustrated housewives.

When David at thirteen ran away with a nineteen-year-old topless dancer on the night of Martin Luther King's assassination, I searched for him in the dingy crash pads that had sprung up in midtown Atlanta. "He got intuh a white Mustang wid a man wid a mustache and a barefoot gurl wid a long skirt on 'n' said he wuz goin' to Wash'nton, Dee Cee," mumbled a filthy stoned youth whom I had finally managed to rouse. "We can't look for your little boy, lady!" yelled an exasperated voice when I phoned the Washington police department. "We're havin' riots all over the place!"

Was the world going up in flames, punishing me at last for my sexual sins?

By the time I heard of the women's movement in 1969, I was living with my third husband. We had met at a summer writers' conference in Colorado, another of the journeys for which I had saved money all year in order to accommodate what I now considered my real, if selfish and despicable, self. My second marriage was ending; David was doing and taking things for which I didn't even know the names; and I was so unhappy, so immersed in despair, that I attended the conference with the conscious intention of sleeping with as many strangers as I could: it was still the only way I had found to break up my misery.

As a married Southern woman in the sixties, I had felt left out of the culture I saw so vividly portrayed on television. But Ben, nine years my junior and a Yale Drama School dropout, had been a real part of it: at Columbia University, he had written pamphlets for SDS, demonstrated for civil rights, and known people like Mark Rudd, Teddy Gold, and others I had only read about in the *Atlanta Journal* and *Constitution.* As a protégé of Robert Brustein (whoever that was) he had been quoted in Brustein's article on the Living Theater (whatever that was) in *The Atlantic Monthly* six months before at the age of twenty-four.

Though he said he liked the way I waited on him, bringing him extra iced tea or milk or refilling his plate in the university cafeteria, he ignored me physically in a way I had never experienced. I didn't yet understand the cerebral approach to sex, and was puzzled when he wanted to talk, about writing, writers, himself, even me. When he spoke in the clipped Boston accent that went straight to the pit of my stomach and made me think of Bobby Kennedy, it was with an intensity totally different from the determined anti-intellectualism of the Famous Southern Poet and all the other deer- and woman-chasin' good ole boys I had known. As far as I could tell, he had little or no interest in guns, pickup trucks, or shooting rats at the county dump. When he told me he had never even had sex in the backseat of a Chevy, the idea of a sexuality that moved directly from high school to guilt-free adulthood titillated my Bible Belt imagination.

On the day Paul moved out, Ben, with the mobility of the privileged, moved in, to live with me and experience the South. Mother, who had received reports of my behavior from Paul, called from North Carolina to cry that I was ruining her life, then drove down to Atlanta to jerk from my beds the heirloom crocheted bedspreads she had given me. As Ben walked her back to her car, carrying a cardboard box holding the coverlets, she begged him (in a subdued way: he was a *man* and a Yankee) not to ruin my good name: it was all a girl had, especially when she was a woman with three children! (How she would have suffered had she known that my third set of in-laws, second-generation Jewish immigrants, would soon complain that I was "not in their class" because I was Southern, a shiksa who, in their view, as the daughter of an ex-Southern belle and a failed

179

Southern businessman, was not good enough for a nouveau-riche Jewish prince.)

But Ben's red beard, L. L. Bean shirts, restrained sexuality—above all, his arrogance—made me feel safe. I was certain he would give order to my messy life. As long as I was with him, I couldn't turn out like Mother, who despite her remarriage seemed crazier every year. Since I now had a half-day job as a typist at Royal Typewriter Company, I could, just barely, afford to get a divorce and marry him.

As a Southern woman, I was used to thinking my own thoughts, keeping my own counsel. Whatever confidence I had in my own ideas came because they went unchallenged. In the South, for a woman to think anything, is cute, or at worst, irritating. Now I swept from the kitchen floor the chipmunk heads brought in by the cats, the dried slugs that had crawled in through the cracks of the old house at night—and listened to Ben rave about my life, my values, the whole region. Sitting across from him at the kitchen table, I watched his sensuous mouth move beneath his red beard, and nodded respectfully. If Northeastern women were smarter than Southern women, as Mother had said, then Northeastern men, being men, must be that much more so.

I still shared Mother's notions about the importance of feminine passivity and charm. When I finally experienced New England women through Ben's Boston family, I cringed at what seemed to me their graceless outspokenness. His mother was skinny, sarcastic, and talked about masturbation at the dinner table. She and her friends' aggressive opinions, gray-on-gray sports clothes, and lack of interest in Revlon combined with the cold wind off the Charles River to tighten my genital muscles into near-frigidity. How could they expect to be loved? Or didn't they care, I wondered, applying more and more perfume in an effort to replace my missing secretions. I didn't realize that such relentless self-assertion, such understated dress, was femininity in the best Radcliffe tradition.

Now while my new love verbally reorganized my life, I looked at his long eyelashes with lust, and unconsciously wrote

SHIT on a paper napkin. I would dream one night that Ben was holding my coat—unlikely, since he didn't believe in chivalry —as the sleeves turned into a straitjacket, binding me fast. Neither of us yet knew that a Jewish prince and the daughter of a Southern belle were too much alike, that we had been brought up with the same expectations of being coddled and indulged, the same training in sulkiness and hysteria—methods and expectations that would inevitably clash. When I insisted that Ben share the housework, he was upset. I had waited until we were wed to ask; I knew better than to make him mad before he was hooked. "The worst year of my life," he later said of the first year of our marriage. But when I suggested that we have separate bank accounts and share expenses exactly, he approved; after all, he was liberated, too, and saw no reason why a man should support a woman—though the other way around might be okay.

Radical ideas didn't threaten my new husband. Indeed, he encouraged them. We would have open marriage, freedom from jealousy, independent finances, role reversal—even marathon group therapy. Though I still couldn't express anger directly, I could at least contemplate it. The end of the decade was near, and something exciting was happening, something that had to do with women. I asked the *Atlanta* magazine if I could write an article for them on the phenomenon. When members of a radical feminist group participated in a panel discussion at the Atlanta Press Club, I attended to gather material. During his preliminary speech, Hal Gulliver, an editorial writer for the *Atlanta Constitution*, made mocking references to the women. I felt that feeling rising again at the back of my neck. The finished article, I thought, was the best I had written. I had spent two months interviewing strange enclaves of outspoken young women, mostly curly-haired Barnard graduates from New York, whatever Atlanta professional women I could ferret out, and my own friends and daughters. With the help of the explicit descriptions in women's-movement literature and Paul's divorce gift of a vibrator, I had just learned to have orgasms at will. When the male magazine editor read my piece

181

with a sneer, then insisted on cutting a paragraph on female masturbation, I suddenly knew what the feeling was—anger.

The Famous Southern Poet had once told me that "the woman has never truly been known in poetry: she either says too little or too much." At that moment, eager to please him, I determined to write what was just right about feminine experience. By 1970, I was wondering for the first time why the Famous Southern Poet, or any man, should have the authority to say what was true of women's lives. I still felt self-conscious, somehow guilty, when a construction worker called out to me on the street; I still wore high-heeled sandals, blue eye shadow, and false eyelashes. But *The Feminine Mystique* had affected me like successful surgery on a person who had previously been blind. Everywhere I looked, I saw more injustices toward myself and other women and found more fuel for my rage. I found that I could hold my uncomfortable new insights away from me —like holding a lobster over a pot of boiling water with a pair of tongs—by putting them in writing. In my poems, I began to use all the words and express all the feelings I had been taught, as a Southern woman, never to express.

At lunch at Aunt Pearl's house, I sat beside Grandmother Lee, Mother, Aunt Billie, Aunt Florance, and Anne, and shuddered in the final throes of ambivalence. The pale camellias floating in a crystal dish, the white tablecloth, the carefully polished silver seduced me in a way I had thought no longer possible. Then Aunt Florance began talking about "black women who won't work for five dollars a day anymore—they're all gettin' so uppity." I looked at the elderly black maid who waited silently, hands folded, in the doorway to serve us, and felt the now-familiar feeling rise at the back of my neck. But I knew, too, that the words filling my mouth weren't proper for a Southern-ladies' luncheon, that if I let them out, they would simply be regarded as another part of my whole inappropriate life, from my too long and unpermanented hair through my messy house to my two-and-a-half marriages and the blue jeans I wasn't wearing that day.

"My house is *always* a mess!" I said, falling into the self-deprecatory tone Southern women use to declaw themselves. Mother and Grandmother Lee looked uncomfortable. But Aunt Florance, a salad fork full of tomato aspic quivering in midair near her thinning mouth, looked at me with a venom that seemed to ooze involuntarily from beneath her executive-wife manners: "Rosemary, you know it's only that way because you and those *bra burners*"—here, her voice rose shrilly—"want it that way!"

"If you're so smart, why aren't you rich?" is a common rhetorical question. "If you're so smart, why aren't you taken care of by a powerful man, and dressed like Rosalynn Carter?" is the unspoken question every traditional Southern woman asks of her less-dependent sister. It was understood that in our family, Anne was the successful member, I, the black sheep—just as Mother was the black sheep among her sisters. But though I felt guilty about my new messy anger, just as I always had about my stickily excessive sexuality, my improper will, I also felt like a kamikaze pilot of Southern feminine experience, shooting forward in the grips of a vision from which there was no return.

Because of her own early ambitions to write, Mother had been proud of my occasional articles in the *Atlanta* magazine. It was my poetry she didn't understand. "Rows-may-ree, you worked three years for thirty-five dollars!" she had exclaimed exasperatedly when my first poem had been printed in *The Atlantic Monthly*. But sometimes she liked to listen to them, especially when they were about animals or nature or something "pretty." But as I read her one of my new poems, one that expressed some of my new rage, she looked at me in terror; I had questioned values she had never dared question, expressed feelings she had never allowed into consciousness.

When I participated in an annual spring literary festival at Louisiana State University, I found that my new work upset other people besides Mother. The poster for the event showed a black-net-stockinged leg raised in a chorus kick, but of the six visiting poets, I was the only woman. The night before I left

Atlanta, aware that I would give a reading the next night with the well-known California poet Robert Creeley, I dreamed that I had to take pizza as refreshments for the event because I was a woman. Though the women graduate students said that my poems expressed exactly what they felt but had always been afraid to say, one of the famous male poets told me drunkenly and angrily that "you just can't write that." When I questioned another of the visiting poets about his work, he smirked, "You wanna fuck, baby?" Back home in Atlanta, I dreamed I was in a school cafeteria with the male poets, and they wouldn't let me sit at their table. When I sent the manuscript of my new poems to a New York editor who had once said he liked my work, I called for his response. "I hated it!" he yelled over the telephone wire; "I felt like I'd fallen down a vaginal orifice!"

The more I broke with the values on which Mother had staked her vague sanity, the more intimidated she became about confronting me directly. "A-nne," she would call my sister and cry, "cain't you speak to Rows-may-ree about leavin' that good man . . . livin' in sin with that boy . . . sendin' the chirren to school with nigras. . . ." Five years later in 1974, a year and a half before her suicide, she would call me from North Carolina to say brightly, "Rows-may-ree, A-nne says you have a book comin' out." I hadn't wanted to tell her, but my sister had done it for me. "Well, what's the name of it?" she asked expectantly. *"A Sexual Tour of the Deep South,"* I answered reluctantly. Another pause, then we both began giggling. "Wel-l-l, I'm goin' to write a book called *The Sensuous Grandmother*, and it's not goin' to have eny of that dirty stuff in it, either!" I recalled that Laura and Darcy had discovered a copy of *The Sensuous Woman* beneath her couch covers on our last visit to North Carolina. I thought of her childlike delight in ten-cent store scents and fake costume jewelry and wondered what she would have been like had her sensual, life-loving self been allowed to emerge.

On my way to New York in 1975, the last time I saw her alive, Mother insisted I give her a copy of the book in a brown paper sack "in case Wayne [her husband] sees it." "Now, if you meet that Erica Jong," she added from the driveway, "you tell her she's re-al nasty-minded!" My heart dipped; she hadn't read my book yet. (When Aunt Grace told Grandmother Lee about it, she said she wanted a copy, too. "But it has lots of words you might not like," I said reluctantly. "Don't you worry," she said in her Sunday-school voice, "I cain't understand those words enyway!")

A week later in New York, I received one of Mother's usual chatty letters in her usual style—as positive and cheery as Pollyanna, with all the *I*'s, which she considered egotistical, unrefined, omitted. This meant that most of the sentences started with a verb: "Worked in the garden all week. Picked beans and canned them. The fuchsias are blooming on the porch...." Then, in the middle of more garden news, one line: "That was some book!"

Four months later at Mother's funeral, the Methodist minister intoned over and over how happy Mother had been in Christ, what Christian joy she had known throughout her life. The only thing true to Mother in the service was the white enameled casket, which, with its metallic gold handles, echoed her taste in costume jewelry. It turned out later that Ben and I had shared the same fantasy of jumping up, interrupting the service with the truth. Instead, we filed past the preacher as he sanctimoniously shook the hand of each member of Mother's family. "You're the son-in-law who's a writer?" he asked Ben. "Yes," Ben replied quickly; "and Melissa was a writer, too, didn't she tell you? She planned to write a book called *The Sensuous Grandmother.*" As our eyes met across the shocked gaze of the man of God, my and Ben's appreciation of one another, though recently diminishing, flared afresh for a moment. But through my flash of gratitude toward my husband, I realized with alarm that Mother and I might have been more alike—beneath her crazy little-girl mask, my rebel compulsion —than I had wanted or allowed myself to believe.

185

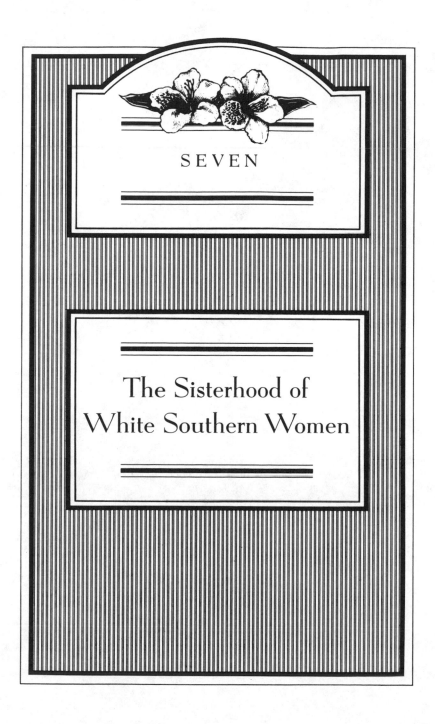

SEVEN

The Sisterhood of
White Southern Women

"I used tuh take me a li'l creem duh minthe—till Mama sed it tastid jes' lak green Maa-lox."

"Thet's thuh way I wuz 'bout Am'retta—till Otis started up 'bout it bein' lak sumthin' a lady alcuh-holic wud drank...."

I was in a restaurant in downtown Macon, eating alone, listening to the two couples across from me. The women had beehive hairdos and wore polyester pantsuits; the men wore what an Atlanta friend called "carcinogenic polyester leisure suits." Both men had paunches, and one sported white plastic-patent-leather loafers with white socks. As the two women discussed after-dinner drinks, the men talked about the chances of the Georgia Bulldogs.

It was 1971. Because I was now "liberated," and married to a "liberated" man, I had a job that meant I traveled alone. For half the school year I visited schools in Georgia and other parts of the Southeast to do poetry workshops with the students. When I was gone, I was gone all week, rushing home on weekends to cook, paste up lists of household chores on the side of the refrigerator, sort out the children's crises, sweep more chipmunk heads and slugs from beneath the kitchen table, and make love to my new husband. Sometimes at the table after dinner, Ben put a cat beneath his shirt, and I imagined he was pregnant. I liked coming home to him, rather than the other way around.

But as I toyed with a tossed salad drowned in a half cup of bright-orange French dressing, I felt anxious, lonely. As I had once feared heights, I now feared being alone on the road in the sticks of the Deep South. I was afraid of knocks on my motel door in the middle of the night, of eating grits and eggs in a café full of construction workers, of stopping at a service station in the middle of nowhere—red-neck eyes on the nape of my neck, the curve of my ass—as I made a trembling phone call to find out where I had taken the wrong road. "Nevah look in thuh barbah shop windah when you walk pas'," I had been told repeatedly as a girl: always, I kept my eyes toward the road, or the sidewalk, or my plate, or the floor. I had been brought up to fear black, white-trash, red-neck—*all*—men; and the way to make rape and mayhem certain, I knew, was to acknowledge their existence or mine.

In motels in Columbus or Columbia, often above a honky-tonk full of soldiers and red-necks, I went to bed with a book at six. As semis sped along the Georgia or South Carolina highway outside my door, or worse, as the truck drivers themselves walked along the corridor near my room, I listened to them drunkenly mumbling "Muthafucka" and "Shee-it, man!" and "pussy," and quivered, certain that my door would be crashed through, that instant violence would take place, if they suspected for a moment that a woman was there alone. In Columbia, a woman moaned and begged in the room next to mine, as though she were about to be killed. But as I frantically dialed the room clerk, I heard her outside the door: "Pleeeze, Quinton, lemme back in. . . ." This time, she only sounded like Mother, pleading with Daddy.

Worse than my fear of rape was my sense of isolation. Lying in a Scottish Inn outside Chattanooga, or a Davis Brothers Motel near Macon, listening to the two-ton rigs whiz by, I would feel the very room revolving, the bed spinning freely out of control, as though I were sky diving or riding a raft over the rapids of the Chattanooga River. At home my life revolved around Ben and my children, but here I had total vertigo, was connected to nothing—truly alone for the first time in my life.

At first I tried phoning Ben. But he didn't approve of the dependency indicated by my call: I was supposed to be free of all that now, he would say sternly, till I hung up, my anxiety still a lead ball in my belly. Sometimes my disorientation would peak, become so complete that I would sob half the night with the deep sobs, as though from some bottomless chasm, I had often heard rising from somewhere inside Mother. The next morning I would drag myself out of bed to go to a new rural high school. I would try to smile brightly at a principal who looked more like a country sheriff as he, in turn, looked at me curiously, if not disapprovingly, and my eyes would ache from my tears of the night before. As I struggled to hold the attention of a hundred hulking, often barefoot students for the next four hours, my head would throb. Only after I ate beans and cornbread in the school lunchroom and sat in the smoke-filled teachers' lounge with women who peered at me suspiciously as they discussed recipes and home canning, could I return, with relief, to the same motel room where I had felt so alienated the night before.

Gradually, the motel rooms, with their color television sets, the orange acrylic bedspreads, the Formica desks with their open Bibles, became wombs, drawing me in. Here, everything was in its place, and dependable. I lay sprawled on the big bed and drank Jack Daniel's from a flask Ben had given me as a gift. I developed a taste for Kentucky Fried Chicken and McDonald's Quarter-Pounders with cheese. The fear, and the feeling of loneliness, like the nausea of early pregnancy, passed. It was as though a new self had been born, the self I was when I was alone. I was strong now, not weak like Mother, and never would be again.

I wouldn't realize—until they were gone—how anchored I still was by husband, children, house, parents.

"She wuz on welfare and ev'ry time she got 'er check, she would come intuh the school hall and holler fur her two kids, a hot dog in each hand: it wuz her treat fur 'em on the day she got 'er money."

I was at a dry, of course, creamed-corn-and-parched-roast-beef-again PTA dinner in the basement of the Baptist church in Walhalla, South Carolina; and the school principal, who sported the regulation good-ole-boy crew cut and paunch, had turned out, not unexpectedly, to be a humorist:

"Wall, they lived out a piece, and wun day when wun of 'er

boys got di-reeah at school, I had tuh drive 'im home. I kept
sayin' 'Whar do yew live?' 'n' he kep sayin' 'Thisaway' or
'Thataway.' I kep drivin' arown in circles—yew kin 'magine the
smell in thuh car, 'cause he'd gone in 'is pants—'n' fin'ly we
came up tuh this ole shack, 'n' he sed, 'Thar's mah house!' 'n'
I took 'im up tuh thuh doe, 'n' she came out, 'n' I sed, 'Lady, yo
boy's sick,' 'n' she sed, 'I know it—why dew yuh thank I sent
'im tuh school whar thar's an indoe bathroom?'

   "In thuh meantime, a dog thet wuz tied in thuh yard by a
rope had run rown 'n' rown threw thuh winduh of a junked car
whut wuz out thar. 'Save muh rope! Save muh rope!' she hol-
lered—'n' I had tuh wind thet danged dog rown 'n' rown threw
thet winduh till I got 'im out!"

He was telling the kind of story Southerners like most to tell,
and the subject interested me. When I had stopped being
afraid, I had begun noticing, for the first time, the Southern
women around me. Since I had married at sixteen, I had spent
most of my life at home in the purdah Southern propriety demands and had thought the experiences of Mother, Grandmother Lee, my aunts, and me unique. But now I saw women
like us everywhere. Without knowing it, I had begun research
on the sisterhood of white Southern women.

   "I jes' take a li'l NyQuil ev'ry night—have fur two years or
more: it helps me to sleep," said Rayline, an anxious preacher's
wife and high-school teacher, in the teachers' lounge in a school
in the mountains of North Georgia. Her voice had the same
high little-girlishness as Mother's, and what she said made me
think of my Jack Daniel's and the phenobarbital Mother now
cried she had to take at several intervals during the night in
order to sleep, even though her husband called her a "drug
addict" and insisted on separate beds.

   At forty-five, Rayline still had a halo of dark curls, a magnolia-
cream complexion; that she had once been very pretty, like
Mother, was clear. But like Mother's, her forehead, the sides of
her mouth were deeply etched by the lines of her constantly
exaggerated feelings. It was as though both of them barely
contained some constant inner violence.

Mother had just had tests by a neurologist to find out about the unexplained pains she had been having in her lower back and down her right leg for the past year. Now Rayline began retelling me, for the dozenth time, about her exploratory surgery: "They never did find out whut it wuz, whut wuz causin' it, 'n' now I still have this twitch at thuh side of muh eye, 'n' my bosoms don't feel right, though I cain't find a lump, 'n' I feel so funny when I git up in the mornin's. . . ."

Like Mother, Rayline had always "wonid to write"; recently, she had shown me her poems. Like Mother's, her efforts turned out to be a puerile arrangement of proper sentiments about her role as wife and mother, and about how happy she was to be a Christian. As a preacher's wife, she bore the onus of setting an example to other women in the community; when I suggested that other feelings might lie beneath the surface, she looked at me with vague apprehension. Did I mean sex, that great Southern taboo that became the metaphor for every forbidden emotion? Like Mother, and all the Southern women I had known, she had never directly experienced or expressed anger. "What do yuh mean?" she asked, genuinely puzzled.

Across the room, Melba, tea-rose perfumed, sixty pounds overweight, in a flowered crepe dress, her piled-up brown hair drifting in tendrils toward her faintly perspiring white neck, snorted. She didn't have much sympathy for Rayline's pains or problems. Earlier, when Rayline had whined about "gittin' oldah 'n' losin' mah looks," Melba had said tartly, "Well, it's bettah than not gittin' older at all, isn't it?" The year before, Melba had almost died in a diabetic coma; now, at thirty-seven, she lived with her parents. After teachers college, she confided, she had tried to break away, to live on her own in a town up in North Carolina, where she had gotten a teaching job, had had her own apartment, joined the local drama group, even had an affair—with a married man, she told me later, when she trusted me. But he wouldn't get a divorce and marry her, as he had promised, and since she had almost died last year, she needed to live with her parents in case she needed to be taken care of.

It was after her close call with death that she had burned the letters from her one lover and put the ashes in a Planters Peanuts jar, which she kept on the mantelpiece in her bedroom. "Whut if I had died 'n' Mama 'n' Daddy had found 'em!" she exclaimed. The idea that they might know of her improper conduct seemed to frighten her more than that she could have died. Later, when I found that Mother had destroyed her best pieces of writing before her suicide, I thought of Melba.

Once, in her twenties, Melba had been called before a local board of education for giving a male high school student a ride home in her car. Now, like Mother, she lived caught in the vise between feelings and society. Near the school was a colorful bar, illegal in a dry county. On Friday nights, mountaineers from twenty and thirty miles away drifted down to get drunk, grab the microphone from the girl vocalist, and create their own lyrics. Would Melba like to go there with me that weekend? No, of course she couldn't. Mama and Daddy wouldn't let her, much less the school board!

It should have been funny. But it wasn't.

There's a certain kind of Southern woman who wears a pastel, usually pale green, polyester dress or pantsuit, medium-heeled pumps, stockings, and, of course, a girdle. Her frosted gray hair lifts rigidly off her neck in a beauty-parlor beehive; her only makeup is a prim slash of lipstick, a chalky powder that gathers in the lines of her face. It is as though she has been frozen in time, and it would be impossible to say whether middle age began at thirty or fifty; in every case, she is permanently 55.6 years old. She is the schoolteacher with twenty years tenure, the chairwoman of the Woman's Missionary Union at the First Baptist Church, the president of the Daughters of the Confederacy, the woman who, like Grandmother Lee, I would least like to know my sexual fantasies. She is Aunt Florance, Darlene's mother, and the women I would sometimes think of as I drove through Milledgeville or Eatonton, Georgia.

Black writer Alice Walker grew up in Eatonton on a tenant farm till she was thirteen. "Those women would act 'nice' to blacks," she said, "but eventually their faces became their masks." She told me that once her mother worked all day for such a woman—cleaning her two-story house; boiling, washing, and ironing her clothes; then raking a yardful of magnolia leaves. "The woman gave Mama seventy-five cents, and she threw it back in her face," Alice said.

Traveling through the South, I found that the masked ladies were as ubiquitous as dogwood petals in April. And though their primary characteristic is an unpuzzled self-righteousness, they often have particular traits adapted to their locale.

In the wild city of Macon, home of Little Richard, Otis Redding, the Allman Brothers, and Capricorn Records, I agreed to board, during my eight-week tenure, with the sweet-looking white-haired mother of a local school administrator. Bertie Mae's immaculate five-room bungalow was crammed with purple bric-a-brac and plastic-and-doily-covered living-room and bedroom "suits." Her distinguishing trait was that, like Miz Lillian, she liked to drink. And her choice of beverage was as sweet as her taste in home furnishings. Every night she churned up in her blender a batch of Daiquiris made from frozen lemonade and cheap white rum. Together we would sit on the plastic-covered couch watching the evening news on her big color TV and getting tighter and tighter. By the time we sat down to our supper of black-eyed peas and cornbread, or fried chicken and collard greens, we would both be pleasantly tipsy, and she would be primed for gossip about her late husband, the women at her church, the people with whom she had worked before she retired.

Because of our proximity in the tiny house, I began to have strange erotic dreams in which she—a fat, white-haired woman with lavender soap in her bathroom—figured. Yet the arrangements were fairly satisfactory; all I was required to do, I soon realized, was follow her drink for drink, compliment her cooking, and listen.

But Bertie Mae had her limit, and it was sexual. After I had invited a male co-worker in for a drink while she was out of town visiting her married daughter, she confronted me the next day after school: "Yew had a *man* in here, didn't yuh?" she accused me, indicating the two highball glasses in the sink. Then, before I could answer: "Wall, yew'll jes' have tuh leave. Besides, yo' car is makin' a spot on mah driveway!" It was true. Right in the spot where I parked my Fiat, oil had oozed onto the concrete she usually kept scrubbed white with Ajax.

Bertie Mae's attitude wasn't restricted to an older generation. Darla, eighteen, had worked as a call girl in Atlanta, but had returned home to Eufala, Alabama, to work in a grenade factory and date her married brother-in-law. Darla's cross to bear was her mother, a Holy Roller, who disapproved of her lipstick and slacks. When I asked Darla if she had ever talked with her about orgasms she squealed, "Lordy, no! She'd kick me clear out of the state!"

"I look to my husband for guidance," Camille, an English-department head, told me seriously. Her husband was a local banker, and "I'm so lucky because he's so *good,"* she added, a taut look crossing her pretty face, as though she imagined that without his discipline, she was uncertain of how she might behave, how low her character might sink.

Susie had a beauty-parlor Farrah Fawcett hairdo and figure to match, was thirty-two, and taught school, yet still lived at home in Savannah with her widowed mother. She hadn't had sex since her divorce four years before. "I got so mixed up about it, I talked to my preacher," she told me, anxiety lines deepening her tanned forehead. "But he said it's not right. So I guess I'll jes' have to keep waitin' for Him"—I couldn't tell whether she meant Jesus or the Right Man—"to come along." In a concession to the times, she added, "I try to jog about four miles a day. I've found that helps a lot." My mind boggled: I had rarely been without sex for more than two weeks—except for birth exigencies—since I was sixteen. Now I knew for sure I never could have made it as a good Baptist!

Linda, elegant braids coiled around her head, stitched pubic hair on one of her stuffed people sculptures. We were at her house on Savannah Beach—a kind of tackier southeastern Provincetown—talking about our Southern upbringings and her divorce after twenty years with a compulsively womanizing man of God. That morning I had been guest speaker at the New Light Revelation Church where her former spouse was minister. Now, in the middle of our conversation, he called me to say thanks—and to ask whether he might see me if he came to Atlanta.

Linda smiled thinly, unperturbed; his behavior, it seemed, was characteristic. She wasn't even interested in discussing it. But as the conversation turned to a common acquaintance from Beaufort, South Carolina, the coastal town where Linda had grown up, there was a hint of Bertie Mae, of Grandmother Lee and her steely Baptist morality, in the air.

Montana had been Linda's sorority sister at the University of Georgia. But a couple of years before, she had gone through a divorce in which her own relatives had been called to testify that she was an unfit mother, citing such behavior as wearing blue jeans and T-shirts without a bra.

"Montana shouldn't have run around on Jim"—her used-car-dealer husband—"embarrassin' him all over Beaufort like that!" Linda stated flatly. "I don't care how frustrated she was. Why, it was jes' as silly as her changin' her name from Mary Aline to Montana and runnin' off to SoHo!"

Was she thinking of what she had gone through because of her preacher husband's skirt-chasing? A few months later, I read in the *Atlanta Journal* that her ex-husband had been arrested and charged with murder. It was alleged that he had driven to a Mississippi trailer park and shot twice at point-blank range the fiancé of the ex–girl friend who had been the corespondent in his and Linda's divorce.

A New York friend said that visiting the South reminded her of nothing more than being in high school again. And from the names given so many Southerners—T.J., Junior, Jim-Bob, and Bubba; Missy, Mandy, Lynn, and Lynn Sue—one would think they were intended to remain perpetual children. But when women in their twenties attached themselves to the same values that had driven Mother, Grandmother Lee, and the masked ladies, they seemed caricatured, out of sync, as though they had just arrived on a spaceship that had brought them directly from another decade without passing through the sixties at all.

Culver was Ben's Southern buddy and, with Ben's tacit approval, my lover. A sensitive good ole boy who liked to read John Donne to me in bed, he was also an imaginative dresser who wore a Red Rose feed cap and one of his wife Mandy's gold earrings in one pierced ear ("I got drunk 'n' got this gurl tuh do it with a safety pin"). When he and Mandy visited Savannah, I met them at their motel room. "Rows-may-ree, scuse thuh way this room looks!" Mandy squealed. "I jes' cleaned the sink, but it's a me-ass!" I peered inside at bicycles, strewn panty hose, an electric iron, even a can of Lysol. "But enyway," she gushed on in the hyperbole to which Southerners are given, "despite the me-ass, we're jes' thrilled tuh death tuh see yuh!"

Looking as though she had been candied, Mandy oozed out of a red-and-white-checked cotton dress with puffed sleeves, red satin ribbons at the neck, and red sandals. Her finger- and toenails were painted ruby red, her long blonde hair hung smoothly down her back. Long uncut hair is still a sexual status symbol in the South. "I wonid to marry me somebody *purty*— a sorority gurl," Culver had once told me, as though it was the finest possession a Southern man could own. Never mind that he had to keep a tube of K.Y. jelly beside the bed in his house in Atlanta, because, he had explained as he had lain beside me, spent, "Thet gal is jes' as dry as a bone—she jes' don't lak doin' it, ah guess!" There had been a note of pride in his voice: in the traditional logic of Southern men, the purity—or frigidity—of his good Southern girl kept him from having to worry about his manhood, and permitted him to spend time in bed with bad women like me.

Once, at dinner at his house, Mandy had called Culver downstairs to have him show her the order in which the ingredients should be stuck on the skewer for shish kebab. "I don't know *why* he wonts tuh have this fancy stuff!" she had complained petulantly. "Prob'ly 'cause Ben's a Yankee 'n' he wonts tuh make a good impression on y'all." At a party at my and Ben's house, she had dragged her husband through the front door incensed when another guest had pulled out a joint and offered her a toke. Now, as we left the motel room, Culver whispered in my ear, "Don't brang out eny dope—Mandy'll have a fit!"

Our first stop was the Pink House, a bar set in an eighteenth-century mansion that had served as headquarters for General York during what we still refer to, in the South, as the "Wawh Between thuh States." Mandy looked perfect, sitting on the couch before the cut pink flowers, the low lights turning her blonde tendrils to candle glow. But when Lonnie, the gay piano player, came over to our table, he ignored her widening eyes, her puckered lips, and talked about his latest trick: "Thuh cutest li'l truck drivah yew evah saw, honey!—met 'im at thuh Gator Lounge. 'Deed, since these friends of yours are frum Etlana, I'll take y'all ovah thyah. But first," he enthused, indicating the gay disco around the corner, "we'll trot ovah to Dr. Feelgood's—jes' lemme finish one mo' tune!"

Gay talk is enough like good-ole-boy talk to be nonthreatening to many Southern men. And some of the motions—bear hugs, ass patting, shoulder blows—are the same, differing only in the degree of overt sexuality. Soon we were being swept down the street, an eager Culver, a pouting Mandy in tow, to walk into a room dark but for flickering purple strobe lights, full of milling men and a few women, and a jungle beat that drowned out conversation.

In a few minutes, Culver shouted in my ear through the sounds of Alice Cooper: "Rows-may-ree, we've got tuh git outta hyah—Mandy's havin' a fit!"

On the sidewalk, Mandy stood fanning herself breathlessly, as though she had just seen a vision too horrible to contemplate. "Rows-may-ree, how kin yew *stand* thet—they jes' don't pay *us* eny 'tention at all!"

One of the benefits of being a liberated woman, I had discovered, was that now I could go—as long as I could find a man to take me—to all the places that had once been off-limits. Lonnie, undaunted, was ready to take us to the notorious Gator Lounge, and since he, Culver, and I all had a taste for low life, Mandy was outnumbered again. "Honey, yew'll luv it!" Lonnie gushed to Culver, ignoring Mandy's sulk. As a gay Southern male, he was at least as good at her act as she was.

Despite her delicacy, Mandy's favorite drink was an iced-tea glass full of Black Jack with a little water and no ice. At the Gator Lounge, she ordered more bourbon and a hamburger, then stomped back to the ladies' room. In seconds, she stomped out again: "Thyah's no *toil*-it papuh in thyah!" she announced, incensed. As though each had suddenly heard the voice of his sacred mother, several drunk sailors and truck drivers reeled from their bar stools and rushed up with paper napkins. With a wordless sniff, she accepted their offerings and stalked back into the rest room.

As Mandy gobbled down a hamburger that looked like a huge greasy sausage on a biscuit, as Lonnie worked on another truck driver, and Culver and I played the pinball machine, tears, the fat, endless tears I had learned from Mother, ran down my cheeks. Because Mandy was there, Culver couldn't give me the Southern comfort—the hugs and ear nibbles and neck kisses— with which Southern men automatically soothe away incipient hysteria in the women with whom they are involved. All he could do this time was whisper pleadingly, "Oh, come *on*, honey!"

Suddenly, Mandy bolted from her chair, looking as though she might choke. "Cul-vah!" she screeched. "We have tuh leave this place! Naow!" As we looked around, we saw the skinny girl in the G-string who had just danced out topless across the top of the bar.

"Did yew see thuh way those boys jumped tew when she said thet about the toilet papuh?" Culver asked admiringly as we hastened out just in time to interrupt a slight black man who was stealing the hubcaps from Lonnie's silver Lincoln Continental.

Culver. I could have brained him. The first time we had gone to bed together, Mandy had called my motel room, just at the crucial moment, to ask, as though it was the most natural thing in the world, "Is Culvah thyah, Rows-may-ree? I need tuh ask 'm sumthin' about BankAmericard." As my lover had sat naked, patiently explaining something obvious to the literate world, what had been between us a few minutes before rapidly diminished.

Now, by using manipulation and hysteria, the methods I had rejected because of Mother's lack of success with them, the means to which Ben refused to respond at all, Mandy had successfully controlled the evening and gained her husband's admiration. Once he had told me that in high school, she had been a Latin scholar; how dumb was she, anyway? Back in my motel room, I called him in his, where Mandy already lay beside him, sweet in a ruffled batiste gown, to yell over the phone, "You can't have it both ways, you know, have a woman like her, and a woman like me, too!" As long as I was so confused, of course he could! But Culver seemed to understand my yelling better than anything I had ever said to him before; if I could have been more hysterical, that probably would have been good, too.

A few weeks before, over enchiladas in a bad Mexican restaurant, he had told me how protective he had to be of Mandy, how fragile she was, " 'Cause if anything evah happened tuh 'er, her mama and daddy would nevah forgive me." That was why he had had to drive her for two hours through a raging rainstorm the Saturday before to the mill town that had just the right color yarn for her needlepoint. An only child, Mandy had, still had, a well-off father who doted on her, a mother who treated her like a Southern princess. Mother had had neither a father who had loved her nor a tender mother, and neither had I. Was this why we were so easily hurt?

As he spoke protectively of Mandy, the fat tears had started down my cheeks, spontaneous, uncontrollable—lymph fluid from an old wound. Culver had been unperturbed. He often made me weep simply by singing and playing on his guitar the Baptist hymns we had both grown up washed in. Southern women, since they so often feel powerless, cry a lot, and Southern men learn early how to deal with it; and the only words they use are *baby, honey,* and *sweetheart.* Whatever their cause,

Culver responded to my tears in the traditional Southern gentleman's way, by taking me home and fucking me through them till they stopped.

The fucking worked as long as I didn't think. But now I was a weirdo, a half-liberated woman in conformityland. I had rejected the choices of Mother and Mandy, and while I was more curious about other Southern women than I had ever been, I also felt supercilious: I had made the right choices, not they.

But if Mother had not failed at manipulation and role playing, if Daddy had been more receptive to it, would I have made them? Once, lunching with Mandy, I had heard the exasperation with which she spoke of Culver; behind her giggles had been the same condescension, the same dammed anger I had grown up hearing in the voice of every conventional Southern woman I had known. Her tone had seemed to validate all my choices of the past few years: I needed, more than anything, not to take Mother, Mandy, and their kind seriously.

Yet I had to admit that that night in Savannah, Mandy had had more power than I did, or at least I felt she did. And it was not the last time I would experience chagrin and loss at meeting Southern women who had clung to, and become successful in, the Southern terms of marriage, material security, a powerful husband, through the old Southern skills.

Once a debutante, always a debutante—there's no such creature as an ex-debutante, I was told.

Missy grew up in Savannah, went to *the* private day school, made a local debut. When we met, she was five years younger than I, but had been married for twelve years to the same man, also a local who had gone to the right schools. They had two children, and lived in the kind of historic townhouse for which the city of Savannah is famous.

Indeed, it is as though the architecture of the town dictates fashion as well: stylish Savannah women are given to wearing shawls, Albert Nipon dresses with gathered skirts, full of rosebuds and little tucks, and in a place where flowers bloom almost

202

all year round, flowers in their curled hair. "Missy is the only woman I know who really looks and acts like a heroine in a Scott Fitzgerald story," a friend said of her before we met. She was referring to Missy's habit of reclining on couches at social gatherings, and pulling a shawl or coverlet up under a face that has the white, white skin that comes from carefully avoiding the sun. Lying there, she did look delicate. "Sometimes I have these *fits*," she said cheerfully; unlike Mandy, Missy seemed aware of her incongruities. "If I get stoned or somethin', I have one; ev'rybody has to come round and hold my hand—else I'll go into hysterics—and then," she laughed, "I don't have to do enythang for the rest of the evenin'!"

Missy taught English at a Savannah high school, but tittered derisively when she spoke of her job: in young-and-monied Savannah, it's redneck to take anything seriously, particularly work. "This summer I'm goin' to check out my genealogy, join the Colonyul Dames; that'll be a trip, won't it, sittin' stoned at lunch with those old ladies, jes' 'cause my great-great-great-granddaddy was a captain in the king's militia in South Carolina? Then jes' stay high 'n' read all of Lilyun Hellman.

"When Beau and I were first married," she went on, "we tried to think of decadent thangs to do. 'Bout the worst we could come up with was drinkin' 'Co-Colas' 'n' eatin' hamburgers in bed. But now there are lots of thangs. . . ."

"The one problem of my life," Beau told me in the voluptuous double-syllabled tones of the aristocratic Southern male, "is avoidin' boredom." A group of us were sitting on River Street, watching an ocean liner move majestically down the Savannah River, its lights flashing in the night like a Southern Christmas tree, only a hundred feet from where we drank our rum and tonics.

Money had given Missy and Beau privilege and beauty, and salvation from boredom. Every weekend, they had soirees and "got wrecked" and swapped or bought a few new antiques. Their living room was hung with good contemporary paintings, which they traveled to New York to buy. New hardback bestsellers lay open all over the house. On the mantelpiece in the library stood a gold-framed photograph of Missy's sister's Indian guru; the year before, she and Beau had traveled to India to visit the sister and her husband at their ashram.

Missy's best friend Clare had just gone to a one-thousand-dollar-a-week fat farm in Houston but had gotten so bored that she had run away to a hotel where she had stayed stoned and drunk and shopped for designer dresses from Nieman-Marcus. It seemed to be the kind of anecdote Missy liked best, one that emphasized "fun" and indicated a lack of seriousness, especially where money was concerned.

Last year, when she and Beau had decided they wanted to "see a demonstration," they had invited Clare, her husband, and her husband's mistress, then had had the maid pack a lunch that included a linen tablecloth, stem crystal, and a half case of Pouilly-Fuissé. They had driven to South Carolina, and near the site of a demonstration against a proposed nuclear power plant had spread the cloth on a grassy hill in a churchyard. Drinking from the wine glasses, nibbling watercress sandwiches and cold boiled crab, they had watched the marchers from a safe distance.

As far as politics were concerned, Beau was still given to comments about "noblesse oblige" and "good-lookin' nigger wenches." A bumper sticker on his navy Mercedes-Benz convertible asserted his positive feelings about Arabs, despite the fact that Savannah was one of the first Southern cities to be settled by Jews and has an influential Jewish population. WASP Savannah was and is a society that rejects anyone without the right ancestors. It is said that when a prominent, but nouveau-riche, citizen was refused entry to the elite Oglethorpe Club around the turn of the century, he built a mansion directly across the narrow street.

The Oglethorpe Club had been the scene of one of Missy's favorite coups: "We went there for dinner, and I was so stoned, I forgot to use a Tampax; when I stood up, the upholstered chair where I'd been sittin' was all bloody; since my dress was black, nobody could tell who'd done it. Beau and I jes' laughed and laughed. . . ."

204

As we smoked more Colombian, drank more rum and tonics, I began to imagine they were mint juleps. I needed to obliterate my sense of being back at E. Rivers Grammar School in the wrong ugly brown dress, my underpants held up by a gigantic safety pin, listening to classmates talk about evening gowns and parties at the Piedmont Driving Club. Beau looked like my best pubescent dreams: the dope and booze had blotted out my awareness of his politics and I had encouraged his kiss in the backseat as the group of us had driven back from River Street. If Mother had not married Daddy, if Daddy had not turned into a drunk and a gambler, if I had worn nice dresses from the girls' department at Davison's department store, if we had not had to move to the country, if I had gone to dancing school and Sweet Briar in Virginia, if, if, if . . . would I now be in a room like this, wearing an Albert Nipon dress, comfortable with my prejudices and married to a man like Beau . . . having *fun* and not painfully liberated at all?

My reverie was broken by Missy's "Lulu" voice. She had told me earlier of her three voices—her own, Lulu's, and Miz Slut's; she had created the last recently when one of her friends had been left by her husband for a younger woman, an "outsider." "Miz Slut says her husban' is out lookin' fah pussy when he says he's goin' out with clients in the evenin'," she purred archly, giving Beau a cross look as he took my elbow to "show you the garden." Even a woman in a designer dress has to hold on to her man; and while liaisons among the right people might be acceptable, affairs with outsiders were not. Now she pulled the shawl up under her chin: "Lulu is tired, Lulu wants to go to bed," she whispered, and closed her eyes, a signal that the evening had ended.

Beau had already told me that I frightened him—"travelin' alone, married three times, and all that." I had been categorized, I knew, something borne out a few weeks later, when I ran into Beau on a Savannah street: "I went to a party last week, wanted you tuh go but couldn't reach you, a girl jumped naked out of a cake, we threw rubbahs all ovah a tree. . . ."

Even before he told me, I knew Missy had not been there, just as I had known at E. Rivers School, and as Missy had pulled the shawl up under her chin, that I was a misfit, and wouldn't be invited back.

The Famous Southern Poet once told me I would have made a good pioneer woman; a friend who was into reincarnation imagined my former life to have been that of a dance-hall girl in a saloon in the Old West.

Both images conjure up what is known in the South as a good ole girl, the female counterpart of the good ole boy—or the kind of woman a Southern man admiringly described as "thuh type yew might find out in thuh woods choppin' wood."

Naturally, if the good ole boys are out in the pickup drinking beer, or in their urban version, creating disturbances in chic Atlanta, or Washington, D.C., bars, somebody's got to be back at the homeplace chopping wood, and it's useful if, as Southern poet Bill Doxie put it, *under that cute pink nipple pounds a heart of raw gristle.*

Grandmother Lee's mother, walking back from school at nine to find her mother's best china butter dish floating in a gutter in the wake of the Yankees, yet trotting on home to feed the chickens, was a good ole girl; so was Scarlett. (Melanie, too tender-hearted, was not.)

Rosalynn Carter, Miz Lillian, Cornelia Wallace, Aunt Thelma, Grandmother Lee, and Tammy Wynette are good ole girls. Mother, Mandy, Missy, the masked ladies, and any woman who voluntarily escaped the Deep South for "New Yawk" were not.

Good ole girls are realistic and materialistic and loyal to the land. Being a good ole girl means standing by your man and not making waves. Good ole girls come sexy or pure, and in either case are respected by good ole boys.

All the women in country-music songs are good ole girls.

Like Susan Hayward donning blue jeans to host a barbecue with second husband Eaton Chalkley in Carrollton, Georgia, I could still play the role, even look the part. But as a self-supporting woman married to a Yankee, I could no longer truly qualify. A good ole girl, and not a good ole girl, I existed in a no-woman's-land. With Culver, I was one; with Ben, I wasn't. Traveling alone, teaching, writing, it was my good-ole-girl toughness that saw me through. But at home as a wife and mother, I reverted again to the hysterical woman Mother had been.

Daily, I had to rev myself up for the struggles of liberation. Though I told myself that Jimmy probably never went down on Rosalynn, I yearned for the easy benefits of the role I had left behind. I now understood too well why so many Southern women clung to their roles, allowed their lives to be defined by the supermarket, beauty parlor, garden club, and a paunchy husband drinking a six-pack in front of a color TV: it was *easier*.

For one thing, good ole girls, since they had denied themselves, could get mad more easily and self-righteously than I could with my abortive therapy, my affairs, my several marriages, my writing, my struggles for liberation. It was as though conformity itself gave them the right to say what they pleased. "George's brother, Gerald, is telling everybody I've been fucking every state trooper for miles around!" Cornelia complained angrily to the media during her divorce. When Billy Carter was asked on a talk show whether he envied his brother, he replied, "Nope. When I thank of envy, I thank of Stella Parton, Dolly's sister. Yuh see, she ain't got much on top." "At least there's an operation to correct my problem," Stella retorted to the media; "I never heard of an operation for a silicone brain!"

Above all, good ole girls are tough. At supper on the grounds of their homeplace in Young Harris, Georgia, Shirley Miller, wife of the lieutenant governor, told me excitedly that "I've got a new hog I'm raisin', 'n' it's near ready tuh slaughtah!" Zell Miller's mother, Birdie, was like a phenomenon of nature: widowed at thirty-nine, left near-penniless with two children in the North Georgia mountains, she had laboriously handpicked stones from a creek to build over a period of years the beautiful rock house atop a hill where Shirley and I stood. "Mountain women are strong," Miller wrote of his mother in his autobiography. "Mountain women are independent. Mountain women

207

are of tough moral fiber." The bottom line might have been that mountain women are asexual: nowhere in his book did he imply that during widowhood she had a life beyond that of children, church, and community.

Yet as I sat on the front porch, enjoying the cool, clear mountain air, I watched a woman in thin white cotton slacks through which one could see her printed bikini panties, in a bare-midriff shirt tied tautly beneath her small pointed breasts, walk through the screen door, carrying a filled beer cup. She handed it to a paunchy man in a butter-yellow polyester jumpsuit, opaque dark glasses, obligatory white plastic-patent shoes, hair held in a ducktail pompadour by what looked like melted Vaseline—"the shuruf uf Lavonia," I heard someone say. Deep in ritual good-ole-boy talk—the words can just about be predicted —he took the cup without speaking. After all, she was only doing what a good ole girl should do, taking care of her man, and looking silently sexy in the style he undoubtedly favored— a style that insists on mascaraed fake lashes, long teased, dyed hair, bra with push-up pads, a style that, in its fulfillment, hearkens north to Nashville, to Tammy, Loretta, Dolly. It's a look that sometimes makes it hard to tell the hookers from the wives.

Conservative good ole girls wear long dark hot-rolled hair, gold hoop earrings, navy polyester pantsuits or dresses, and may have long legs and fantastic figures. The most conservative wear Rosalynn Carter hairdos, kept permanented and off the neck, dark Nelly Don dresses, and plain, but matching, dark pumps and pocketbooks. ("I offered to do Rosalynn's hair free," a chic Atlanta hair stylist told me, "but she turned me down. Just wanted to keep getting that weekly shampoo and set at that little shop in Albany, I guess.") Successful good ole girls, that is, those with the most powerful husbands, wear killer, or keep-off, diamonds. Never do good ole girls wear anything that looks vaguely *Vogue*-ish; and they wear blue jeans only literally down on the farm.

"Teachers are ladies with drab hairdos," wrote a fifth-grader in one of my classes. Most of the teachers I met in teachers' lounges conformed to his description. "Don't they ever get down?" whispered a fellow visiting artist, coughing on smoke. Indeed, the room was a sea of tense teacher faces, tense teacher hands raising cigarettes to tensely pressed red mouths. But some teachers, I discovered, were barely disguised good ole girls of the sexy variety. Whether they lived in a middle-sized city like Charlotte or Savannah, or in a rural town where the one restaurant was inside the one service station, the good-ole-girl teacher was often the most glamorous woman in town.

Sherry wore her L'Orealed auburn hair in a congealed side sweep, and had had a nose job the year before. The surgery had been inspired by her intuition that her good-ole-boy husband was about to leave her for "a dumpy woman with platinum hair and a silver Mach V." It had all started when "he would dip snuff out on the golf course with the boys, tryin' tuh be Billy Cartah or sumthin', then come home and try tuh kiss me." But Sherry, a good ole girl of the classy variety, was having none of that: "I knew sumthin' was up when he started complainin' that my underwear was the wrong color—*she* prob'ly wears black, or purple, or sumthin'!" She still wore her killer diamond—"at least he gave me sum good jew'lry"—and assorted gold and jade bracelets. With the pragmatism of the authentic good ole girl, she awaited the sale of the house, when he could "have his wimmen 'n' his ole guns," and she would have some cash. That he began, with typical good-ole-boy sentimentality, sending her red roses at school *after* their divorce, didn't make a dent, and only added to her image as a femme fatale. A frog can only see what it can eat, I had read somewhere. All Sherry had to do now was find another man to take care of her, and like a frog going after a fly, she would succeed. It was the one thing she, I, every Southern woman I had ever met had been bred to do.

Sherry made me think of the single-minded woman I once had been. Was that the twinge I felt when she came by my apartment one night? She wore black high-heeled sandals, a black cotton dress decorated with pink flowers, and pink satin bows, and carried a Saturday-night special in her Pappagallo purse. "Sometimes I wear it in a shoulder holster," she explained; "but tonight"—she planned to cruise local prospects at

209

the Plantation Club—"I wanted to look pretty." Just coming out of the sloppy sixties, I craved skirts, earrings like small ivory roses, even the ankle bracelets some Southern women had never stopped wearing. Had Sherry, with her sure, if limited, sense of direction, shown good sense in avoiding liberation altogether?

When I learned that my sisters in Valdosta or Fort Valley or Macon were indulging in the Sin—that they secretly led sex lives as complex as my own, sans my struggles with guilt—I felt chagrined: ever since Mother and Daddy's early attentions, I had considered my sexuality excessive, indeed, "my cross to bear." But here were women who were living out the Pleasure Principle without having been liberated at all. "Do what you want around here," said a Charleston woman who, in her own words, had "slept with every man in town—just don't tell it."

Debbie, a married teacher in Fort Valley, described to me the details of her affair with the visiting artist who was my friend —letters routed around the local postmistress, who might iron and read them, hidden phone bills and cars obscured on side roads, trips to motels in the next county. Her sister-in-law and best friend, Peaches, preferred picking men up over the CB radio of her Lincoln Continental, then leading them to the next Holiday Inn. Regardless of their age, Southern women still talk like high school students in the girls' bathroom; though they had known each other since grammar school, and were married to brothers, Debbie and Peaches had only recently discovered that each played around.

Today they and their close friends cover for one another just as the good ole boys always have. "'N' then she called and said, 'Rush ovah to mah house and tear up all those lettahs from Otis in the left-hand top drawah of mah dressah 'n' flush 'em down the toilet 'fore I get there with Stuckey. . . .'" recalled Debbie of a woman friend's crisis in cheating on the husband-to-be she had only recently lured from his first wife.

In the South, "Your Cheatin' Heart" is not just the name of a song by Hank Williams. My own family, aside from Mother and Daddy's guilty lusts, had been true Bible Belt repressives, but some Southerners, even churchgoing ones, appeared to take the Sin less seriously. Hypocrisy is rampant; passion and its demands, pleasure and one's right to it, are unwritten laws. "I get moralistic after a few weeks at home," says a Charlestonian turned New York journalist, a third glass of Jack Daniel's tinkling in her hand; "all people do around here is party." Or as a Hollywood scriptwriter homesick for his South Carolina home put it, "Those folks really know how to *live*...."

I was learning to live, too, and at times learning how unlike my Southern sisters I was fast becoming. But like an actress long trained in one role, I could still fall back easily into the part. With a woman friend, I attended a family wedding in Mobile. My friend was astonished at how quickly I established rapport with the poker-playing, country-club mother she had fled the South to escape. Yet all I had done was plug into ritual good-ole-girl talk. The bride was a cousin from an unpopular branch of their family, and also the old date of a gossipy male friend of mine. When I mentioned that the man had claimed that the bride, delicate and frilly in her tiered pink organdy, had had an insatiable desire for being tied up and fucked in the ass, my friend's proper mother had chortled, "Why, ev'rybody knows Betty Lou's a nym-pho-main-ee-ac!"

It was a moment when my friend's mother and I recognized the frequently barbaric nature of Southern feminine relationships, the domination—despite the women's movement—of loyalty by cattiness and opportunism. It's a cruelty that starts in high school, when it sometimes even manifests itself physically. At Tucker High, I had heard of the girl in the next county who had been raped with a croquet stick by her girl friends at a spend-the-night party. A man in the North Georgia mountains told me what had happened to the girl he and his buddies had taken into the woods for a youthful gang bang: "All thuh boys' gal friends came roarin' up in a pickup and threw 'er— screamin' 'er lungs out—intuh thuh back of thuh truck by her hair."

Because of sexual competitiveness, there are still limitations on how open most Southern women feel they can be with one

211

another. Relationships with men follow even more rigid ground rules: the unisex attitude valued in California and New York hardly exists; difference, kept warm by a climate in which flowers bloom year round, is still viewed as a sexual lubricant. One of my problems with Ben, I would later realize, was that my attempts at Northeastern straightforwardness always came out garbled by Southern dissembling. "You may be too independent for the good ole boys," he would complain, "but you're too dependent for me!" But I was still a bit of a good ole girl; and like Grandmother Lee, the good ole girl still regards candor with, or trust in, a man—much less a husband—unwise, even just plain dumb.

It is an attitude that has its Southern male complement, instilled well before grade school. "I am the horn on a rinosiros . . ." wrote a fourth-grade boy in Macon; "I catch up with my victom . . . feel me perce her body . . . feel her smoth guts as they ose around me . . . feel the thump of her heart slowly die down." At thirty, Culver still felt that only misguidance or sheer stupidity could lead a woman to expect that relations between men and women could be anything but devious, manipulative, and ultimately, male controlled. "Don't yew know wimmen aren't s'posed to trust men!" he exclaimed when I complained of a mutual male acquaintance's deception of his lady. As Ben and I, caught up in the backlash of the sixties, painfully discussed the affairs that were a part of our "open" marriage, Culver mumbled disgustedly that we had "broken the code"; privately, he recommended to Ben that he beat me up.

Yet acting on the territorial imperative that includes the right to take sexual care of one's buddy's woman, he found it honorable to pursue an affair with me as soon as he sensed dissension in the air. It is an attitude that lends a homey and incestuous aura to relations between the sexes. The extended family, such an important part of Southern life, extends, too, to friends; and the best friends—aside from brothers and cousins and second cousins—are *old* friends. Within this network, some women become old friends—and sexual property.

As in the extended family, such relationships can become cross-generational: a few years later, my friend Claudine, daughter Darcy, eighteen, and I would burst into giggles when we realized we had all slept with the same slow-talking Macon blues guitarist who had also been Culver's best buddy in college. The Southern woman who sleeps around finds that as long as she does so within a certain group, her value within it is enhanced; while outside it, she is seen, at best, as consorting with the enemy, at worst, as devalued, a slut.

Another piece of good-ole-boy property is his cowboy boots; a sign of a good ole boy in good standing is that he wears them in the summer. As Culver sat on the side of my bed, pulling his on, country singer Willie Nelson's voice on the radio moved him to mention that "if ole Ben came in thuh room right now, he'd be doin' right to shoot us both." He was speaking out of the Southern connection between sex and violence. As the writers of country song lyrics know, Southerners prefer to take their sex life—or death—seriously. The notion that one might get shot in the process intensifies the pleasure.

Like the region it represents, country music is a closed system; the philosophy expressed through its words is one of fatalism, inevitability. The role of the woman as temptress and angel is clear, as is the man's wretched need of her, which is why a Southern man, so vulnerable in sex, can't afford to let down his macho image at any other moment. It's as though bedding down with a woman is like bedding down with snakes with a potential for instant penis paralysis; because of this anxiety, good-ole-boy talk is often peppered with references to "big fat dicks" and that ultimate insult, "he looks lak he's lookin' tuh git it in the ass." During a six-hour car trip I took with two good-ole-boy poets, the conversation was one part Polack jokes, two parts sex talk.

That Culver was a poet and an academic had done little to change his diction or his mores. "It's only natchrul for a married man to git a little *strange,*" he told me, employing the term Southern men use to refer to uninvolved sex, "but if I ever caught enybody with Mandy, I'd kill 'im!"

Why did I feel devalued, unanchored, as I clasped my bra? Was it because Ben wasn't there, shooting *him,* and wouldn't be even if he knew? Jealousy might be uncivilized, but it sure was flattering. But that couldn't happen, because, in the first place, Ben was one of the first men I knew who didn't own a gun. "Thet Ben, much as I lak 'im, is strange," Culver went on. "Why, bet if he knew, y'all would jes' have *words.*"

Culver considered my women's lib talk "sumthin yew do 'cause yew need a man tuh dom'nate yuh." As I traveled to my jobs in Southern schools, I saw "I'd nevah let mah wife out alone lak that" in the eyes of every man I met. Any woman who comes on too strong, who appears to be taking too good care of herself obviously needs "a good fuck, baby!" She needs it to "take the starch out," and though the starch might make it more exciting, it's better if she never gets in that overly upright posture at all. Hookers sometimes get more positive feedback from good ole boys than career women: they remind them of their wives, and at least they're usually in the right position— prone. Or as one Southern man described his ideal woman, "She always wears dresses 'n' bends over a lot."

Yet a slight resistance to being tilted is desirable. "Don't yew know yew're s'posed to hold off?" a blond ex-Vanderbilt fraternity man told me. Though he usually had the kind of Southern manners that make a woman feel she's being bathed in melted butter, or Joy perfume, he felt driven to complain that I wasn't following the rule that goes "Let him chase you till you catch him." Never mind that he was holding me down on the couch kissing me on our very first date; he found it puzzling that a woman might use a man as a sex object. When I pointed out that there might be inequity in his opportunity to insist, my necessity to demur, he repeated, "I don't know why—that's jes' the way it's s'posed to be!"

There's no one stubborner than a Southern man clinging to his male prerogatives. It was the seventies; yet a handsome deep-sea diver and cocaine smuggler explained the double standard to me as though it had been invented yesterday. "When I married my second wife, she understood that I get to run around, she stays home on thuh yacht, tends thuh kids 'n' thuh business. On thuh other hand, she's got a Coupe DeVille, can write as many checks as she wants. And I know she's a good girl, she won't cheat on me." I must have looked skeptical; he felt

214

called upon to enlarge: "Me and my good buddies—at least, thuh Southern men *I* know—consider it a point of honor to take good care—I don't mean halfway, I mean good care—of our wives and kids. Why, we'd work ourselves intuh thuh grave to do it. And I think that's a preet-ty good deal, don't you?"

He was pulling on an epauletted baby-blue work shirt that matched his long-lashed eyes, white cotton Landlubbers, tennis shoes with no socks; because he worked on the docks every day, his ankles were a smooth jet brown. The night before, he, like the Famous Southern Poet, had insisted we make love without my diaphragm: "I make real pretty babies—'sides, you know I'd take care of you," he had whispered, caressing me at the same moment in an unbearably delicious place. The reason I had not put my diaphragm in earlier was because he liked to "surprise" me, that is, come over any time he had the notion; and once he was inside my apartment, few moments lapsed between talk and the sex during which he whispered elaborate fantasies involving cruel pirates and ravished maidens, which recalled almost exactly, if more lasciviously, my own daydreams at eleven.

Now he guzzled a third Saint Pauli Girl, grabbed his sea cap, kissed me through his blond beard: "Gotta go, sweetheart, gotta big deal, big meetin'!" I thought of his wife on the yacht outside Charleston, managing four kids from his two marriages, writing checks, being a good girl—doing without him, or anyone. Why oh why oh why did my stomach turn over anyway? Why did I still like Southern men at all? And why, when Culver said I needed a man to dominate me, even when he recommended that Ben beat me up, did something correspond in my groin, as though he had pressed the well-trained Southern-woman part of my brain? Like Mother, I still craved the haven, the prison that Southern women call success.

"All Southern men are romantics," Culver had told me. "They read *Ivanhoe* back in plantation days." That he also approved of his best buddy, Stoney, who had received a Bronze Star for "shootin' a bunch of yella niggers over in Nam," didn't completely ruin his charm for me. Ben didn't believe in chivalry, and it hurt.

It was as though I was addicted to being called "sweetheart," "baby," and "honey," to having doors opened for me, to being taken out to dives or dinner without always picking up half the check, to being played the guitar to and sung to, to being complimented on everything I wore, every way I smelled, every way I combed my hair, to being licked up the backbone and in every possible crevice, to being cuddled, doted on, toyed with, adored, dominated. The men I was meeting now were better lovers then the brutal bumpkins I had fucked as a rural teenager: they had retained the earthiness, but had more style. "Goin' down on thuh cut" is what Southern blacks call sucking pussy, and Southern men don't mind doing it, nor do they share the more effete male's aversion to menstrual blood and anal sex.

Never mind that a Southern man calls every waitress and barmaid the same sweet names he calls you in bed, that his well-trained eye for other women strays constantly while you're out with him. His *Weltanschauung,* his fear that, as a Louisiana man put it, "every woman really wants a big black schlong," and, more than anything, his love affair with mortality, make him make love as though he might be called home by his Savior at any moment—and into immediate account for his skill at pleasing women. It is this feeling that every time might be his last that makes making love with a Southern man—despite his frequent evasiveness, oppressiveness, even downright cruelty —lovemaking, instead of fucking.

Daphne, who even at night wears straw picture hats decorated with rayon roses, lived for three years with, and was married for one month to, a Southern man diagnosed by his psychiatrist as a bona fide psychopath. Though she moved from one Georgia town to another to escape him, he still flies to the city where she now lives to visit her unexpectedly in the middle of the night. Despite the plantation bonnets, Daphne is a well-educated young woman who at one time ran her own business and renovated her own house. Yet she says, "There's no way in the world I could resist Noble. He's the best lover I've ever had, could ever imagine having."

I heard the bell in my brain ring again, the one that was connected to something in my belly, and the sound conjured up

216

images of the Famous Southern Poet, the sea-captain-turned-cocaine-smuggler, the blue-eyed blues guitarist, who had raped me, he said in apology, because I smelled so good. Indeed, I even loved Ben, my one Yankee lover, as much for his long eyelashes, his articulate charm, the way he looked in a white linen suit, a shirt emblazoned with purple flowers, as for his intellect or his goodness.

Yes, charisma is the middle name of scads of Southern cads. Gene was a handsome charmer who had been unfaithfully married for years to the kind of young woman who still—in the sixties—wore white gloves and carried calling cards. Despite his widely known lecheries, he knew how to stir feminine sympathy for his plight: in his backyard, he built a stone chair to face the bedroom window of his former wife, who, in the Southern way, still lived next door in the house they had occupied together. "So I can sit 'n' watch thuh lights go out when she's up there with somebody else," he explained, indulging in the ready self-pity that lies just beneath the skin of the Southern male psyche.

A fortyish University of Georgia professor fulfilled a lifelong desire when he had an arrowed heart with *Mother* inside it tattooed on his groin. Unrequited love, even if it was once unwanted love, is another sentiment Southern men don't mind wallowing in; and being yearned after, after the fact, is an ego trip to which Southern women early become addicted. Indeed, every Southern femme fatale requires at least a few beaus who are still hopelessly in love with her to keep her femininity intact, and Southern men seem more than willing to oblige. Fifteen years after our affair, the Famous Southern Poet and I shared a podium for a poetry reading in Atlanta. "I honor thuh past, Rosemary, I honor thuh past," he whispered to me, his eyes swimming with an inebriated light. "Do yew know what I mean?"

Southern men are suckers for big straw hats, perhaps because they make them think of plantation days, which gives Southern women another reason, aside from the hot sun on hair and face, to continue wearing them. Culver had been pinned to Mandy

217

in college; but one day in the students' lounge, he had seen "a beautiful dancer in a big hat." In the case of Southern male lust, whatever attitude will do the job—that is, disarm, charm, seduce—is shamelessly called up:

" 'I've got tuh have that,' I tole my buddy, 'n' when he said he knew 'er, that he'd arrange it, I went near wild! Well, he went over 'n' talked to 'er, 'n' she said only if I got rid'a Mandy. So I went tuh Mandy 'n' said I thought we should cool it for a while. Course, she went bananas. But I didn't care 'cause I had tuh have me that li'l gal.

"Well, we did it on this li'l cot at my buddy's apartment, 'n' her period started right in the middle of it. But I was wild about that gal! Thuh next mornin', I went down tuh thuh drugstore tuh get 'er some Kotex, 'n' while I was payin', I looked down 'n' saw thuh dried blood all ovah muh shirt sleeve.

"But she didn't lak me all that much, so after a while, I called Mandy agin. She was 'bout to git engaged to this boy from Sea Island—he'd already give 'er a big di'mond. But I was a desprit man, horny as hell! It took me 'bout nine straight hours of talkin' to git 'er back.

"So yuh see," he concluded with a flourish and a dig at what he called my "man hatin' ": "Southern women may 'go bananas' but we men have feelin's, too!"

There's no doubt about it, Southern men have, and freely express, "feelin's." Add to that their desire to excel as lovers, their vulnerability to, even expectation of, female moods, and one begins to understand their charm. They seemed to regard the anger I expressed in my poems as something akin to the harmless temper tantrums indulged in by Scarlett O'Hara. When Gene recently asked what I was writing, I said, "Something about Southern men." Putting his arm around my shoulder, he replied soothingly, "Honey, don't you worry—we'll know you didn't mean it!" It is a protectiveness, an expectation of fragility, that can be as addictive as magnolia blossoms or Jack Daniel's. "I've got this hyuh unreg'stured gun," said Earl, the bourbon-drinking husband of a teacher in Macon, when I confessed at dinner that I was not happy about my third marriage, that yes, maybe even Ben's Yankee background had something to do with the differences between us.

"Yew jes' take it, 'n' drive right up tuh Etlana, 'n' ring his doe bell, 'n' shoot thuh bastard!" he advised, as though it were the obvious thing to do, "then jes' drive right on back 'n' throw thuh gun intuh thuh Chattahoochee. . . ."

He was carving, placing on my plate another huge slab of bloody meat, pouring my glass half full of straight Jack again. When he noticed that, despite my anger with my estranged spouse, I looked doubtful, he added supportively, "'N' if yew don't wanna do it, honey, I'll do it fur ya!"

That his own daughter had been raped by a black who had slashed her thighs with a needle in a New York subway station the year before when she had been sent there to school at eighteen, had added to his reservoir of instant good-ole-boy rage toward niggers, Jews, Yankees, Arabs, gooks, chinks, Polacks, fags, and other unknowns. It was a hate from which I, as an increasingly aware human being, recoiled. Yet as he spoke, a corresponding quiver of violence, some obscene connection, ran through me, too.

His wife, who was from gentle Virginia, looked abashed; this was not what she expected from the visiting poet. Earlier, because of my interest in literature, she had brought up Charles Dickens. "Who's thet?" Earl had demanded. "Is he a membah of thuh gun club?" Now he tenderly showed me Polaroids of himself, holding aloft by a bloody snout the wild boar he had just shot in the North Georgia woods.

"I don't see how eny man could have this little lady, 'n' not treat 'er right!" he said as I departed, looking down my dress with eyes narrowed by bourbon, and totally overlooking that a year before I had published a book of poems crammed with castration images and rage toward Southern men.

Yet Earl knew, and I knew, that on some deep level, we understood each other only too well.

219

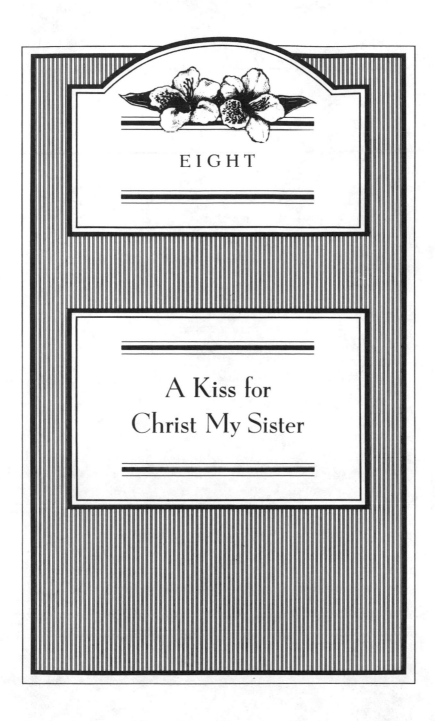

EIGHT

A Kiss for
Christ My Sister

"Why don't you jes' git on in bed with us?" Debbie suggested one night when she, her lover—my co-worker—and I had spent the evening talking and drinking in her motel room. The sexual tension was not just Mother's, Daddy's, or mine, I was beginning to realize; the whole region was drenched in it. ("I walked around horny all the time," says a New York editor of the period when she lived in Macon as the unhappy wife of a state legislator's son.) As Debbie pulled my wrist and slouched back giggling, I thought of Mother's guilt-etched forehead, her fuchsiaed lips tight on her coffee cup, her old trousseau slip dripping lace from beneath her dress, and felt sad. Beneath *her* dress, Debbie, who obviously suffered no such anxieties, wore a frilly peach garter belt.

I could see why my Western friend liked her. I did, too, though I wasn't quite as ready for what she suggested as I would be later. But I knew that had I been, Debbie wouldn't have called it, if she referred to it directly at all, bisexuality, or homosexuality, or anything other than "partyin'," "gittin' down," or whatever happened to be the local slang for what occurs under the influence of alcohol. Just as what one does in New York doesn't count, neither does what one does while imbibing Black Jack or Johnny Walker Red.

"Edith Head gives good wardrobe," suggests graffiti in the women's room of an Atlanta pub. In a place where every woman is brought up to flirt and seduce, an acute awareness of the competition is inevitable; if Southern women look and smell good, they look and smell good to each other, too. Add to that their fondness for physical affection, or "sloppin' sugah all ovah each othah," and it begins to feel as though men are simply used to hold at bay an attraction that could spill over into overt sexuality at any moment.

Like most Southern women, my sister, Anne, and I still spent hours over bloody marys in the middle of days spent shopping for sexier and sexier clothes, the perfect plum eye shadow for the perfect plum dress. Regardless of age or politics, we lolled through indolent afternoons in chaise longues, indulging in what we called our "obsession with men." Yet we know this is only the female version of good-ole-boy talk about guns, hunting dogs, pussy—that it has more to do with each other than the men.

My first lapse in an "obsession with men" would come later —after Mother's suicide, my and Ben's divorce—during six months spent in Savannah with my woman lover, Jane. Since she was aggressively indifferent to relations between men and women, we had to make do, aside from our mutual interests in the literary and visual arts, with gossip about recipes, decor, clothes. After making love in a room that looked much as I imagined Scarlett's to have looked—O'Hara green walls, pink chaise longue, high mantelpiece—we liked lying back among mounds of white ruffled pillows, leafing together through the latest issue of *Vogue,* or gorging on novels that were as decadent and sweet as Godiva chocolates.

It was a totally feminine world that, while delicious, began to nag: what was missing—like the penis that was not resting against my thigh—was the man on whom to project this heightened sensuality. Later, because of Jane, I would sometimes miss breasts: she had helped me realize what women give to men. Aching for the mother I had thought I hated, lonely for the daughters who had recently left home, without a husband for the first time in my adult life, I loved burying myself in her plush flesh, found solace in her salty sweetness, in the knowledge that every sensation in my body could be echoed exactly in hers.

Yet it was not a world into which I always easily fit. "How can you go out on the streets dressed like that?!" Lola, Louisianian-turned-New Yorker, would storm at me a year later. We were stepping out onto 110th Street on the Upper West Side. I had thought this beautiful woman, with her dark hair, her intense features, her Southern origins would make a good substitute for

Mother, despite the fact that she was ten years younger than I. I had noticed that her dresser was as chaotic as Mother's had been, its drawers stuffed with torn papers, its top littered with dusty eye shadows, broken lipsticks, notes on the backs of old laundry tickets.

The first time we had made love—at her mother's house in Baton Rouge—she had told me that her mother, too, had given her forced enemas as a child. As our hands touched in the gap between the guest-room beds, I had felt a rush of connection, relief. But since then I had had sexual fantasies in which she and my dead mother became one—Mother's face overlapping her's, Mother's dark curls obscuring her straighter black hair, her hands holding my wrists to the bed as Mother's had.

Was her anger, so much like Mother's pent-up rage, part of my attraction, too? Her black hair flying, she stomped the sidewalk in her tough boots. "You just dress that way to please men!" she went on vehemently, her lip peeling back like Mother's. Yes, I had to admit that, like the Cosmo girl, I had had looking sexy to men in mind when I had donned the black cotton sundress, stuck the fake pink azalea in my hair. It was a mind-set I didn't think about; it just *was*.

Was she really complaining about my failure to take sex between women seriously? But my attitude was just a regional one that she had left behind in Baton Rouge parish. Southern men find lesbianism "cute," even titillating; just as it's better to have more guns, hound dogs, houses, cars, and money, the gluttonous good-ole-boy mind assumes that if one woman is good in bed, then two must be better. Queen Victoria, I read somewhere, refused to pass a law against lesbianism because she couldn't believe women would do such things. A similar attitude exists in the South.

In Savannah, one of the many gay high school students I met looked, with her lush red hair falling past the white middy blouse, touching the ass of the navy middy skirt that was a part of her Catholic day-school uniform, like a French pornographer's dream. Southern lesbians are almost as likely to indulge in makeup, girly frills, as their straighter sisters, who, in turn, tend to view lesbianism as simply an extension of the physical affection already rampant among girl friends, or as part of the maiden-lady syndrome. Eccentric Southern ladies are a tradition; unmarried women have always shared houses and lives.

In Chattanooga, Azalea (or 'Zalya, as her lover, Cookie, called her) wore a ruffled cotton skirt, a mutton-sleeved blouse. She had the black, black hair, the white, white skin often the mark of young Appalachian women, and would have looked delicate but for thirty extra pounds. She was losing them, she explained, at the rate of three a week at a salon where she was pummeled, loofahed, wrapped in Saran Wrap. She felt a sleeker image would be better for her work as a real-estate saleswoman.

Azalea would have grown up on a farm in Tennessee, but her daddy had gambled it away in a poker game just before she was born. "Mama says that while she was havin' me, Daddy was lyin' up drunk with a woman over in the next county." Her mother was the martyr Azalea was determined never to become; like me, she had turned off her love for her parents early.

Cookie, blonde and fatter still, was a computer programmer. When she and Azalea had been fourteen and fifteen, they had had crushes on the same boy and at a spend-the-night party had begun making love, each pretending the other was the boy. Cookie's fair head was bent over a dress she was making for Azalea, yet she beamed as her lover spoke: "We used role playin' as an excuse for sex for years"—it sounded like girls dancing together so they could later dance with their boyfriends—" 'n' went on that way for years, even when I was married for a while. . . ."

"Fin'ly, we jes' admitted that we loved each other, liked havin' sex," Cookie spoke up, "and it was frightening!"

Azalea smiled beatifically. "We still don't call ourselves dykes, or enythang like that. Though Cookie mos'ly has fantasies about women, I still feel that way about men." Earlier in the evening, she had described her crush on a male co-worker, as Cookie had clucked indulgently: what if Azalea, stoned on mescaline, had holed up in an Atlanta motel with five men the weekend before? What if she did "get crazy" every full moon and go out looking for a prick?

"We've been through so much together," Azalea concluded, "that nothin' can come between me 'n' Cookie now."

Before I met them in Savannah, a friend in Charlotte had described Jane and her lover, Delta, to me: "They look like they're made of feathers and old lace." In Dr. Feelgood's, Delta held up the skirt of her gray nun's habit. "It's lined in cerise silk. A lover who was a nun made it for me so we could go to bars together and get free drinks." Her frizzy blonde hair pinned into a knot at the nape of her slender neck, she sipped her sloe-gin fizz as though it were Kool-Aid. Miss Jane had long, slender legs thrust into tight jeans stuffed into cowboy boots, full breasts that showed at the open neck of her work shirt, and an elfin haircut; though I'd never known one before, I knew she was the epitome of the Sarah Lawrence girl.

In the South, lesbianism is usually visceral rather than ideological; high school dropouts fall in love with debutantes and college graduates; gay bars and parties are for cruising rather than intellectualizing. But Delta and Miss Jane had the kind of background that predisposed them to sexual politics; privilege and education had given them an elitest view. They saw lesbianism as a means of living free of the rigid rules that control the lives of most Southern women.

"I was in high school during the early sixties." Delta laughed. "I wanted to be an anarchist when I grew up." Though they hadn't known each other as children, she and Jane had both pretended that they were crippled, and had deliberately walked with a limp: "We wanted to be different."

If their goal was to become bona fide Southern eccentrics, they succeeded early. Delta, daughter of a wealthy Mississippi doctor, had been kicked out of Duke, then had gone on to Sarah Lawrence. During a summer in Ireland, she had joined the Tinkers, a group of Irish gypsies in revolt, and had even married one of them. Flying back to the U.S. in brogans, lice in her pretty blonde hair, she vowed to live the rest of her life in a tent, which she promptly pitched on the Sarah Lawrence campus, along with a sign reading, DELTA PITCHES HER TENT/ IN THE PLACE OF EXCREMENT. When the Irish gypsy came to claim his bride, Delta drove him west in her van and left him ecstatically working as a ranch hand "in some place in Montana—I don't know whether he ever got a divorce, whether we're still legally married, or what. . . ."

In the meantime, she had become involved with Miss Jane, who had graduated from Sarah Lawrence a year before her and was in New York writing—and once appearing in—porn films, then working "as a flunky for Norman Mailer; I had to fuck his paunchy buddies. But he didn't like me much—I was real skinny then, and he said I didn't look like a real woman!"

Because they were both still fucking men, Delta and Jane went together to get IUDs: "Delta would come to my apartment, I'd have a man there—and I'd go out to the top of the stairs in my robe and go cra-zee!"

After a while, they left for Mexico in Delta's van. "We were goin' to do the Alice Toklas–Gertrude Stein thing," Jane explained. "We didn't have any mirrors, and after a while, it seemed like Delta's face was my face. We got bored and decided we wanted to live in a Southern seacoast town. So we looked on the map, saw Savannah, and here we are!"

Miss Jane's Savannah house looked like the dreams of two sensuous women: peach- and butter-colored walls, furniture that looked like soft sculpture, cushions embroidered with their own nude forms. The walls were hung with Delta's paintings; one represented an enormous baby doll, its torso stuffed inside an open suitcase, its head detached, lying alongside. Did she experience the same severing of mind and body, separation of intellect and sexuality, that was fast becoming my constant gut-gnawing conflict?

As their houseguest, I lay in the green bedroom amid the white ruffled pillows, admiring the floor that Miss Jane had hand-painted in an exact replica of an old-fashioned patchwork quilt. Drifting off to sleep, I dreamed vaguely of small breasts beneath translucent Indian shirts, of pubes as softly mounded as my own. Because I knew they had an "open marriage," I half expected one of them to tiptoe into my room at any moment. "We're all sexual beings; who we relate to sexually is our choice," my sportsy new woman therapist had recently told me;

"but you'd never sleep with a woman: it would threaten your image of yourself as a femme fatale."

Despite my fantasies, I couldn't have imagined that two years later I would be divorced from Ben—and lying beside Miss Jane in the green room.

Even when the coupling stopped short of sex, some Southern women seemed to have forged bonds more permanent than marriage. In Savannah, identical twenty-year-old twins lived upstairs in the house where I roomed. Lily and Lilac held jobs as cashiers at the same famous seafood restaurant. "We've always worked at the same place," Lilac told me, "ever since we left home at fifteen."

The twins shared a new turquoise Triumph, wore their hair in chic French twists, and had sleek black boyfriends. The last is unusual for white Southern women, who, once they break with tradition, seem to feel free to break it in almost any other way. Though she had never been married, Lilac had a sweet three-month-old daughter who rarely seemed to cry: "We were goin' with brothers, rock musicians, when I got preggies. One of 'em wanted tuh marry me, but I already had Lily, so why would I wanna do that?" She giggled. "We take care of 'er together—yeh, havin' the baby's been fun!"

They made me think of two pretty little girls playing house —till their mother came to visit. The third day she was there, Lily came to my door: "I hope we didn't keep you up last night. Ma's an ex-drunk, 'n' she got down with some wine 'n' was goin' on at us for hours." I thought of the masked lady I had seen coming and going with them—plump, permanented, proper, her pocketbook stuck securely under her arm, just as Mother's had always been. "We're gittin' her outta here jes' as soon as possible," Lily went on in an irritated tone I recognized as one I had often used with Mother.

A few hours later, the three plus baby emerged, Lily carrying her mother's suitcase, Lilac the infant seat. The older woman walked stiffly in her polyester pantsuit, patting her frosted pale-orange curls as though to be sure they were still in place. I thought of her pregnant twenty years before with the daughters who now hated her, of Mother and how I had loathed the hysteria I had never understood.

Looking straight ahead, her double chin wobbling, she carefully lowered herself into the Triumph, and tears rose in my eyes. Like Mother, she had given her daughters, through her weakness, a kind of callous energy, or what Mother had always called my "stubbornness."

And because of it, she, like Mother, would end up alone.

Over the years, Anne and I would sometimes laugh that our relationship would outlast those with husbands, children, friends, that we would ultimately end our days together, two crazy old ladies, arguing over who would do the dishes. It was a joke that had been started by Mother long before, when she, Anne, and I, pregnant with David, had lived peacefully together. In those days, despite her drab job, our poverty-level existence, she had frequently still laughed her thin, girlish laugh.

Now I thought of Azalea and Cookie, of Delta and Miss Jane, of Lily and Lilac—of all the moments I had spent in bed with a man when I had felt, even during our shared pleasure, that he was in Massachusetts while I was still in Georgia. And the fantasy of a life shared with a loved woman seemed as soft, simple, pleasant as the scent of biscuits rising from a Southern oven.

Yet I knew the reality of that fantasy wasn't easy for every Southern woman who wanted it. I had heard of the South Carolina girl who had been shipped off to the state mental hospital when she had confessed her strange desires to her high school counselor. I had seen Earl's daughter, Earline, wearing her usual Sears, Roebuck overalls, stumbling so drunkenly down the steep stone stairs of a gay bar that I feared she would fall and bash her skull. And Lola had told me how, in love with her younger sister, she had at last fled her feelings, Baton Rouge, and her huge network of powerful female relatives.

In the Basement, an infamous Savannah gay bar, Lacey asked
me to dance on the tiny raised dance floor. At 160 pounds, in
work boots and Levi's, she looked rough, tough, and dangerous
—more like a man than a woman. "Let's dance slutty," she
murmured huskily, sticking her thick thigh between mine, then
complained, "Girl, I hope yew kin kiss better than yew kin
dance!" When I explained that I had come with Miss Jane, that,
indeed, I favored men, she said, "Whut?! Yew lak one a' them
thangs pokin' aroun' inside yew?"

Lacey had been poked around inside, too. She had been
raped at fifteen and had given birth to a daughter. She had been
raped again at twenty-four by four black men who, abetted by
her brother, sought to prove to her that she was a woman. Not
only raped, she said, but kicked, beaten, bloodied: "I'll never
forget thet night—sumthin' happened in muh brain—'n' the
po-leese didn't keer: I wuz black, wuzn't no virgin, 'n' I wuz
gay. . . ."

As we danced, her voice, against the music from the jukebox,
became more and more like a talking blues: "After I los' muh
mama, Daddy sole muh bicycle fur whiskey . . . I los' the fers'
gurl I loved. . . . On thuh night befo' her weddin', I put hickeys
all over thet gurl's body . . . it didn't do no good. . . . Fur a long
time, I tried tuh git over it . . . let mens have sex wid me. . . . 'N'
I love muh li'l gurl . . . muh li'l gurl-chile. . . . So don't call me
gay . . . don't call me straight . . . don't call me nothin' . . . jes'
call me Lacey—Lacey in Search of Love."

Savannah is a small town, especially for gays. I knew from
Miss Jane that Lacey was a high school dropout who had lived
her whole life in the same city, that she wrote poetry, that,
despite her tough image, she insisted on keeping her own
clothes on during sex while she pleasured the woman she loved.
She made me think of a gentle but mannish Atlanta woman who
told me that her first pickup after she came out as a lesbian was
a waitress who she fumblingly discovered was a man in drag.

A few nights later, I came home late to find Lacey sitting on
my steps. "I tried tuh choke Beth," she sobbed, " 'n' I jes' know
she's called the po-leese!" I thought of the slight, refined-look-
ing white girl with whom I had last seen her. "I tole her she

231

didn't kiss worth shit, 'n' she got mad, 'n' I jes' saw red. . . ." Her broad shoulders shook as I put my arm around them. "Oh why oh why oh why do I hurt thuh ones I love? . . ." Her gasps seemed to tear from someplace where confusion was as endless as Mother's, as my own.

A few days later, she came back with Beth, bringing poems to show me. "She fo'gave me!" she said excitedly. "She fo'gave me! Kin yew believe thet?"

Lacey—Lacey in Search of Love. I would never think of her as anything else.

Two years before I met Lacey, I had telephoned a school for women wrestlers outside Columbia, South Carolina. I was working in the city for a week, snow had fallen, school had been shut down; I imagined the women wrestlers would make a good story and called for an appointment. When a deep, yet feminine, voice answered to say that everyone else was away, but that I could visit if I wished, I suddenly envisioned the desolate location of the school, on the outskirts of town, near Sesquicentennial State Park and the state mental hospital, and hastily said no thanks, another time. Vaguely ashamed of my fear of someone who, after all, was just a woman like myself, I hung up.

Once, when I had still feared flying, I had run for a tiny commuter plane on an airstrip outside Gulfport and had been airborne before my stomach had had time to turn over in its usual takeoff fear. Now, it was as though I was on another uncomfortable journey from which there was no turning back. I had a career, a handsome husband, a lover in New Orleans, dresses that cost more than $17.95, yet I felt like a chameleon on a plaid rug, a fly caught in flypaper, my cat with the bone in her throat. It was as as though I were whizzing down a narrow highway at night, with no shoulder, no headlights. When would the Bible Belt God I had known since childhood strike down his recalcitrant daughter? And what were the limits to my greed?

I had to admit that the traditional Southern women I met retained a certainty about place and role that I had lost, however voluntarily. Indeed, a few of the archetypes seemed to get away with having it all: good-ole-girl Dolly Parton married early, and is still married to Nashville paving contractor Carl Dean; country-music star Porter Wagoner facilitated her career; and her "friend for life," Judy Ogle, lives and travels with her. But Cornelia Wallace was uppity, and claims to have been brutalized by her crippled husband. Gloria Carter Spann was arrested for playing her harmonica too loud in the McWaffle Restaurant in Americus, Georgia, and has a son in California's Vacaville prison. Martha Mitchell truth-told too much, and died alone.

When I called the school for women wrestlers, I was looking for strong Southern women, role models, and the only ones I could imagine at that time were literally muscular. That strength, of course, was not the strength for which I was searching. Nor would I easily find it. What I would find instead was that every Southern woman who didn't fit easily and cleanly into the role of little girl, masked lady, society woman, or good ole girl suffered drains of energy, creativity, and sometimes—as in Mother's case—even sanity.

While I might feel like Zelda, struggling for identity, yet driving myself mad, some Southern women had already crossed the line. Anne reported that after Mother's exploratory spinal surgery in an Atlanta hospital, she obsessively complained that the nurses were watching her through the TV set in her room, listening through a bugging device as she talked with visitors. Miss Peggy, a seventy-year-old redhead, rode her bicycle up and down the street in front of my window in Savannah, stopping occasionally to giggle that "Daddy's goin' to fine me a fine man tuh marry someday!" Betty the Bag Lady had gotten her name from her perpetually carried shopping bag; it was said that—at sixty, her sparse hair dyed orange—she still made her living by giving blow jobs behind the bushes of the Savannah parks where, in warm weather, she also slept.

Estelle, a fiftyish maiden lady in Mobile, worked at two jobs as a bookkeeper and accountant and had a big bank account stashed away. Although she still hoped to marry "someday," she lived alone in the dank mansion that had belonged to Daddy. "I'm always in sech a hurry," she moaned, pushing a grimy rag across the edge of a mahogany end table, "I nevah kin git thangs clean aroun' hyah!" It looked hopeless to me: dust, bits of torn paper, undescribable litter seemed to cover every surface. I remembered Mother, hurriedly blotting her lipstick on the nearest matchbook or bill from Georgia Power, in her effort not to miss a bus or burn the beans. I thought of her dresser top with its broken and tangled costume jewelry, broken lipsticks and compacts scattering pale powder; and of my own teenage room shared with Anne—the wrinkled clothes piled in the corner, my own scraps imprinted by Tangee, the half-empty jars of Noxema. Was being a terrible housekeeper one of the few forms of rebellion left to Southern women who would remain little girls, just as anorexia nervosa is one of the few recourses left to teenagers threatened by impending womanhood?

"Lawdie me!" Estelle declared to the friend who had brought me to visit. She had just come back into the room, watering what looked like a set of wilting elephant's ears from a tarnished silver coffeepot. "Yew didn't let thet gal intuh thuh bathroom, did yuh?" But it was too late; I had already seen the five captive Siamese cats, the array of cat turds, the mildewed pink douche bag. " 'Stelle lets them cats sleep with 'er at night 'cause she gits off on 'em sprayin' in 'er hairdo," whispered the friend cruelly.

But 'Stelle, with an obliviousness I was beginning to envy, didn't notice; she had just brought out a basket containing the traditional Southern amusement. Holding up a dimming yellow photo, she explained, "Thet's Daddy! Isn't he thuh handsomes' thang?"

My concept of time as multilinear was common to Southerners, it seemed—yesterday as real as today, more real than tomorrow, with reality held in relatively low esteem.

"Don't you think Northern women have more depth than Southern women?" a New Yorker, unaware that I was a native of Georgia, asked me at an Atlanta dinner party. What she really meant, I think, was "Don't you think Northern women are more rational?"—or, as Mother put it long before, "can talk better." What my dinner partner didn't understand was that in the South, feeling and experience pass immediately into theater. The ability to analyze, synthesize, articulate—qualities so admired in Northeastern literati circles—are just not that much in demand, indeed, are avoided, as though they might clog up direct expression. Just as we automatically filter from our minds any less-than-colorful information, any hazy abstraction that might interfere with a good anecdote, we also filter out everything that doesn't make for good drama.

Intrigued with the sound of the words, Brecht named his song "Moon of Alabama" without having visited the Southern United States; truly, Southern town names ring like lyrics—Natchez, Eufala, Tuscaloosa, Mobile. The landscape, too, contributes to a less-than-intellectual approach. The way light falls on a shack in South Georgia forms the perfect setting for a scene from Tennessee Williams. Charleston, Savannah, New Orleans, with their decadent rococo avenues, are automatic stage sets. Walking streets named Hibiscus, Flamingo, St. Phillips, St. Julian, I sense myself to be in a state of grace, of pagan permissiveness.

Indeed, folks from all over come to New Orleans each year to act out their fantasies during the four days of Mardi Gras. Hatchet-faced men from New Jersey pose as cloistered nuns; WACs from South Dakota lie down with French Quarter bohemians; members of a Houston motorcycle gang lie in a circle on Bourbon Street, wearing backless black leather pants, while a member in high black headdress and high drag walks over their bare buttocks in black stiletto heels. But the rest of the South, if in slightly less flamboyant fashion, acts out its myths and fantasies all year round.

Inconsistencies. Incongruities. Eccentricities.

Camels, I read somewhere, had once been imported to Georgia in the hope they would thrive on plantations and farms. Those humped beasts, trotting by columned houses, through cotton fields, could not have seemed stranger than some of the forms through which Southern women expressed their conflicts.

In younger women, the form taken was often simply caricature, a cartoon of traditional attitudes such as innocence, coyness, and masochism. A Savannah doctor's daughter who still wore braces was given the annual "Miss Blow Job" award by the local gay community after she had worked for a time as a barmaid in Dr. Feelgood's. "Thank y'all fur comin'," she drawled demurely in acceptance. "You'd look mighty funny with it!" she later replied to a man who said he wanted her body.

A sixteen-year-old black girl described how she picked up boys: "I be walkin' down Broughton Street"—the local black hangout. "I sees some good-lookin' bloods; I looks over at 'em, then cuts muh eyes. 'Hey, Mama!' they says. 'Whut's yo' name? Whut's yo' numbah?' 'N' I sashays on by, lookin' straight ahead, *re-el* soft, 'n' says it *fast:* 'LIZA! 234-6718!' "

At a Savannah high school, a black boy who habitually wore a tuxedo to class remarked that "women are like cars: they has tuh be kep' in good shape so yew kin drive 'em." When I asked whether anyone in the class agreed, a beautiful black girl with her hair drawn to one side, a magnolia blossom behind her ear, lowered her eyes and raised her hand. At the end of the class, she turned in a poem called "Boots":

Boots.
There are all kinds of boots—
dress boots, ladies' boots—
but what I like best
is to drink the sweat
from a man's work boot.

Sometimes women break totally with one part of the pattern, leaving other parts completely intact. Practicing the drums in her Upper West Side apartment, hanging out at rock concerts in order to write her spirited music pieces for *Viva* or *The Village Voice*, novelist Blanche Boyd was still the same eccentric Southern girl who had been kicked out of Duke in the early sixties for hypnotizing people ("They made a rule about it after I started doin' it.") and wearing a trench coat with nothing on under it ("They said girls couldn't wear pants—and I sure as hell wasn't goin' to wear a dress!").

"People in New York think I'm a barbarian because I'm from the South," Blanche admitted, "but the first time I saw television, I knew I would have to leave Charleston. Yes, there's a part of me, the Southern part, that can't live here; another, that can't live there. So I'm forever in exile." But I noticed there was an enormous box of Estée Lauder—Southern panacea for everything—on her dresser top: "Mama sent it to me from South Carolina," she said. And when she answered the phone, she murmured "Yes, Mama . . . yes, Mama . . . yes, Mama . . ." in the same conciliatory tones I had so often used with Mother, with exactly the same attitude with which I had put on the brown dress on my way to New York in my effort to please her.

Susan went to court in Charleston to maintain her maiden name after her marriage to Glenn, but supported them both so her thirty-five-year-old no-good good-ole-boy husband could "find himself." Each morning on Beaulahland, the rented South Carolina plantation where they lived, Glenn, blond and charming, and often as not nursing a hangover, lounged in the pure-silk robes he favored, while Susan, plump and proper in her Jonathan Logan dress, trotted off to her job as a junior administrator. Glenn's mother had lived for forty years in the same house in Prosperity, South Carolina, but had never unpacked the cardboard boxes in her dining room. Which, Susan told me in her aristocratic Charleston accent, explained satisfactorily, to her mind, why "Glenn is thuh way he is—'sides, whayah would I evah fine such a good-lookin' man agin?"

Often, it was as though something valuable had been permanently lost in the struggle to break with convention. Melody had managed a live-music nightclub and published a country-music newspaper. She had kicked Kris Kristofferson out of bed after she met him at a party, she claimed, " 'Cause he was jes' doin' a numbah on me." Atlanta is full of beautiful, beautifully dressed women, but with her long blonde hair and frame, Melody looked special—the perfect example for a woman's-magazine piece on "How to Look Rich Even If You're Not." "Just before, or after, an involvement with a new man, I go crazy—shoppin' and shoppin'!" Or did she mean "shopliftin' and shopliftin' "? She had told me how constantly broke she was and of the method she had devised for stealing the books and magazines she needed. And when would she repay the twenty dollars I had loaned her the month before? Her long blonde hair was smooth-looking, but her hand shook when she lit her cigarette. It was as though I had momentarily glimpsed a psyche as chaotic as Mother's, as mine.

Since I had met her four months before, Melody had moved three times, from one man's apartment to another. *Rushed to the hospital with a kidney infection,* read the note she left on her door at the time for our next appointment, supposedly an interview with me for her country-music paper. Funny, we had talked on the phone just a few hours before. But talking to Melody, I was beginning to notice, felt slippery in a certain familiar way—like, I suddenly realized, listening to a Southern man tell his Southern lies! Had I come into contact with the female version of the garden-variety Southern-male sociopath?

Melody and I would never keep our appointment and would only run into one another, during the next few years, at funky events like the Atlanta premiere of the Sex Pistols, or the Capricorn Records annual picnic in Macon, both peopled by characters so much more extreme than ourselves that I lost interest in asking her for the twenty dollars or why she hadn't shown up. Indeed, in the midst of solid-gold razor blades on chains, safety pins through cheeks, and hair frizzed a half foot in the air, we hugged and kissed and promised to "get together soon."

By then I had been thinking for some time of how breaking with tradition in the traditional South left women morally de-energized, with only a deficit out of which to responsibly handle the freedom for which we had fought. Once the limits were broken, there seemed to be no others. It was as though kicking over the traces, in a culture where women are expected to nurture, yet traditionally are deprived of nurturing, required such energy that even the unbroken rules tumbled in the wake of those broken, giving rise to the bizarre, if imaginative, behavior to which Southern women are prone.

Amanda, from Tennessee, attended business school and lived with her boyfriend in Atlanta. When she and her roommate quarreled about a trip he planned to make without her, she waited till he left town, then drove around the rural areas outside the city, collecting live turkeys in the back of her Ford station wagon. He was a turkey, she had decided, and as a farm girl, she knew just how messy turkeys could be. Depositing the gobblers in her soon-to-be–ex-friend's apartment, she moved out, leaving a message he would never forget.

Later, Amanda traveled around the world alone, working in a hand laundry in London, losing her luggage, passport, and money in the middle of India. "Amanda's jes' a good ole girl!" the folks outside Memphis chuckled when they heard. Before long, she managed to get back to the hills to marry a high school classmate whose farm adjoined the one she, in the meantime, had inherited. She sounded like a sixties version of a friend's legendary Aunt Hester: also a Tennessee farm woman, she had simply lifted her long skirts and spread her legs when she needed to piss; she had long ago stopped what she called "war-in' them drawers."

Branch, too, was no slouch at resisting local mores. We had met in a tiny school in North Georgia when I was there to teach poetry for a week while Branch, a talented painter, served as artist-in-residence. But back in Atlanta, I soon heard that she had lost her job when she moved out of her room in the lunch-room lady's house to live openly in the small mountain community with a bricklayer from Shreveport. Not long after, she lost a similar job after she attacked a fellow artist, a photographer from New York, when he insisted on taking pictures of her class in action; charging his camera, threatening to break it, she had grabbed his hair and pulled. "You just don't like me because I'm not Southern—" he had yelled, "but I am! I am! My great-grandmother's from Virginia. . . ."

"Too bad," she said a long time later with a laugh. "He didn't know we barely consider Virginya—much less Wash-in'ton, Dee Cee—South at all! And he was right," she went on; "I didn't like 'im. The artists in the project lived in that big apartment together, and from the very first day, he tried to git pushy, askin' me if I wanted to read his journal 'n' all."

For Branch, New York–pushy would repel. Despite her cropped blonde hair, her constant Levi's, her hefty look, she was still a private Southern lady to the core. True, she had been married, a mother, lived communally, and traveled alone in Italy, Japan, Korea—where, knowing no Korean, still in her jeans and T-shirt, she had picked up a ferry boatman and spent the night with him in his bunk. But that had been away from home and had happened elsewhere than in the deepest Branch.

It was the deepest Branch who wore denims during the day, Dior and John Kloss gowns at night. "I never want to make any man feel that way again," she declared. "That's why I never show mah ankles in daylight." Yet in every way other than her inflexible rage, her twenty pounds overweight, Branch, with her translucent skin, her snow-blonde hair, was extravagantly sensual. The bedroom of her Atlanta apartment had pomegranate walls, rose-embossed antique drapes, a brass bed covered in tasseled melon satin coverlets—the interior of a womb just before menstruation, I thought every time I walked through it. At dinner parties, she served Rosalynn's Eggplant Pudding, peach preserves she had put up herself, pound cake flavored with lemon and vanilla, coated with a buttermilk glaze—all on dishes from the collection of Blue Wisteria that had begun with her grandmother.

It was the Blue Wisteria, perched on a molding around the high-ceilinged dining room, that almost came between us. At the end of a long rowdy dinner during which eight of us had drunk quantities of Myers rum, then wine, a friend and I began dancing to the stereo. "Don't kick yo' foot up like that, Rowsmay-ree!" Branch remonstrated sternly, the mask of some long-dead member of the Daughters of the Confederacy congealing her downy eyebrows. "You might break Mama's china!" I sensed that it was the impropriety of my dancing like a chorus girl that was the real offense, but I also knew that Branch was known for abruptly ending lifelong friendships over what seemed minor matters. A group of artist friends with whom she had once alternated communal dinners had decided to break down her taciturnity by tickling her on the rug; Branch had sunk her teeth into the hand of one, and leaving a bleeding bite mark, had slammed out forever.

She had ended a marriage and her life as a young mother as abruptly. During her first year at the University of Tennessee at Chattanooga, Branch had had sex for the first time and, as I had dreamed of it happening, had become pregnant. It was a traditional Southern love story: secretly married, she hid out in a cheap furnished apartment while her young husband lived in his fraternity house and dated other girls because "people would know if I didn't." After the baby was born, they bought a house and furniture with the dowry given them by Branch's father. A year and a half later, Branch walked out, without money, clothes, or baby.

"I'll git you a maid," her distraught spouse yelled after her, thinking it was housework that was driving her mad. It was, partly, but more, too. "I beat the baby up a lot, and I was afraid of what I might do—she had so many bruises that I had to check 'er out before I could take 'er to the pediatrician for a routine checkup."

The possibility of violence, from within or without, had never been far away from Branch. Indeed, it was our shared scars, plus our mutual sense of being malformed, that sealed my and Branch's friendship. Together, we would laugh about events that made more insulated friends recoil. T. J., holding the pillow over my face years before, had not been unlike Branch's daddy and her brother, Frank, out on the boat: "Frank didn't like some 'smart-assed thang' I said to 'im in front of 'thuh boys'—so he turned aroun' 'n' kicked me in thuh chin. Blood was pourin' ev'rywhere, but I could hardly get Daddy tuh turn thuh boat back around so I could get tuh thuh hospital." After she had had the gash stitched, she had gone to the Memphis police department, made out an assault charge, and left town—fast. "Against her own brother!" her family raged.

241

I understood, too, when a few months later they made up. Though the same leeway doesn't exist toward friends, practically nothing, much less a little spell of violence, incest, or alcoholism, is unforgivable in a true Southern family. What *is* unforgivable is running off to New York, California, South America without looking back—or breaking with "blood," as Branch had done with her daughter, as she had almost done again with Frank.

Branch had been crushed when her grandmother had recently told her from her deathbed that she could never forgive her for "leavin' thet chile." This time, despite Frank's continued bad habits, she had had the good sense to make up: "When I went to visit, he threw an iron skillet to thuh floor so hard it shattered—jes' 'cause his second wife, Lottie, didn't have thuh supper on thuh table on time. . . ." But she was glad, she said, that he had recently gotten probation for bashing in both a man and his pickup with a tire iron: "It would've ruined his business —'sides, he's family."

Family. Most of Branch's whimsical paintings portrayed fantasy families in fantasy situations: *The Frog Family on Vacation, The Frog Family Goes on a Picnic.* . . . Aside from art and the domestic arts, Branch's eyes lit most quickly at mention of ancestors. For despite its violent core, her own Tennessee family was established country-club elite. Her golf-playing mother, for whom her daddy had sold one of his farms in order to dry her out at an expensive Houston alcoholism clinic some time before, had for years been an officer of the Daughters of the Confederacy. Branch, wearing circle pins, had once been a junior officer, making her grandmothers and her daddy proud. When she visited her paternal grandmother in Louisiana each summer during her teens, there had been concern over who she should date: ". . . Not that crop duster—he's not in our class. . . ."

The last time Branch and I talked, she said quietly that she wanted to give up the part of herself that liked bricklayers and ferryboatmen and crop dusters—even the part that had earned her her regional reputation as an artist. She had given up her Levi's for navy slacks and had dusted her fair lids with pale-blue shadow. She wanted to wear good little dresses, she said; if she was not too ruined, marry an upstanding man; or maybe just go back home, get back into the Daughters of the Confederacy: "If only Mother would die—I love bein' with Daddy, 'n' I could have a little house on his land. . . ."

As she spoke, I felt dismay. I knew her choices mattered to me because I had not yet fully made my own. I understood too well how she felt, that it had been her nonconformity that had caused her pain, not her early deprivation, her own lack of nurturing. She and I were each like a photograph I had seen in a book of freaks: smiling, wearing a sunsuit, Betty Lou Williams of Albany, Georgia, lay back against a flowered couch, displaying the arm, leg, torso of her embedded twin; X rays had revealed another woman's head trapped within her body, explained the caption.

Branch and I felt that our creativity, our adventurousness, our achievements—all the qualities that would have been assets had we been Southern men—were burdens, deformities, keeping us from the self-esteem we so desperately needed. And the sheer effort required to keep going in the direction of independence had created, for both of us, a fascination with our phantom psyches, with the women we would have been had we followed the paths laid out for us. "I'm afraid that if I ever went home to Charleston to live, I would become a Republican, just like Mama and the other members of my family," confesses writer Blanche Boyd. Indeed, trying to bridge both worlds required such energy, took such a toll, that Branch and I—and every other Southern woman I met who tried it—ended up feeling like Karl Wallenda, crossing the Tallulah Gorge in North Georgia on a tight wire on a windy day.

In Greensboro Janeene and I sat up till early morning, talking about ways to keep from being blown away. We were both, by Southern standards, high achievers, near or over forty. Yet we were each living through an identity crisis more severe than any we had known as high school cheerleaders. Janeene had recently been divorced from her husband of many years; I felt divorce coming on. And we were both playing the game long practiced by good ole boys: besides Ben, I had a twenty-five-year-old lover in New Orleans; she had a twenty-seven-year-old boyfriend—and keeping him down on the farm while she worked like a dog was taking its toll. *KEEP FUCKING BOYS/in perspective* would make a good poster for women our age, we laughed over our Jack Daniel's.

She kept a picture of Rita Hayworth, looking dissipated on her way to an alcoholism clinic, on her refrigerator door next to Gloria Steinem's telephone number. Taking a little nip in the afternoon is acceptable even in Plains, but too many little nips can become too much of a habit. A friend had described "a wonderful new diet—you'll lose ten pounds in a week—but you can't drink the first three days; jes' take some Valium, honey, and you can stan' it. . . ." That one might live three days un-medicated wasn't even a consideration. Two afternoons that week we had gone to her spa—steaming, whirlpooling, turning limp beneath massage. Janeene was round, even lush, but with her Clairol blonde curls, her carefully applied lashes, her floaty batiste tops, she looked like a slightly more delicate Dolly Parton.

"Revlon depends on women like us!" she laughed when I teased her about the amount of makeup in the bathroom of her architect-designed North Carolina home; creams, blushers, glosses, pencils, in every conceivable form and color, tumbled from shelves, covered vanities—more than I had ever seen in one place outside a department store. But she knew, and I knew, the makeup was necessary to the flirting we were ex-pected, and expected ourselves, to do. "I hate to go out to dinner with Southern women," my New York literary agent complained one evening as we ordered in Alfredo's. "They always flirt with the waiters." It took me a moment to realize she was talking about me—that what seemed to me to be nor-mal behavior, that is, deference and smiles for men, seemed to her to be artifice.

It was a kind of artifice that had served Janeene well: during her twenties, she had posed as Ezra Pound's niece in order to visit him in Saint Elizabeth's Hospital, outside Washington, D.C. Her collection of their correspondence had recently turned out to be worth thousands. It was the kind of thing one would expect of her: her talent for turning everything to publicity and profit had given her regional literary power for years. When her father later died, a friend amusedly observed that even his obituary sounded like a publicity piece for Janeene.

Earlier in the week, Janeene had taken me to visit her mother —250 pounds in a purple print dress and purple feather earrings, greeting us in a house filled with purple plastic flowers, purple kitchen utensils, purple couches and chairs. It was both Bertie Mac's and Grandmother Lee's favorite color, and the fat woman with her rouged cheeks, her permanent wave, had just the kind of look Mother would have warmed to. "Janeene's all tore up about thet boy," she said to me confidentially, meaning Janeene's former spouse, not her boyfriend. We were all drunk again, and Janeene had just screeched at her mother that all her problems with men had started when the older woman had slapped her hand when she had put pebbles inside her vagina at three. She had told me how her daddy had had her "dress up like a whore, my boobs pokin' out of my dress," at fifteen, in order to take her on the road with him to sell dental equipment. Now as he came through the back door, charming and inebriated in a vaudevillian straw hat, I understood why Janeene was still Little Janeene, even at forty-five.

Now, as we sat drinking at three in the morning, she got down to the nitty-gritty, or what she called "my breakdown." A few weeks before, a crew had lived at her house, from which she also runs her publishing business, for seven days to film her à la the Louds of California. It was definitely cinema verité: all week the cameras had followed her every move, including her fight with her young lover when she discovered that he had been seeing a woman nearer his age, even her hysteria and tears. But at the end of the filming, she had donned her white satin dress, her new white feather coat ("a six-hundred-dollar divorce gift to myself") to attend a dinner in her honor. Driving home, she had passed her lover's house, and fantasizing him in bed with the other woman, had swerved her car around, squealed to a stop, then stomped to the back door to put her fist through the glass panel.

Blood had spurted everywhere—down the front of the white satin dress, all over the white feather coat. When her naked lover hastily opened the door, she broke all his mother's china against the kitchen walls. And despite the fact that everyone in Greensboro knows her, she gave a false name at the emergency room, where, still wearing the soggy coat, lying back to have her wrist and forearm stitched, she had looked over at an orderly who had a stump instead of an arm. "Hey, man," she cried, "I'll bet you're the best fuck in town!"

A Southern woman like Janeene seems akin to an Act of God. Yet could any of us get that strong without also being mutilated? For some Southern women, there was no question of backtracking—even if going forward meant irreparable loss. "When people ask, 'How did you have thuh guts tuh do this or that?' they don't understand that once the forces have been set in motion—once the veil has been ripped from your eyes—there's no choice but goin' on. . . ."

Ben and I were staying at the Chelsea for a few months, and I was talking with Montana in, of all places, a little restaurant in the West Village called Montana Eve. Wearing jeans and a boy's plaid shirt, Montana had bicycled up from her SoHo loft. As we embraced, I noticed that both her hair and smile were still sunny, but there was a hint of wistfulness beneath the latter. "So good to see you—well, lah de dah dah 'n' all that!" she gushed breathlessly, at thirty-five, the same Southern girl who still gave our mutual friend Linda their secret sorority good-bye.

"When *The Feminine Mystique* was published, I was pregnant with my first baby," she was saying now, "but I couldn't let myself read it: I knew I would get too stirred up." As a sorority sister and cheerleader at the University of Georgia,

Montana had been interested in art, and felt weird, but had tried to conform by wearing the plainest Peter Pan collars, crew-neck sweaters, and plaid skirts she could find, and by dating the most regular boys. When she married one of them, she moved with him to Beaufort, South Carolina, population 9,444, where he became a used-car dealer, just as her daddy had been in Athens, Georgia.

After a while they bought a run-down plantation house and had two more babies. "It was that house I loved more than anything else," she said wistfully, and she didn't have to say more. I had already conjured up the cool, high-ceilinged rooms, the spiral staircase on which one felt elegant even taking down the laundry, the feel of paint flecking against one's fingertips as one leaned against a decaying column. And best of all, the steps where one would sit barefoot after supper, drinking a bourbon and water, looking up at the stars through live oaks dripping Spanish moss—listening to nothing but the voices of frogs and children playing and one's own deepest self.

Perhaps it had been this listening to her deepest self that had started the change: "Somethin' was happenin' that I jes' couldn't seem to stop, like one of those old-fashioned butter churns, churnin' me up inside," she went on, describing the way I had felt almost every day of my life. "The more I got into my paintin', everything I read, everybody I met, agitated the churnin'. And I jes' had to have the guts for it."

Beaufort is the town that, a dozen or so years ago, drove physician Don Gatch out of town after he reported to national media the horror of medical facilities available to local blacks— a town where he claims crosses were burned in his yard, where he and his wife were shot at as they drove by in their car, where he says he was finally imprisoned on trumped-up charges of drug abuse and homosexuality. It is not a town known for its liberal views, and one of the things Montana had to have the guts for was a divorce trial in which her own friends and relatives were called up as witnesses to prove her husband Jim's charge that she was an unfit mother.

A favorite aunt testified that when she had visited, Montana had stayed up late, and when she went back into the room, Montana had fallen asleep with her mouth open, her ashtray on her chest, "jes' lak she'd been drinkin' or sumthin'." Another witness declared that she wore blue jeans, and often appeared to be "warin' less than she should on top." Then there were the affairs that had embarrassed Jim all over Beaufort. And two hours down the road in Savannah, Montana had met Delta and Miss Jane. "They tried to make me out to be a drunk and a drug addict and a sickie and a slut," Montana said, "but even Jim thought bringin' in my affair with a woman would be too perverse."

After she lost custody, she went to Savannah to live with Miss Jane—"All that summer I was crazy with pain, not sure at all I wanted to become a lesbian, it's a wonder she could stand me" —then to Connecticut to spend time with a woman friend. The friend was a psychiatrist whom Montana had met in Beaufort after the psychiatrist's lover had dumped her, pregnant, off his sailboat in the midst of a romantic year-long cruise; shell-shocked, she had stayed in town a couple of years to have her baby and practice: "She understood what I was goin' through. But it took a couple of years to lick my wounds, pick up the pieces—to realize that after losin' my children, nothin' could ever hurt me again." She had changed her name from Mary Alice Allen to Montana, just to try to forget the whole South, everything. Because she was tall, rangy, freckled, folks often took her for a Westerner, a look she accentuated with the Levi's and high-heeled purple suede boots.

She did make me think of a pioneer woman, a good ole girl who had struggled through barbed-wire fences. Was that what we—Blanche, Branch, Janeene—all were? A couple of years later, Montana and I would have shared Miss Jane and a New York filmmaker who at first thought we were each "adorable," but who vowed, after the two of us, that he would never "get involved with a crazy Southern woman again!" But I already felt close to her, listening to her talk about how she was happier now, living in SoHo, getting a bit of recognition. Besides, she said hopefully, she had just met a new man, "a real Southern gentleman, the old-school type. I met 'im on my last trip home!"

At last I was meeting other Southern women who were struggling with the same conflicts, but the air felt painfully thin, as though we were breathlessly trying to communicate as we climbed side by side up Stone Mountain. One of the ways I could deal with the thin air, I found, was to concentrate on women who were still struggling to achieve what I had left behind, or on women who had survived, but not as well. Chatting with a black waitress in Vidalia, Georgia, learning that her whole ambition was to marry the ordinary-looking white man who managed the short-order restaurant, I could feel, for a moment, condescending, successful. It was an ugly kind of arrogance akin to feeling well off when one sees a cripple or hears of a friend's bad luck, and gives one the kind of permission to relax described by a New York woman when a man fell to his death on the sidewalk at her feet: "My first thought was, Oh, good, now I have an excuse to start smoking again!"

I was like a sex kitten who had learned to talk, and the energy it had taken had depleted me for almost everything else. That I had struggled to become something beyond the Southern man's ideal of "a woman who wears a skirt and bends over a lot," that I worked, traveled alone, and made my own money, gave me license for ignoring my disintegrating third marriage, neglecting my teenage children, drinking Jack Daniel's, and sleeping around when I was out of town. But by looking where I had started, I could feel good about myself once more.

Sometimes as I drove down Highway 441 through the middle-Georgia town of Eatonton, I passed the local factory at 3:30 P.M., just as the workers were leaving their shift. From the perspective of my overcomplicated life, I enjoyed a fleeting image of an anonymous existence in the tiny town, of running away from home, family, career, beginning a life described by shifts, meals, television, church. Once I would have dreamed myself cradled in the gentle arms of Jesus, carried to a white cloud, lifted out of my stress; now I saw myself walking down Main Street, carrying my lunch pail, mindlessly thinking of what would be on TV that night. It was a fantasy as romanticized as the one I used to relieve myself in the midst of my and Ben's increasingly bitter quarrels. Inspired by *Belle de Jour,* I momentarily became Catherine Deneuve, reclining in my couture dress in an elegant Paris apartment filled with cut chrysanthemums.

Yet when my friend Robert John told me the story of his sister, Faith, I knew I was still as much like her—a part of the world of the barely survived—as the worldly woman I aspired to become. Faith and Robert had grown up in Elora, Tennessee, "population fifty, with one cement-block café with a bare bulb over the door." It was 1956; she was sixteen and pregnant; even if she had had the money—or hadn't had the religion—abortions were illegal, and her boyfriend had left for the army:

"I was nine, 'n' she told me first—wringin' her hands 'n' sayin' 'Oh, Robert John, what'll I do?' Then she told Mama, 'n' the cryin' 'n' sobbin' started. The upshot was that she had to go live with *his* mama in Harvey, Illinois, so they could git married when he came home on leave." Harvey, he went on to explain, was a suburb of Chicago where everyone from Elora went when they wanted to make money. "Folks would say, 'Go up tuh Harvey 'n' git you a job.' It was a regular little Appalachia, set right in Illinois. Of course, it didn't work out. But she stayed up there and worked as a waitress 'n' I don't know what all. Then she got pregnant agin, this time by a married man. She had tuh depend on me—I was up there by then—'n' her high school chum, Duck, who had come up there tuh work, too."

Robert dug into a box of photographs, and brought up one of Faith and Duck at fifteen, standing in front of a ramshackle porch, their arms about one another's waists. Faith wore a printed dress with a draped bodice that accentuated her bosom; Duck had on what looked like a Girl Scout uniform that was a size too small and saddle oxfords without socks: "Even back then, Duck wore boy's clothes 'n' all, 'n' she was gawky as hell!"

Robert, seventeen, was just beginning to realize he was gay, though he didn't know exactly what gay was—and if he was in love with a boy, then Duck must be in love with Faith. "I asked Duck if she knew what queers was, 'n' she said 'Whut do they do?' I didn't know no better than her, but I said 'Suck each other's pussy, 'n' if you wanna make Faith feel better, that's

250

whut you should do tuh her.' Duck looked real surprised for a minute, then said, 'But I wouldn't wanna git them hars in my mouth!'

"Duck was known for bein' stingy, but one day she came in with a bag of groc'ries 'n' said, 'Faith, honey, here's a little sumthin' for you, 'n' you don't have tuh pay me back, either.' Then she dug intuh her bag and came up with a carton of Camels. Well, you don't know whut that meant then, we was all so poor. But poor Faith, she jes' burst into tears."

Faith gave up her second baby for adoption; she had worked for almost nothing in a lawyer's office because he said—if she also slept with him—he would arrange it in a way that she could keep track of where it had gone. In a few years, she married a marine, and they lived in trailers wherever they went. Robert pulled out another picture, this time of a svelte Faith, wearing a Dorothy Lamour–type sarong bathing suit; smiling triumphantly, she stood posed in front of a trailer beside which stood a scraggly palmetto tree. Had the marine been to her what Paul had been to me?

"Then she got sick, some kinda female trouble; Mama said a doctor had messed 'er up inside, 'n' she was laid up in that trailer for years. Mama would write 'n' say, 'Faith can't drive, Faith can't walk no more, Faith's goin' tuh die. . . .' But now, she's doin' fine, 'cept for gittin' religion agin, becomin' a Jesus freak. . . ." He held out the most recent picture, circa 1974: Faith in a trim pantsuit, bubble hairdo, posed before the Elora Café, just beneath the bare bulb over the doorway—a glorious visit home, the victory of sheer survival. Nothing more. But nothing less.

"I wuz nursed by my mama till I wuz four years old—Lawd, that woman did ever'thang to git me off the breast. . . . Well, after my daddy passed, my mama went out tuh work, 'n' I wuz raised by my gran'daddy. We slep' in thuh same bed till I wuz twenty-two or twenty-three. I'd always put muh leg over his, 'n' he'd jes' pat it, 'n' I'd go tuh sleep—spoiled, Lawdy me! I wuz

jes' a bitty baby. Why, I set in his lap till I wuz fifteen years old.
Well, after he passed I had occasion to sleep with Mama: I put
muh leg over hers—'n' you know what happened? She patted
me on thuh leg, jes' lak Gran'daddy. As Mama always says,
no-body laks tuh sleep alone. . . ."

A black history teacher in middle Georgia had told me the
story of his life. But it was from Robert that I learned a Southern
boy could grow up as a Southern girl. On his family's dirt farm
in Tennessee, he liked to dress up in Faith's dresses and high
heels and, on a Sunday afternoon, swing in the porch swing,
watching the traffic move down the highway and through
Elora. "Wuz thet yew?" the kids in the fourth grade would hoot
the next day, "warin' thet red dress 'n' them shoes?"

Some Sundays, Cousin Kenny, twelve, an ominous toy gun
and holster at his hip, came to visit in his cowboy suit. Inevitably, he would get a handful of lard from the kitchen and insist
that John go with him down to the woods beyond the pasture.
"But I don' wont to, Kenny," John would plead, "it makes me
feel lak I hafta shit."

Cornholing, in the rural South, doesn't imply homosexuality:
like fucking a cow or a pig, it's just a little something among the
boys. ("No wonder you couldn't get off," goes a Southern joke
about a man who tried to fuck a pig. "You picked the ugliest one
in the bunch!") Still, the one who gets repeatedly cornholed is
bound to be called a fairy. Soon the boys at school would let John
go down on them, by the creek, behind the gym, but never
spoke to him in the school hall except to chant things like, "Thar
goes John, the softest cheeks muh balls ever laid on."

Maybe if he did what they were always laughing about—that
is, got some pussy—they would accept him. Out by the town
dump, he asked Velma, the school slut, if she would let him do
it. "Cain't tuhday," she replied mysteriously, inscribing an enormous *M* in the dust at his feet. Too intimidated by the tough
girl to ask, he wondered mutely what she meant. Was she a
'Morphadite!? Through years of front-porch anecdotes, he had
heard awe-filled references to the person of two sexes. Years
later, he realized Velma had probably meant Menstruating. But

by then it was too late: he was used to being queer, a sex object for men.

It was 1974 in Savannah, where I now spent time teaching each year, that Robert John told me his stories. We sat out on the steps or in the porch swing, listening to the crickets, sharing a bottle of cheap wine, drawing up images from the past in the desultory way Southerners favor. "I ain't never done nuthin' fast, honey," I heard a black woman say as she walked past in the dark. Indeed, Savannah is a city where time seems slowed. "Somewhere between Guatemala and New York," Robert described it. "It's as though you really have more time here."

Aside from slowed time, Savannah—and Charleston and New Orleans—are known for their blurred sexual distinctions. The voluptuous vocal tones of men named Hodding and Eban and Derek III, the intensity of their interest in antiques and ancestors, sometimes makes it hard to tell the hetero- from the homo-, or even bi-, sexual males. It is as though the cities themselves are so soft, so womanish, that every impulse toward feminine caricature is fed.

I had heard of Dawn, the legendary Charleston transsexual who was said to have wandered the streets pushing a carriage containing a black baby that she claimed was her own child, fathered by her chauffeur after her sex-change operation. At Mardi Gras in New Orleans, I had met Russell, who sat on an overturned garbage can as though it were a throne, wearing only a sheet draped like a toga, a pair of torn panty hose, a lot of thick blue eye shadow, and the kind of pocketbook favored by Mother and the masked ladies. "Oh-h-h, I luuuv that hat!" he exclaimed as I walked into a bar wearing a pink felt cloche I had picked up at Woolworth's—drag queens are more appreciative of the nuances of style than any Southern woman I have ever met.

Miss Latrice Boudair sat on my couch in Savannah sipping sherry in sleek black satin trousers, black silk shirt, alligator-green pumps. By day, she preferred dressing as an effeminate boy: "This shirt was a steal, honey—ni-teen ni-tee-five—'n' *so* dee-vine!" I had to admit that Latrice had good taste, and she appreciated the fine arts. Because I was a "poetry teacher," she had come by my apartment with a young poet who had just finished a manuscript.

As the friend read from his poetry, we both sat, rapt. Then Latrice said she had to rush back to the low-rent motel where she lived because her weekend husband, a marine from a nearby base, had come into town early: " 'N' you *know* how a man is, honey. Peter's not used to havin' a re*la*tionship, 'n' I jes' have tuh git over thyah 'n' reassure 'im. . . ." And probably, she didn't want to miss her soaps: "Every drag queen really wants to be a suburban housewife," my lover in the French Quarter had told me.

At our first meeting in Dr. Feelgood's, Latrice had worn a red satin shirt, a midi-length black skirt, and black ankle-strap high heels. The next time I saw her, she had just come out of jail— "False charges, a'course, darlin' "—and twirled a silk shawl around her shoulders as she spoke; in her hair was a huge white flower. "I'm on the rag, you know," I heard her say to the sailor at the bar. I had already heard how Latrice—a twenty-seven-year-old black man—made a couple of hundred a night by picking up tricks, giving them the same story, then satisfying them in one of the two ways women have traditionally used during their periods.

"I knew he really loved me," I heard one drag queen tell another, "when he turned me over and saw that I was a man, and did it anyway."

Robert John had once been a drag queen, too. Today he is a divorced father, a vegetarian who wears nothing but faded T-shirts, drawstring cotton pants. After he had accumulated money, dresses, poodles, antiques, houses, madness, the bubble had burst. For six months, he had withdrawn to a fifteen-dollar-a-month dirt-floored hut in a village in Guatemala, living off bananas and avocados, occasionally taking the Valium sold there without prescription. Makeup, wigs, dresses, and parties like the one for which he hired a cruise ship to entertain his

Savannah friends all night with booze, dope, a live band were things of the past.

Robert liked to say that he had been liberated by *Ms.* magazine and introduced to heterosex first by Delta, then Miss Jane: "Delta brought me one red rose the next morning. I called all my friends, who couldn't believe I had actually slept with a woman!"

In 1977, Robert and Miss Jane were married in an Episcopal ceremony performed by the bride's priest-father. The party following the wedding—reminiscent of past decadence—featured a house overflowing with white orchids, the scent of Colombian, a cerulean-blue wedding cake, naked guests in a pool. As the three of us sat at breakfast on the morning of the wedding—I was a houseguest; by then we were all family—Robert asked Jane whether she recalled when, the night before, her mother had asked if the cake would have cabbage roses: "You said 'What are cabbage roses?' and I started to say 'Don't you remember that velvet dress I had with the cloth flowers at the hem?' "

It was hard for me to imagine Robert, with his shock of dark hair, his black beard, in a dress. But I had seen the color Polaroids, and he had had a lot more panache than my women friends or me. "It was hell staggerin' along these brick sidewalks in high heels—'specially early in thuh mornin' when I had a hangover," he laughed; then he said more seriously, "Dressin' like a woman made me feel sickish—all those garter belts 'n' things. I wondered if real women felt the same way."

What were the shivers of recognition I felt as he, Latrice, and friends spoke? And why were my feelings sadder, more intense than those I felt chatting with the B-girls and Korean hookers at the Lamp Post, where the jukebox had music to suit every sailor—Greek, Italian, Norwegian—who might dock? Was it because the drag queens caricatured everything I as a Southern woman had been brought up to become? Because they had embraced the least-free aspects of being female? Or because I had long felt, because of what I fantasized as my embedded penis, like a man in feminine disguise?

255

A woman artist friend had had a man's face skillfully painted on her belly, her pubic hair becoming his beard, then had had color slides made to preserve the work. "I was hallucinating—seeing women turning into men everywhere," she said. Had she only been seeing the reality of our situation as nonconforming Southern women?

Just over the bridge that crosses the Savannah River into South Carolina, a neon sign whirls continuously, like an enormous Fourth of July sparkler. Fireworks are legal in South Carolina, and Looney Luke's is one of the places where folks stop to buy them. Besides the Japanese fireworks, Looney Luke's sells souvenirs of the Deep South—the chenille bedspreads woven with life-size color peacocks, fringed velvet pillows that read MOTHER in raised red letters, miniature Jack Daniel's bottles with a Confederate colonel trapped inside, plus peach liquor and baskets of pecans, and something a visitor from New York called the most obscene artifact he had ever come across: "Pistol Packin' Mama" is a small plastic doll with huge hard tits clothed in a sprayed-on sweater, a miniskirt of polka-dotted cotton; when one presses her wobbly head, with its painted-on blue eyes, an enormous penis pops out through the slit in the skirt.

The more independent I became, the more I felt like the doll with the hidden penis. It was only my marriage, the fact that I was still emotionally, if not financially, supported by a husband, that gave external propriety to my life. Yet with our mutual adulteries, my growing commitment to my work, my deepening obsession with other Southern women, even that seemed to be going down fast. Sometimes I would arrive in Atlanta on Friday night, after driving three or four hours from wherever I had been, to go out with Ben to a movie or dinner with friends—and would burst into tears, or at the least drink too much, out of sheer fatigue, the intensity of what I had experienced during the week.

Every summer now, Ben and I went to Boston (where his mother still took him for walks to tell him how his father couldn't accept our marriage) and Cape Cod. When we visited friends on John's Pond on the Cape, Laura, fifteen, and Darcy, fourteen, decided after dinner to canoe out onto the lake alone. At first Ben and I sat talking with our friends. Then I realized there was no moon, that the lake was pitch, a monster's dream, that they had been gone a very long time. I couldn't breathe through my panic and could tell that even our hosts, familiar with the lake, were alarmed.

At last they arrived, terrified themselves at the risk they had taken. "We couldn't find our way back, everything was black!" Laura gasped in my arms, shaking; "Mother, we couldn't tell where we were at all!" Would this be their lives, going out into dark places where I would have no power to guide them?

With whatever energy I had left from work going into my disintegrating marriage, I had little left for my daughters—they had become the staples of my nightmares: Darcy, her nude body delivered to the front door thrown across a steamer trunk; Laura, staring at me desperately through the window of a passing taxi, the glass so thick that there was no way we could communicate. David had left home to lead a life that chronically depressed me—I imagined giving up makeup and sex to pay for my failures with him. Darcy had written a poem that began,

> I'm standing in the men's room
> of the Standard station
> and suddenly I think of Mother . . .

Laura had pushed for early admission to college in order to leave home at fifteen. All of them, I knew, were lonely.

On Father's Day, over Ben's protest that it was a sentimental indulgence, I called Daddy from my brother-in-law's house on Cape Cod. "I have tuh go tuh thuh hospital for tests," he said tearily, " 'n' I'm so scared. . . ." From Anne, I learned that a malignancy had been found, a cancer that had already entered his brain. "He cain't talk, Rows-may-ree," his wife said when I called his hospital room. "When he heard yo' voice, he started cryin'." Was this the father whom I had once hated with a cold, hard hatred? I was shaken. Had Daddy once felt the way I felt —helpless? Had my whole view of him been colored by Mother's?

Mother had learned of Daddy's terminal illness and wrote me tearful letters recalling the romantic figure who had played love songs on his saxophone, who had worn his felt hat at such a rakish angle—her most romantic beau, who was now abandoning her, taking with him his unrequited love, the last proof of the belle she had been.

Everything was too complicated. I couldn't control it.

Pus dripped from the forsythia blossoms. Ben confessed that he hated the labia-pink azaleas that covered the South each spring; that he resented the house where the bugs came in through the cracks despite the crown moldings, the hundred-foot pines, the coral goldfish pond—indeed, that he craved the whole gray-brown ambience of the Northeast.

Driving back to Atlanta after our third summer up East, we stopped at the Francis Marion Hotel in Charleston; the broken air conditioning, the mosquitoes biting us all night kept us from making love, seemed to presage something sickening. Ben had finally admitted that he didn't like my having the lover in New Orleans, that I must choose; nor could he any longer accept my one-night stands.

I had tried to find it amusing when he had contracted scabies from an ex-nun with hairy legs. But when he had had an affair with an Atlanta city planner, I had fantasized slashing her too-pretty face with a razor blade. And when he had brought a secretary home from his office to sleep between my flowered sheets, beneath my yellow chenille spread, I had been so enraged that I had told her off at a social gathering. Later, when she had been found axed in the skull in a strange apartment, a V clipped out of her forehead, I had felt guilty, confused, as though I had been partly to blame. Mother, in North Carolina, Daddy, in his hospital room, seemed far away. But the evil they had seen in me at three was manifesting itself as surely as I had known it would.

The hot, slippery end of August slid into September in Georgia. In a week, I would begin my residency at the women's prison in Milledgeville. In a month, Mother would be dead. In three months, I would be forty.

I didn't yet know how crazy I could become.

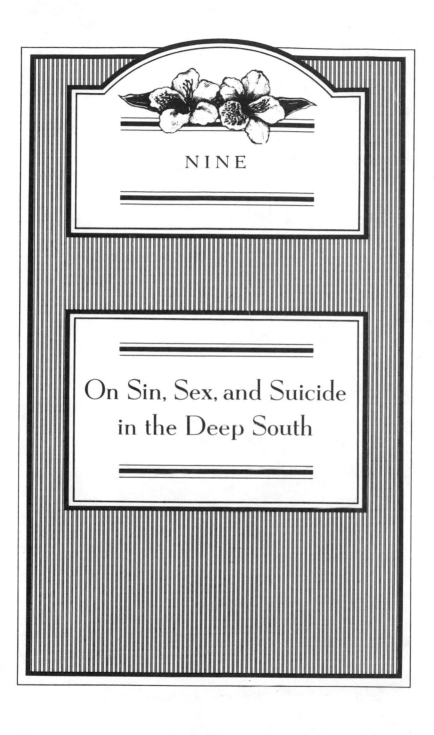

NINE

On Sin, Sex, and Suicide
in the Deep South

ANYONE WHO ENTERS THIS BUILDING IS SUBJECT TO
THOROUGH SEARCH

*"Whut's the Blood Night? It's whut the womens in the Macon
county jail says they does tuh yew on yo' firs' night hyah. . . ."*

ANYONE BRINGING WEAPONS OR ALCOHOL ON THE
PREMISES WILL BE PROSECUTED

*"It's a juke joint—yew know whut a juke joint is; it leads yew
roun' 'n' down 'n' down, a Juke Joint in Hell!"*

ANYONE DISRUPTIVE OF THE PEACE OF THIS PLACE
WILL BE FORCIBLY REMOVED

I sat on the bench in the lobby beside a slight black girl who
trembled visibly. "Are yew new, too?" she had asked before she
told me about the Blood Night. Now, as I said in what I hoped
was a convincing voice that I was sure it wouldn't be that bad,
that the women in the Macon jail had undoubtedly been teasing
her, her child's eyes clung to mine. I pushed back my own
fantasies of her coming search and invasion, of her skinny legs,
already rigid with fear, pried apart. She looked about Darcy's
age, and I noticed that she had one carefully cultivated and
painted long fingernail, that she clutched what was apparently
her one possession, a broken toothbrush, in a greasy piece of
Saran Wrap. When the locked door opened and a muscular arm
beckoned me through, the girl shuddered, as though I had been
torn from her.

As I was led through the day room over damp concrete floors, past peeling green walls, a lone chair or couch bulging dingy stuffing, a tall hefty woman with her T-shirt rolled up to her shoulders to display a big tattoo of a dripping heart and dagger called after me: "Hey, foxy, where'd yuh git those rags?" "Saks Fifth Avenue," I called back, suddenly embarrassed that two weeks before I had been on Fifth Avenue, that I had money to buy new clothes, that I was free. But she grinned. "Foxy!" she yelled again. "Hey, muh name's Peggy—maybe I'll see yuh around!" The skinny woman beside her, her own blouse open to her navel to reveal an enormous rose tattooed between her small white breasts, eyed me suspiciously. "Is she new?" I heard her whisper.

A woman in a Muslim headdress held out her hand as though we were at a tea: "Queenie is my alias. They say I'm a kleptomaniac, but I want to start a charm class." Each of Easter Sunday's toenails was painted a different color—blue, yellow, black, purple, red; I painted my toenails, too, so I took off my boot and we compared colors. A girl across the room wore jeans that had been cut off at the knee, the remaining fabric made into elasticized ruffles that fit her ankles, each part embroidered and reembroidered. Around me was hair dyed in more colors, arranged in more exotic ways, than I had ever seen in one place.

Chain Gang Candy had told me that she was thirty-four, but in her short brown cotton dress, her brown oxfords with white anklets, she looked like a chunky teenager. Doris, fat and depressed-looking, wore scuffed purple velour bedroom slippers and clutched a copy of "The Upper Room," the same Methodist tract Mother religiously read. Peggy, who had spoken to me in the day room, sat on my other side, grinning.

An hour before, when I had been introduced to my class, I had quickly learned that they were more interested in my midi-length batik skirt, my Italian boots, the color of my nail polish —in the facts that I, too, had had a daddy who drank, had dropped out of high school, been brutalized by a man, married more than once, and was a mother—than in my identity as an artist who would help them do something called "write poetry."

"The bes' thang 'bout bein' in here is thet there ain't no mens," volunteered Candy, thinking, since she had heard my life history, that I would understand instantly. "Ole One Eye—he's thuh warden—we all hates him—and a few a thuh guards, theys thuh onlies' mens we see."

"When I see a man agin, I won't say 'Hi,' I'll say 'Good-bye'!" quipped Jewell, who had murdered the man who had married her when she was fifty, then cheated her out of her meager savings and molested her teenage daughter. Almost every woman in the group, I learned, had been incarcerated for a crime that had to do with a man.

Versie had been indicted for writing bad checks. "And thet wuz caused by a man, too," she joked. "If thuh man at thuh bank hadn't called the po-leese, I wouldn't be hyah!"

Easter Sunday laughed about the way she had run all the way home from the party to get her daddy's shotgun, then had run back, leaping gullies and fences, to shoot her old man's new lady over the fruit punch. Nor was there any stigma in killing or wreaking revenge directly on one's husband or lover: "I knew he wasn't goin' to look at no Frigidaire," declared Candy, explaining why she had thrown the Clorox in her husband's eyes.

Like most Southerners, they could turn horror stories into comedy. "Yep, I come home, heard thuh record player goin', thuh back doe slam; he didn't have no shirt on, his thang stickin' out lak a poker—" related Maybelle. "I TORE THET PLACE UP! Next thang I know, I woke up in thuh Macon county jail. . . ."

Tearing places up seemed popular. "I heard 'bout muh husban' bein' with that other woman, so I went to the fact'ry where they wuz workin' 'n' TORE thet place up!" said Peggy. "Then I moved muh stuff out tuh Mama's 'n' that night went down tuh thuh river 'n' wuz drinkin' wine 'n' feelin' fine—till I got home. 'N' there he wuz, hidin' behin' the porch swing. 'N' before I could get holda muh gun, he's pulled his out 'n' shot me in thuh leg, 'n' that's the las' I saw of thuh son of a bitch! I don't know why they put *me* in here," she mused, "since *I* wuz thuh one thet got shot. . . ."

265

When Easter Sunday had talked about shooting her rival, and Candy had described her revenge on her unfaithful spouse, I had recalled too clearly my fantasy of slashing the city planner's face, my first impulse after Ben had told me about the secretary between my flowered sheets. In a way that seemed driven through every sinew, I wanted to tear up his manuscripts, rip his books apart, throw his belt buckles through the window. Yet was tearing things up, even if one ended up behind bars, better than cancer, alcoholism, or other forms of self-punishment? Doris dolefully confessed that though she was the mother of six illegitimate children, most of them by a white police lieutenant in the middle-sized Georgia town where she lived, she didn't like sex all that much: "I always thank of a movie, or sum book I've read." When her children had been born, the white doctors and nurses in the public hospital had censored her, saying, "Somebody's crossed the color line. . . ." She had accepted their scorn and the responsibility for the children as her own and had been properly grateful when the white woman for whom she worked as a housemaid had given her leftovers and old clothes. She had lost that job because she drank: "When I fin'ly went to a clinic in town, I told one of thuh counselors thuh name of thuh daddy of my chirren. She promised not tuh tell, but she did—'n' he got me picked up on 'sturbance of thuh peace, 'n' I laid up 'n thuh county jail with thuh DT's till I come here. . . ."

Despite her momentary rage, Maybelle passively accepted her lot, too. This time she spoke in a low voice, as though she were still in the past: "Muh man, he laks to eat at two or three 'n thuh mornin'. I alwa's cook fur him then. 'Course, we makes our livin' sellin' moonshine, homebrew. . . ." She seemed to have forgotten that she had told us earlier that she was here because he had let her take the rap. "But we lak to drink gov'ment stuff. In the mornin', I take a quart of beer—it heps me do thuh housework, heps thuh day go by. . . ." Her voice became dreamy. "Late in the afternoon, I takes me a pint of vodka, it heps thuh night go by. Then later, we likes a glass of red whiskey—" She stopped for a moment, then added, " 'Course, he's got another wo-man livin' with 'im now—he don't lak sleepin' alone. . . ." I tried not to think of the hand-scribbled verse she had secretly handed me:

> *The sun is setting and*
> *I want time to fly by.*
> *Sitting and waiting—*
> *waiting to die.*

There are virtually no middle-class, and few white, women in prison in Georgia. But Frankie, fair, with long brown hair, had been to Georgia State College for a year. She had been shot in the stomach when she had pulled her own gun during a raid on her drug dealer–lover. My fashionable Atlanta hair dresser, it turned out, had been her connection for skag. But she, too, was subject to the apathy, the lack of self-acceptance that pervaded the institution. "Isn't this too perverse?" she whispered, showing me a love poem she had written to another woman. "Is it all right to write things like this?" When she told me that she was afraid to masturbate in her dormitory because of the older women's demands that she "control yo'self," I thought of my own conflicted sexuality, the policing of Mother and Grandmother Lee.

Virease was a grandmother, too, but she considered us all to be sexually entrapped. "That p'leesman in Macon wan-id a 'bortion on his gal, but I wouldn't do it 'cause he wouldn't pay, so he planted thet catheter, 'n' hyah ah is," fumed the fifty-six-year-old black woman; "so hyah I is, roastin' away in this Juke Joint in Hell!"

At the John Milledge Motel, $24.50 for a five-day week, I had a room complete with old-fashioned dresser, lumpy white chenille-covered bed, air conditioner that didn't quite work, and the all-important color TV. A Milledgeville friend told me that Jayne Mansfield had once been a guest there, that, as a teenager, he had peeked through the curtains of one of the one-story concrete block building to see Jayne, a muscular man at her side, spread out in all her dyed-blonde glory. As I checked in, I thought of Jayne, decapitated in a car crash on a dark road outside New Orleans, a sex object with an IQ of 150, a woman literally split body from mind. Of Flannery O'Connor, living out her last days before her death from lupus in the farmhouse across from the new Holiday Inn. Of Mother, sobbing into her pillow in her dormitory at the Georgia State College for Women a half mile away. I wondered what would happened to me, freak of cunt and brain, in this place that murdered women.

Each night as I drove back from the prison, Mother, in her white middy blouse, her navy pleated skirt, Daddy dreamily playing his saxophone on the roof of the military school across the street, were ghosts that hung among the magnolia blossoms, the live oaks dripping Spanish moss. But now the faces of the women from the prison draped themselves on the hood of my Fiat.

"We can let you work in the prisons now," the woman administrator at the state arts council had said after the publication of my notorious book of poetry. Artists and criminals, a psychologist friend had told me, have the same peculiar swirl in their fingertips. Indeed, as I drove, I felt raw, stunned with connection: working at the prison was like watching a movie that, while a cartoon, revealed a harrowing truth. But the identification I felt seemed to have more to do with our common situation as Southern women than with our acts of rebellion. The only difference between the prisoners and myself, it seemed, was my ability to separate fantasy from action, to envision alternatives and act on them. Holding on to our chastity or a man, meeting the Southern standards for feminine success—standards that contained little leeway for feminine adventurousness, creativity, or thrust—niggled our brains like matters of ultimate importance.

For despite their violence, the incarcerated women were the most conventional I had ever met. Like Mother, they totally accepted society's valuation of themselves and had little or no awareness of their right to legitimate anger. As I listened to

Doris berate herself for not having found a good man to look after her and her children, I also heard Mother—originally a privileged belle—obsess about her failures as a woman. And was Maybelle's "gov'ment stuff . . . heps thuh day go by" the same as Mother's phenobarbital—even my shopping and Jack Daniel's? The forces that had broken Mother's sanity—the conflicts I had observed in even the most striking and achieving Southern women—existed, magnified, in the inmates of the prison.

When I had worked in a training school for girls, I had noticed that many of the misdemeanors for which the teenagers had been incarcerated—sexual promiscuity, staying out all night, running away from home, all of which fell under a charge of being "uncontrollable"—would hardly have been important enough to punish in boys of the same age. Like those girls and the women in the prison, my sister and I had suffered from the consequences of our gender. Since I had been a teenager, I had had the emotional responsibility for three children, and what felt as draining, three husbands. When Anne had scored brilliantly in science on her S.A.T.'s, Mother had refused to let her discuss a scholarship to Emory University on the grounds that she wouldn't have the "right clothes."

It was as though our priorities had been tilted, our energies dispersed disproportionately into activities designed to gain the security of male approval. Anne and I had always mesmerized ourselves with dresses and perfumes; at the prison, the beauty school, where women sizzled, colored, bewigged themselves, was the most popular spot in the building. One night the women were shaken down for weapons in fear of a riot, and I understood the stake in keeping women trivial. Walking down the dim stairwell, I imagined myself dragged into a dormitory, held hostage. But when I saw a woman with a *Glamour* magazine under her arm, I was reassured: how could revolution take place while someone read a fashion magazine?

And how would it feel to come from a family in which time spent in prison was as common as time spent in certain schools? And how was that unlike the way Southern women accepted their imprisonment by their roles? Indeed, the prison *was* a

269

kind of school, a school for the disenfranchised. I thought of a cat I had seen, pregnant, walleyed, wild with hunger, amid the garbage cans of Little Italy in New York. According to Ben, I was a bleeding-heart liberal; from the perspective of middle-class white-male privilege, he was as hard-nosed about the women in the prison as he was about the bums I still had a hard time stumbling over on the Bowery. "They're there because they want to be!" he assured me.

I had agreed to sell the house where I had lived for twelve years, and we now spent weekends packing and looking for an apartment. But all that had begun to seem unreal, far away, actions taken through a fog of fatigue. It was the life in the prison that was real. And my paranoia had come back; when I stopped at a rural service station full of burly red-necks, I sat on the toilet in a ladies' room in which the door wouldn't lock, expecting assault at any moment. One weekend in Atlanta, walking out of a department store, I imagined that a car's backfire was a mad man, shooting specifically at me. One night as I lay in my room at the John Milledge, reading *Against Our Will,* by Susan Brownmiller, I listened through thin walls as three men cursed and shouted, planning what I was sure was rape and murder, but was probably only armed robbery.

At the prison, I now identified with the women in their resentment toward the prison officials. They wanted to give a reading of their poems, but the state office was giving me flak. (Despite the quality of their poems, the Georgia Department of Corrections had refused to print them in an anthology because they had not been written in a manner that "could have been used as a crime-prevention tool.") The grass is too green, wrote Flaubert. It hurts my eyes. Life at the prison was too raw, assaulting my last notions of what it meant to be a Southern woman.

Doris asked if I would bring her a box of Argo laundry starch, "Thuh kin' with thuh big red letters." She liked to eat it—"better 'n fudge." As though she were describing a preference for French over pumpernickel bread, Virease rambled on about how she used to eat "light clay—not thet red kin'...." Easter

Sunday talked about eating newspaper: "I wuz pregnant 'n' had a cravin' fur it. So I tole muh man, 'Go out 'n' git me a paper.' 'Whut fur?' he says, real surprised lak. I says, 'Jes' go git it.' When he got back with it, I tore off thuh white part 'n' wetted it down 'n' salted it—'n' it tasted jes' lak fish!"

I had become comfortable with the way the women joked about anything from vitamin deficiencies to mutilation. "Why do women always look down on a guy who doesn't have all his limbs?" asked Frankie, whose drug dealer–boyfriend had had a wooden leg. "Well, I don't!" exclaimed Peggy. "Once I wuz datin' a dude with no arms and only one leg, 'n' that's why I stole his car: I knew he couldn't run after me! Hey!" she went on, "read that poem again, that good one—the one about jerkin' off!" Peggy had the ready sexuality of her look-alike, Janis Joplin. When I had read "The Ballad of the Lonely Masturbator" by Anne Sexton, she had wiggled empathetically in her chair: "Hell, I might write my own poem about it!"

But the conversation had turned to Inez Garcia, the Chicano woman who had been convicted of murder in California after shooting the man who she said had raped her. The women were indignant, just as they were at the mention of Patty Hearst: "If she wuzn't white 'n' rich, she wouldn't be gittin' treated as good as she is." Doris, happily embroidering, said she had seen Joan Little on "The Merv Griffin Show." Indeed, she hoped to write such good poems that she could get on, too. After all, Nikki Giovanni had done it—why not she? When the voice over the loudspeaker announced medication time, Virease was describing how, despite her second-grade education, she planned to write her Very Own Secret Life Story, which would Tell the Truth about a number of Very Important People in Macon, Georgia. . . .

As I walked down the stairwell and through the doors the guards unlocked for me, I thought of enclosure and resignation and hope. In the prison yard, a tiny frog hopped at my feet, the crickets raised September-in-Georgia voices. It was their hope that bothered me most. Leaving the prison for the "outside" now seemed vaguely dangerous, as though those inside were

271

secure, safe from their own passions, while I floated dangerously free. Was the comfort I felt there just an extension of the apathy they experienced daily—and one of many possible forms of suicide?

As usual as I drove through the main part of town, my parents' faces overlapped, for a moment, the too-bright impressions left by the women in the prison. With relief, I opened the door to my motel room, poured a glass of Jack Daniel's, and plumped down on the lumpy bed to watch the "Tony Orlando and Dawn" show.

The phone rang, and Anne's voice said Mother had taken an overdose of pills.

Over the years, Mother had often written Anne and me threatening suicide, giving frantic instructions on what to do in case of her death. Most had been dismissed as artifacts of her madness. But when Anne found the recent one in which Mother begged to be buried in Georgia, beside her beloved father, rather than in North Carolina where she had been so unhappy, she called me, desperate. With the same adamant propriety with which she had counteracted my wish that Mother be buried in her favorite red dress, Aunt Florance had insisted that no change in funeral plans was possible. Anne's husband came on the line, interrupting her tears: "I've reread the letter: Melissa says she would *prefer* to be buried in Georgia—it's not a definite last wish."

I didn't quite believe him, and I knew Anne didn't, either, but it was easier to give in to his firm male reassurance. Our anguish at what we felt to be our last betrayal of Mother—worse, our sense that, even in death, she was powerless, impotent—went unspoken. It would take nine months for the pain that would engulf me to gestate. First, Daddy had to die, I had to have my fortieth birthday, my third divorce.

My next teaching job was in Savannah, where I lived beside the ocean in an old motel shaped like a showboat. One week Darcy

—agitated and unhappy, in a mood in which I had seen her more and more frequently—came to visit by Greyhound. She had quit school, and at fifteen was living with a dark, brooding boy in whom I saw a potential for violence that Darcy wouldn't acknowledge. That night I noticed with a chill that she kept a glass of water beside her bed, just as Mother always had.

The next morning, when we went out for brunch, she wore an old fur jacket over the same orange midi, the same orange suede boots she had worn to Mother's funeral; she looked exhausted, as from some inner struggle. Over the restaurant table, she poured out the fears that had risen in her since her grandmother's death.

When I rose to go to the ladies' room, I looked back at her. Like Mother at her age, she was heartbreakingly beautiful. The image of her creamy valentine-shaped face, surrounded by thick dark curls that reminded me of Mother's, tore through me like a knife. Would Mother's madness—her propensity for pain and self-destruction—slash through generation after generation?

Or would I be powerful enough to save my daughters—and myself?

Ben and I now took turns visiting one another, and the spaces between our weekends were longer. One Friday he made the five-hour drive from Atlanta to Savannah; we had just lain down together when the phone rang. Anne again, wearily: Daddy had died—"He kept saying 'My coffin, my coffin, give me my coffin, so I can lie down and die.'" I recalled how he had looked at Christmas, not long after Mother's death—his thick black hair lost to cobalt treatments, his eyes vacant—as though some vital connection, some dream of life, had gone with her.

As Ben and I walked along the crummy beach, the waves were an anesthetic, lapping my shock. A woman from the motel crossed our path. "My father died," I said. "Yeah," Ben added petulantly, "that means we can't go to Hilton Head tomorrow."

The next day I flew to Atlanta for the funeral, then back to Savannah to have dinner with Ben. Instead of taking the high-

273

way, the cab driver drove along a dark back road, past deserted warehouses; trapped in my revived paranoia, I sat frozen, released only when I saw Ben waiting for me before the Savannah Hilton. That morning, as the preacher had described Daddy as being "as comfortable, as easy to be with, as this old Bible," I had wanted to throw myself across his casket and speak the love I had never admitted. Now, more than anything, I wanted to be cuddled, cosseted, held in Ben's arms.

Instead—me still in my high heels, the black dress left from Mother's funeral—we walked up and down the cobblestones of River Street. As had been frequent during recent months, we couldn't find a restaurant Ben found pleasing. At last we drove to a bad Italian restaurant on the other side of town. Ben had fallen into one of his moods; during the meal he barely spoke.

He didn't feel like making love that night, he said back at the motel; in fact, he felt more like killing himself. I lay as hollow as one of the shells on the beach. Everything in our marriage had been politically right, but emotionally wrong; though I knew he needed something, I didn't know what it was or how to give it.

The weekend was over, and except for six more bitter months, so was everything else.

My last residence of the school year was in Rabun Gap, Georgia —in the heart of *Deliverance* country, and twenty miles south of the town in North Carolina where mother had donned her blue nightgown and swallowed the pills. With four other artists, I lived for six weeks in a stone lodge in the Appalachian Mountains. The air was cool and crisp, watercress overran the creek, and the gurgle of its water soothed me as had the ocean waves. At night, we made a fire, and told stories, and played darts.

The lodge was only two hours from Atlanta and every Friday the others fled for the city and friends. Ostensibly to write, but really to avoid the frustrations of weekends at home, I often stayed over. On one such weekend, the lodge was to be used for a retreat; I would have to find a motel room. As I got into my car, sheets of water fell before my windshield. Rabun County, I had been told, was the second wettest in the country.

I had heard of an old-fashioned motel ten or twelve miles away. As I turned off the highway onto a shallow road, I suddenly found myself looking into the graveyard of a Baptist church, the distant, rain-shrouded mountains. Beside the graveyard was the motel—tiny cabins with front porches and tin roofs. A chill beyond that caused by the rain ran through me: when I was three or four, Mother and Daddy had decided to take a weekend trip to the mountains, North Georgia, yes, Rabun Gap!

I remembered the rain that had begun during the long drive in Daddy's Ford, how, as I had sat in the front seat in Mother's lap, it had poured down our windshield just as it was doing now. In a motel room that looked like a playhouse, the three of us had slept in one bed, me in the middle, an aluminum pitcher of ice water sweating on the bed table. I had felt comfy and safe between them: Daddy had made jokes, and Mother had laughed.

But had the endless rain, thumping the tin roof of the cabins, presaged Mother's tears, the endless disappointments of years to come? Indeed, was this the same place where we had lain together, me happily holding my beautiful young parents captive for perhaps the last time? Suddenly, I realized there was no one I could ask, that there had only been three people there, and two of those were dead.

Looking out over the gravestones, the cabins, the mountains, I felt disoriented, anxiety jumbling my thoughts. I only knew that I didn't want to stay in that place, and turned my Fiat back toward the highway, where I slowly drove toward Clayton, the largest town in the area. As though to give myself time, I stopped at a service station, where, as a burly mountaineer filled my tank, I stared blindly at the smiling stuffed animals that decorated his window. Back on the road, rain thrashed about my headlights, and I tried to force from my mind the "sentimental, self-indulgent," as Ben would call it, image of Mother's new grave, lashed by the water thirty miles away on a winding dirt road I couldn't find if I wanted to. It was as though I had only fully realized my parents' deaths moments before.

Passion: it was suddenly the only thing I could imagine that would obliterate the void within me. In Clayton, I parked on main street between two pickup trucks, jumped the gushing curb, and rushed into a phone booth. At first the rusty telephone was silent; then I heard the ring in my and Ben's apartment. "Well, of course, I'd be glad to see you," Ben said coolly when I cried that I'd changed my plans, that I wanted to come home, that I wanted to lie in his arms, that—more than anything—I wanted to sleep with him; "but you had already made your plans, and now I have some, too. . . ."

The click of the receiver was a shell in a chamber, the cock of a gun. I ran across the flooded street to a one-room department store; from the racks, I jerked down a blouse with a bird stenciled across its front, a garishly flowered cotton skirt. In the dressing room, the cloth was so cheap that it bent at the creases as I pulled it over my hips; the chartreuse-and-turquoise parrot stretched across my breasts, oversize and malevolent. I remembered how Anne and I had frantically shopped the day before Mother's funeral; neither of us had had black dresses, and in the Saturday-dressing-room frenzy of chic Atlanta shops, we had giggled in hysteria. I thought of a Saturday a decade before, the three of us shopping together: in the dressing room, Anne and I had given one another secret looks across Mother's body—her drooping breasts, her swelling belly—as she had struggled into an outfit much like the one I now wore. Our bodies, our psyches, the look had said, will never be such a mess, the kind of mess I was this moment: in the mirror, but for my long hair, I was Mother—my face her death mask.

I rushed out into the wood-floored store, bought a pair of Jonathan Livingston Seagull knee socks from a sales clerk who looked at me curiously, then drove to the most modern-looking motel in town and checked in for two nights. My hand trembling—from the cold?—I poured myself some bourbon, flopped down on the bed, and dialed the number in New Jersey of a man

I had met once on a plane. From his office as director of computer operations in a large corporation, he gave me mechanistic, yet lascivious, instructions for masturbating. The vision of death—Mother's, Daddy's, my own—rhythmically faded as the contractions moved through my thighs, calves, toes.

A high school student in Savannah had told me about the Route Three Wrecking Crew: "We go out in a pickup, hold iron pipes out thuh winder, knock them mailboxes down as we go by. . . ." With my and Ben's divorce, I felt as though I had been hit in the back of the neck three times—being motherless, fatherless, husbandless became one lump of grief. Numbness dissolved, pure pain rushed in—a pain that seemed to swell and throb against my very body outlines. At moments throughout the day, and when I woke at night—once I was lucky enough to fall asleep—it started up like a physical cancer; I imagined it pulsating against my very fingertips, stopped only by the limits of flesh from emerging. Tears, which had always welled easily to my eyes, were like tiny futile leaks, the night sweats of a major disease. My beloved azaleas, I had been told, were deadly poison: my guts grabbed as though I had been eating them.

Was this what Mother had experienced all her life? That thought was less bearable than any other. One morning as I woke, I lay for an hour, everything I knew of Mother's existence working its way through my psyche; it was as though I lived for sixty minutes the sixty years of her conflicted life. When, another morning, I woke to the phone's ring, the voice of an acquaintance telling me that a young student had killed himself, it seemed nothing more than part of some inevitable fabric.

Anne, who saw people die almost daily at the hospital where she worked, thought she received messages from Mother in her dreams; she was tortured, she said, because she had read that suicides exist after death in a tormented, restless state. But now she was worried about me, too. With horror, she noted that I had begun using Mother's exact anxious gestures, speaking in her same hysterical voice. I had inherited her electric typewriter; when I tried to type, the keys jammed. Writing of Mother in my journal, I inscribed, with a slip of Pentel, " . . . my suicide at sixty . . ."

In a companion dream to the one I had had of Mother a year before her death, in which I had laid my child's head across her satin blouse to find one breast missing, her chest tightly bandaged, I now dreamed myself, single-breasted, so scarred by mastectomy that I would never be sexually loved again. I woke picturing clitorectomies, lobotomies, every literal diminishment of women.

Anne had told me of an operation called pelvic exoneration, in which the vagina and anus are removed, leaving the patient stitched and sexless as a Barbie doll, her excretory functions taking place into plastic pouches attached to her abdomen, her sexual functions taking place not at all. Was that what Mother had felt—wounded, infinitely childlike, a doll with no outlet for her passions? Would the dissonance within me remain trapped, as hers had, for the rest of my life?

Ben had never believed in marriage in the first place, he now said; we should either remain married and have separate apartments, or divorce and continue to live together. In either case, we would still be lovers, he would even give me an Alfa Romeo. The night of the day we signed the papers, he sent me yellow roses, but in a week, moved out anyway. I was no longer civilized, much less interested in civilized divorce.

On what would have been our sixth wedding anniversary, we went to Culver's house for an evening of country and gospel music. Ben had just given me an ironic gift, my copy of the divorce papers. At first I sat drinking Jack Daniel's, listening to the maudlin lyrics, the pensive guitar tones—the usual fat tears running down my face. Most Southern men like to be photographed with their guns whenever possible, and when the musicians brought theirs out for an impromptu Polaroid, I playfully twirled Culver's pistol on my finger.

Culver and the others, drunk themselves, and used to a little Saturday-night violence, looked on unperturbed. But I could see in Ben's eyes his fear that, in my anger, I might really shoot him. I knew the limits of my potential for violence; he didn't. I enjoyed for a moment an obscene feeling of power. But my hoarse voice, as he drove me home, frightened even me. I felt as though I was possessed. Yet whose rage was it that poured from my mouth—Mother's or mine?

For the first time in my life I began bleeding between my periods, great gushes and clots of blood that seemed to pour from my endless wound, indeed, that flooded out onto the puzzled doctor's hands as I lay on her examining table. And now there was no husband to cling to in the night, to tell my shuddering fears that the pain inside me had turned to a literal cancer. In fact, talking to or sleeping with Ben was what seemed to bring on the tide. As we argued over the phone, I would feel the dread dripping begin between my legs. I had once been the kind of woman who wanted her husband to pick her up after a difficult dental appointment, to lean on his arm, to take comfort in his warmth. Now my foot shook on the gas pedal; I had to wait for my nerves to calm; there was no one at home to call.

Although Ben had left me to pay the whole rent, I was glad I lived in a featureless luxury apartment. It soothed me, in the same way my new clothes and hairdo did. I now craved the kind of little dresses and pumps Mother had always admired. I had had my long hair cut and anonymously curled; I even prayed to the Bible Belt God I had known as a child. I was like Branch, traveling into the future with her mama's china. But Jesus had left the Main Line, and my mother's legacy was her madness.

Waylon Jennings sings a song that goes, "I've always been crazy, but it's kept me from going insane. . . ." What I didn't yet realize was that what seemed like breaks in my sanity were really just the first signs of an anger that had been so long dammed that it had taken Mother's death, my third divorce, the loss of youth, house, and children, to release it. Without my crazy mother to give me sanity, my cool husband to restrain me, even children at home to need me, I was unanchored—but also, for the first time, free to totally indulge the terrifying real me.

A man in Wyoming had told me that, after his divorce, he had taken up skydiving because no matter how depressed he might be, once he had jumped from an airplane, he was exhilarated. If I was going to destroy myself, I decided, I might as well do it in the most pleasurable way possible. And if there was one thing besides violence for which my background had prepared me, it was sensuality, even dissipation—for as every Bible Belt Southerner knows deep inside, true salvation lies in licentiousness. Or, as country singer Johnny Duncan suggests, "Johnny Walker Red to tequila in bed just might do it. . . ." I would give myself over, I unconsciously decided, to the all-engrossing, pain-obliterating, personality-reducing sport of emotional and sexual skydiving.

Rabun Gap, *Deliverance* country again. The construction worker I picked up two nights ago at the mountain bar is still here beside me in my cabin with no phone, a half mile down a dirt road from the nearest neighbor. Menstrual blood, where he has gouged me through my period, smears every rudimentary piece of furniture.

The first night he saw the rifle beneath my bed; the next morning he told me about the gang bangs in the mountains to which he had been a party. Now, as he rouses, he sees through the window that snow is falling between the hills. "Yew cain't go back to Etlana today," he growls authoritatively. "Yep, we gonna stay in hyar all day 'n' drink thet last bottle o' George Dickel."

I hear in his voice his barely contained rage at having failed, during our entire debauch, to maintain an erection—never mind that just before we met, he had taken a half-dozen Valium: he was a man, wasn't he? He rises on a beefy elbow and looks down at me, a smile playing beneath his full beard, across his rawly handsome face.

"Yew know those wimmen whut wuz murdered in Rabun County? Wall, I'm the one whut done it. . . ."

I had emerged from the cabin in Rabun Gap alive by pretending to think his threats were just mountain good-ole-boy talk, by hastily pulling on my sweater and jeans, despite his standing behind me, his bearlike arm bent momentarily around my neck, by telling him that a woman friend was coming to take me to breakfast, by soothing him again about the Civil War ("If Gen'ral Lee had only . . ." he had obsessed the night before), by telling him that I would get in touch soonest, but that I was too old for him anyway. "Wall, jes' so you ain't older 'n muh mama," he had said grudgingly as I helped him with his down jacket, pushed him toward the door, just at the lucky sound of a four-wheel-drive vehicle putt-putting up the snow-covered dirt road.

But now I found plenty of people willing to pick up on my fantasies of self-destruction. Culver, sitting on the side of his and Mandy's bed in their house in a wooded area outside the city, polished his rifle and mused, "Yew know, I could jes' stick this up yew, pull thuh trigger, throw yo' body out in thet gully. . . ." A television personality in Savannah seduced me by telling me about his collection of guns: describing the characteristics of each, he rubbed first his thigh and then mine with a tenderness that suddenly dissolved as he brusquely shoved his prick into my ass, amyl nitrite beneath my nose till my brain felt like it would burst. . . .

Savannah. A black panther, fangs bared, rises inches from my lashes.

I hadn't noticed the tattoo on his bicep when we tore our clothes off the night before. I had only been conscious of his baby face, his long-lashed blue eyes, the black speck in the iris of one of them, the way he had kissed me, open-mouthed, as we had danced at Dr. Feelgood's.

Now I remembered what he had told me—that he was twenty-two, a dealer, an ex–heroin addict—that he had joined the army to escape imprisonment for robbing a jewelry store.

That, and the way, before we had fallen into bed, he had carefully placed his open switch-blade knife over the head-board.

Atlanta. The Black Panther and his Italian Buddy. The Italian Buddy has a cleft in his chin, tattoos on both biceps, I notice as he climbs into bed with us.

"Mama Mia! She is so beoootiful!": he licks his lips and gestures with thumb and forefinger. Two sets of hands roaming my body, the Black Panther kissing me open-mouthed, his Italian Buddy fucking me.

I feel like I've died and gone to heaven—until they nearly get into a fistfight, until the Black Panther's threats send the Italian Buddy to sit naked, dangerously brooding, watching from a chair as we fuck.

Until the next morning when the Black Panther tells me that the Italian Buddy had been in prison on a charge of being in the car with a friend who had shot a woman in the side of her throat and shoved her body from the speeding car.

Until I recall what the Black Panther had murmured as he had pressed a forefinger inside me: "I want to see you bleed, baby, *there.* . . ."

If Mother had wanted to kill me, why not my lovers?

I soon found others willing to help, too—sailors from foreign ships, marines from a nearby base, ex-felons, and drag queens and pool sharks and B-girls and drug dealers—dozens of people caught in a nether world similar to my own.

There was cocaine and Quaaludes and angel dust and amyl nitrite and dope, and, of course, liquor. There was discomania and dive life and punk rock. There was group sex and kinky sex and sex with women and sex with boys younger than my son, David. I was a forty-year-old belle with a belated dance card, but this time the follow-through went further than the dance floor.

"Have fun," my therapist had said as I left Atlanta. In Savannah, where I had moved to teach for six months, I lived with my first woman lover and slept with more men that I had in my whole previous life. Total dissipation, I found, was more fun than the local diversion of touring old houses. For half a year I didn't read a newspaper, watch a television program, or go to a movie. Instead, I sat on the porch at dusk and drank wine and smoked dope and talked. There were others, I learned, who had always felt as misplaced as I had. There was Miss Jane and Robert and Latrice Boudair and Delta and Lacey in Search of Love. And where I might have felt fear or repulsion, I often experienced empathy. When the Black Panther cried that he would rather kill himself than spend forty years in the steel mills like his father, the blue sparks burning out his sight, his criminality made perfect sense.

I felt the same camaraderie I had in the prison, the camaraderie of the disenfranchised. It was as though my search for the obliteration of pain through risk and pleasure had taken on the character of a spiritual quest. A veil had been pulled over my sight that made me feel I was never in real danger at all, or at least that it was insignificant in terms of my own inner violence.

It was a life so romantic, so bohemian, that I began to forget about Ben, Mother, the Famous Southern Poet, E. Rivers School —every middle-class standard with which I had futilely tried to conform. Gripped by pleasure and intimacy, I found it hard to think of deprivation or loss. In the same town where, ten years before, vacationing with Paul, I had looked into a hotel mirror and wanted to die, I started to live.

A fat black diva, a man in drag, madly pantomimed across the stage that "I've got eyes, eyes, eyes, yes, eyes, eyes, eyes in the back of mah head. . . ." Probably because of the Baptist church, we had never had proms at Tucker High School; now dancing slow and sleazy at Dr. Feelgood's, a purple strobe curling and flickering against the flamingo walls, I felt, for the first time outside of writing and teaching, like myself. In a place where men were men and sometimes women, where bisexuality seemed to be in the water supply and every kind of sexual act took place in the ladies' room, my parents' crazy sexuality, my traumas at their hands, indeed, what I experienced as my own mixed-up sexual identity, seemed trivial, even insignificant.

It was an atmosphere in which strangers proposed to one another every possible sexual conjunction. "Don't worry, we'll take him with us and I'll give him a blow job," said a man who had propositioned me after I told him I was with someone else.

The spirit of the hermaphrodite I had seen at sixteen was every-where. "This place is everyone's fantasy come true," breathed a man beside me.

Even in Dr. Feelgood's, every familiar face eventually had a name, a niche—mine, I learned, was "the schoolteacher." "A hustler," whispered Robert in response to my question; "goes with men or women." The young man leaned up against the wall, eyes half closed, as another man caressed his nipples through his open work shirt. He seemed curiously familiar—with a start, I realized he reminded me of my own undeter-mined and dreamily passive past self!

Cleveland. The Black Panther again. We're lying on a motel bed, watching *Taxi Driver*. Blood smears the color TV screen; we're stoned on angel dust, just as we have been since I arrived two days before.

I'm imagining the Black Panther ordering French wines, in Gucci loafers and cashmere sweaters—in other words, civilized. Though he's still cross because I wouldn't do heroin the night before, he says he likes my fantasy.

His Sicilian Best Buddy, lounging across from us, just out of prison on a drug conviction, has three tattoos, high cheekbones, and an angelic expression. Every time the Black Panther fucks me, he gets to fuck me, too. The rule, I quickly learned, was that the Sicilian Best Buddy was never to kiss me on the mouth. I also learned that I had little choice about being shared.

We're just starting up again when a third buddy bursts into the room: "Nazzy wuz shot in thuh leg bustin' that drug supply house! We gotta get outta here, *fast.* . . ."

Exactly, my brain unexpectedly echoes.

Indeed, what *was* I doing there? As though I had recently been blind, I began to see danger. When a twenty-one-year-old pool shark, both of us drunk and laughing, carried me up wet stone steps fifty feet high, then swung me out over the parapet, I looked for a split second at the cobbled street below and saw my skull cracked, my brains splattered. A man I had picked up at Dr. Feelgood's ("Burt Reynolds's nephew," he had said. "Muh mama Albertha wuz a Reynolds.") looked more dangerous in my apartment than he had beneath the strobe lights; and when he suggested things in bed that repulsed even me, I knew something was changing. When I almost married a Jesus freak who thought I wrote because I was possessed by demons, when I had, at one time, skinned knees and a smashed thumb from two different accidents that had taken place while I was drinking, I knew things had gone too far.

Yet if it had been my *Looking for Mr. Goodbar* year, why did I feel saner than ever at the end of it? Instead of killing me, following every impulse, breaking with everything I had been taught, doing things Mother would have feared to even speak of, had somehow released a new self. I was like a terminal-cancer patient who had spent her last savings on a vast pleasure trip, only to come back broke and cured—or at least in remission.

Years before, I had read *A Burnt-Out Case* by Graham Greene, and though I had not known why, had identified with the title and the protagonist. Now I understood that I *had* been a burnt-out case—that the energy I had used to repress myself, to even minimally fulfill the roles of wife, mother, and mistress, had drained me in a way that made it seem as though I had lived almost my whole life with a low-grade depression. Energy eaten up by conflict and struggle was something I had observed in the most interesting and achieving Southern women I had met. And if this had been true for us, with our toughness, our opportunities, how had it been for thin-skinned Mother, or any woman less stoic than Grandmother Lee?

At first my new health simply felt like dissipation turning sweeter. As I lay in bed between a lover and the young man we had picked up in an Atlanta gay bar, I dreamed we were three mice sleeping together in a shoe box full of leaves, the boy dressed in a red puffed-sleeve dress, like Hunca Munca in a Kate Greenaway story. When the same man and I went to bed with his black woman lover, she and I talked about new fashions and sexual preferences as our shared man lay back and smoked dope; since her family in South Georgia had been patronized by people like my grandparents, going down on her—indeed, pleasuring her in every possible way—seemed like the least I could do.

Ironically, by sleeping with women, I learned that I wasn't malformed at all. With what seemed like a *whoosh,* the image of my embedded penis was gone; through intimacy with women more aggressive than myself, I found out how traditionally feminine I was, and also how little that had to do with true womanliness. I was light, floating free, like a woman just after surgery for, as an aunt had described it, "a cyst in mah womb as big as a grapefruit!"

I had lost, in traveling, the expensive black dress I had worn to both my parents' funerals and out to dinner with Ben on the night of our divorce. The bleeding that had started after our separation had ended on the anniversary of Mother's death. My new life, it appeared, had been like my new thumbnail—growing pink and strong beneath the old.

Each morning, in my apartment in Atlanta, I sat in the four-poster bed Anne and I had shared as children, drinking coffee, thinking of myself, and Mother. Mother, who didn't learn to drive a car till she was over forty. Mother, who, till the end of her life, felt she couldn't leave her house without the permission of her husband. Mother, who felt guilty for any form of self-assertion, from stating a preference for a certain dress to a sales clerk, to serving toast rather than homemade biscuits at breakfast. Mother, who had never once stayed in a hotel or motel, or eaten in a restaurant, alone.

After Granddaddy Carroll's death, I had suggested to Grandmother Lee that she might go abroad like Aunt Pearl, who, after major surgery at seventy, wearing the same mid-calf black or navy crepe dresses, the same laced black pumps favored by Lee, had traveled alone to Hong Kong. "But, Rows-may-ree," she had protested in the same tone in which she had vetoed my suggestion that she might remarry. "Don't you know she's six months older than me?"

"It's not Hard Shell"—Holy Roller—"is it?" Lee had asked Anne anxiously as she drove her up a winding dirt road to visit Mother's grave. Just as it would have been a social diminishment had Mother been buried in her favorite red dress, it would have been less than proper had she been buried in the wrong kind of Baptist churchyard. "No, no," Anne had reassured her, thinking how even in death, propriety was the most important aspect of Mother's life. Her heart had turned over, she told me later, when she had seen the small tombstone again: MELISSA RUTH CONNELL (HUGHES) HIGDON, 1915–1975, WIFE OF J. WAYNE HIGDON—the only inscription, the least and last part of her identity.

Seven sexless years after her divorce from Daddy, Mother had had a brief affair with the "wolf" at her office. Wringing her hands in what had become a characteristic gesture, she had sobbed out to Anne, seventeen, her horror at having broken one of the Ten Commandments, plus the graphic details of her fall. (Anne, just out of a period when, as a member of Crusade for Christ, she had carried her Bible everywhere, had begged her to stop: "I couldn't stand it," she said, "thinking of Mother with her legs in the air when I couldn't yet deal with my own sexuality.")

Had Mother ever consciously dreamed, even for a moment, of acting out her lush sensuality free of fear of retribution by her Bible Belt God? To free my repressed feelings of love and longing for my dead mother had required, for me, an emotional and literal bisexuality; would Mother have been saved had she been able to express her love for her mother through the love of another woman? Had she, too, ever wanted to run away, leave Anne and me behind, find a room somewhere, lock herself up with trashy novels, tinned sardines, a typewriter, and forget about being pretty or good? Indeed, had she given up being a ruined Southern belle for simply being ruined, would she have been freed from the demons that gnawed at her, the madness that had spelled her death?

On the dresser across from my bed stood one of the more romantic photographs of Mother. In a draped white satin evening gown, she holds her perpetual roses; already, at eighteen, she had begun plucking her brows in the thin thirties fashion she would favor throughout her life. It gives her, despite her beauty, a slightly anxious look. As I sat in bed, I could see my face, reflected in the antique shaving mirror, beside hers; since the picture is black-and-white, our difference in coloring was less obvious.

At the age Mother had been in the photo, determined to rid myself of the distortions inflicted on my teenage body by David's birth, I had done exercises on her rug. Mother had gotten down beside me, and as she had tried the exercises, a great *whoosh* had come from her vulva. I had turned away disgusted. She was so out of shape that she couldn't even raise her legs into the air. I wanted to disown, as I had so many times, my mother's body.

Now, as I did sit-ups each morning, I knew there was no getting away from it—the body that was mine was also hers, had lived in hers, came from it. If my hair was redder, finer, my stomach flatter, my nails clean and pink as a cat's tongue, the petiteness of bone, the roundness of flesh, the shortness of hands remained, and would. And I thought how rapidly, at my age, she had ridden her psychic roller coaster downhill. If my body contained so much of her, what of my mind?

In a restaurant in North Georgia, I had recently watched a family near my table as I ate alone. A young man in a chartreuse polyester jump suit, a plump but pretty woman in a cotton housedress, a toddler, and a baby that was obviously newborn. It was the woman—cuddling the baby on her shoulder, consoling the toddler—who mesmerized me. I had remembered that among Mother's clippings had been a "Dear Abby" column giving advice on how to get along with one's grown children. And far deeper in my gut than the fried chicken I had just swallowed, I had suddenly known that Mother *had* loved me, that the smiling young mother, adoringly holding me up to be photographed, and the contemptuous shrew, taking pleasure in my humiliation, had been one, and that I had distorted the good in order to reject the other.

Yet despite my rejection, I had spent my life, till recently,

doing exactly as Mother had been taught to do, had done, putting my relationships with men before my relationship with
self. Indeed, I had even married certain men because they
promised to be as rejecting, as unloving, even as physically
cruel to me, as she had been. And my whole relation to them,
my dependency and resentment, had been handed down to me
by her whole cloth, like a barely worn dress. Anne, in our little
divided family, had been "on Daddy's side," and, significantly,
has only been married once, has never been beaten or threatened with a gun by a man. But I had been Mother's grudging
ally, and she had so early placed her own filter of rage and need
over my vision that I had never been able to view any man
objectively.

It was a filter that had distorted my view in many ways. After
Mother's suicide, her second husband—distraught over an
event he had been unable, or unwilling, to understand—had
developed a malignancy much like Daddy's. Within a year he
too was dead. At the funeral with Anne, I remembered his
mountain prejudices, his insistence on male supremacy, but also
his often gentle puzzlement, his confusion, at his crazy wife's
histrionics. "Once I rode tuh Macon with 'Lissa 'n' Donald,"
Grandmother Lee said after Mother's death, "and 'Lissa
whined 'n' fussed thuh whole way—it was no wonder that pore
man drank!"

People were the same, but now I saw them differently. At a
family dinner, aunts Florance, Grace, and Lovie were sad, soft
women whose faces had been freed of some harsh veil. "Isn't
she the purties' thang?" they exclaimed of Darcy. "Jes' lak
Melissa!" And of Laura, now in New York at NYU: "'N' *she's*
thuh smartes' thang! But she's not still cuttin' that beautiful red
hair, is she?" Without Mother's pain to color the event, they
were no longer monoliths or monsters, only permanent-waved,
repressed, and aging women, much like the masked ladies I had
met everywhere.

Except for Uncle Bobby—who asked, puzzled, "Who wuz
that who used to come with yuh, your son or your husban'?"—
no one mentioned Ben or our divorce, though Anne had told

me that after our separation, Grandmother Lee had said, " 'Lissa was afraid that boy wouldn't treat 'er right." She had spoken of it as the only kind of tragedy, aside from the will of the Lord, that she knew—that is, male induced. It was her eighty-sixth birthday, and she was more willing than usual to speak of the past. "You know, I was jes' as happy feedin' the chickens, tendin' the calves, as I woulda been doin' enythang else. Why, when the mailman came ev'ryday, it was a big event! I was lucky. But Mr. Carroll—he was sixteen years older'n me —he did get senile. I think it's only men who get that way," she added with her usual sexual chauvinism.

"Whatta ya workin' on now, honey?" Uncle Bobby asked, patting my shoulder. When I answered something about Southern women, he patted me again: "Well, jes' don't make 'em all out Scarletts, honey—let some of 'em be Melanies!"

Melanies. Unfortunately, there had been too many.

In an Atlanta restaurant, I noticed a chubby woman with short red bangs staring at me from another table. As I passed to go to the ladies' room, she rose: "Rows-may-ree, don't you remember me? Dolly, frum Tucker High School!"

Suddenly, I recognized through the fat cheeks, the bangs, the girl who had been on the cheerleading team with me, who had always cried as she sang in the church choir, who, everyone said, during a summer's absence had been sent away to the Florence Crittenton Home for Unwed Mothers. "I married Randall Reeves," she bubbled. "Do you remember? He ran aroun' with Leroy Matthews, that boy who went with Wanza, that girl with the big hips"—indeed, Wanza's wide ass wobbled in my memory. " 'N' my brother, Bud"—one of the nice boys I had rejected out of my preference for the rough ones—"is a commander in the navy. Stoney died of a heart attack. 'N' you should see Crystal—she looks like she's a thousand years old. . . ."

Dolly's voice wound down, her plump face matching it. "And me—my kids've left home, I'm jes' gettin' fat, don't know what tuh do next. Goin' through one of those *Passages*, I guess. . . ."

Between jobs, I stood in the state unemployment office behind a white woman of about my age. She wore an expensively cut dress, respectable pumps, but lace dripped beneath her hem, the chignon at the back of her neck barely contained her curls, her nostrils rapidly flared in the same way Mother's had when she had been on the verge of hysteria.

"It's hot in here, isn't it?" I asked. She turned, grimacing exaggeratedly, her lip curling down like Mother's. "I *hate* to stand in this line," she wailed, looking beyond me, beyond the blacks gossiping behind us, even the institutional green walls, as though she was trapped in what she considered to be her own private degradation.

She was Mother—fragile, too finely bred, out of sync, resisting competence, dreaming that because she was female, had been a belle, justice was a man to take care of her. Blanche DuBois inside her own mad head. The princess still on the pea.

But, I was slowly beginning to realize, not me.

I had come to the department of records for the birth-certificate copy I needed for a tourist card to Central America. I stared, disconcerted, at the Photostatted names and ages of my parents at the time I had been born—nine months after their elopement, a year during which they had still lived at the peak of romantic love.

As though a button had been pressed, images fought in my mind—the need to romanticize them, rage at their suffering. But in that moment, something fell away, too. I suddenly knew that my young parents, no matter how I may have wished more for them, had simply been two more sad idealists, smashed by the Depression and their Bible Belt upbringing. Nothing more, nothing less.

"Every once in a while it dawns on me that we're in Guatemala!" the man with whom I was traveling would marvel later. It was the way I was beginning to feel about my life. My parents' suffering was not, as I had imagined at five, my fault. Just because Mother had killed herself, I didn't have to.

And though the cost had been enormous, I had at last managed something Mother had never dreamed possible—a life outside the role of wife, mother, mistress, or martyr.

In New Orleans, in what was once the slave quarters of the Corn Stalk Inn, coffee is brought out on a silver salver; clear yellow birds flit beneath the bougainvillea. In Atlanta, where I once rode the bus down Peachtree Street to the Carnegie Library, where I yearned after the dresses in the girls' department at Davison's department store, my butcher dresses like Porter Wagoner, my shoe repairman is an overweight Elvis look-alike. But mostly the city could now be anywhere, temperate, urban. "What's your sexual preference?" is a query as frequent as "Where do you go to church?" "Are they playing 'Home on the Range'?" a visitor asked when he heard the chimes at the church across the street plunking out the Baptist hymns that still wrung my gut. Many of my friends are relocated New Yorkers, Midwesterners, Californians; my daughters are Atlantans, rather than Southerners.

It's my several marriages that such friends find hardest to understand. "Why did you marry them?" asked Suzanne, a physician from Detroit, as puzzled as she had been at my story of Cudden Lily's choice to stay in bed for thirty years rather than openly confront her father. It's not a question a Southern woman of my age is likely to ask: for us, a husband, the married state, had been necessary to identity.

Is it a contradiction to remain in the South after all that has happened? A tolerance for ambiguity may be a hallmark of the Southern mind—and however liberated, I'm still a Southern woman. Spanish moss, honeysuckle, kudzu spread their filaments deep into my brain. If anything, I'm like a ranch woman in the West—driven crazy by snow and isolation, yet mesmerized by such dazzling beauty. Despite everything, I'm still afflicted by what Southerners reverently call "roots"—a feeling that early in my life became the fantasy of myself spread-eagled, facedown, going into, through the earth, the very taste of Georgia clay filling my mouth. The way sunlight hits red dirt is as radiant to me as the blues of the Caribbean—besides, my mother, grandmother, great-grandmothers are buried beneath it.

Yes, the way I feel about being a woman in the South is the way I feel about the oleander that blooms in June: though it's said that the sap, even brushed against one's skin, is toxic, I carelessly break the branches, stick the ravishing flowers into my hair. . . .

April. Savannah. The city is a woman, from her cavernous houses, through her veils of pale gray lace, to her labia-pink azalea.

A bunch of them blaze pink in a jar on my worktable. I have a chenille bedspread with a peacock on it, and a cedar chest given me by Grandmother Lee. A small green lizard that glides across the kitchen floor when I walk in barefoot. I have two pretty cotton skirts and a pair of good boots. I have Mother's typewriter, a stack of white bond, a bottle of Gallo Chablis Blanc. . . .

Breathing magnolias, I pass verandahed houses in which I glimpse, through white-veiled windows, cool high rooms like those in Grandmother Lee's house when I was ten—white doilies, high mantelpieces, tall chairs and beds. I have on my green gingham dress again, my starter bra with the blue ribbon, my baby-doll shoes. I think of my boyfriend, Troy, his dwarfed brother, Saxon, my best friend, Barbara, and the Holy Roller church next door. I think of Mother, of Grandmother Lee, of Grandmother Annie, of Anne. I think of Jesus and Culver and the Famous Southern Poet and my son, David. . . .

Two black toddlers, their hair in cornrows, do the twist inside Hula-Hoops. A black father walks a baby girl in a pink dress shaped like a tutu. Another, in his Sunday suit, walks two paces ahead of his teenage son, clapping his hands rhythmically, strutting in a way echoed exactly by the boy. Two sanctified women, still in their white dresses and gloves, rock on a porch and fan themselves.

"I wish I had a nickel tuh put in thet slot ma-cheen!" sings out a young voice behind me. "Hal-lee-lu-ja!" shouts an old black man as I pass.

I have no parents, husband, children, money. I walk down the street, ready to begin my life.